JUMPMAN

ALSO BY JOHNNY SMITH

*The Sons of Westwood: John Wooden, UCLA, and the
Dynasty That Changed College Basketball*

*Blood Brothers: The Fatal Friendship Between
Muhammad Ali and Malcolm X*
with Randy Roberts

A Season in the Sun: The Rise of Mickey Mantle
with Randy Roberts

*War Fever: Boston, Baseball, and America
in the Shadow of the Great War*
with Randy Roberts

JUMPMAN

THE MAKING AND MEANING OF MICHAEL JORDAN

JOHNNY SMITH

BASIC BOOKS

New York

Basic Books
Hachette Book Group
1290 Avenue of the Americas, New York, NY 10104
www.basicbooks.com

Printed in the United States of America

First Edition: November 2023

Published by Basic Books, an imprint of Hachette Book Group, Inc. The Basic Books name and logo is a trademark of the Hachette Book Group.

The Hachette Speakers Bureau provides a wide range of authors for speaking events. To find out more, go to hachettespeakersbureau.com or email HachetteSpeakers@hbgusa.com.

Basic books may be purchased in bulk for business, educational, or promotional use. For more information, please contact your local bookseller or the Hachette Book Group Special Markets Department at special.markets@hbgusa.com.

The publisher is not responsible for websites (or their content) that are not owned by the publisher.

Print book interior design by Amy Quinn.

Library of Congress Cataloging-in-Publication Data

Names: Smith, John Matthew, author.
Title: Jumpman : the making and meaning of Michael Jordan / Johnny Smith.
Description: First edition. | New York : Basic Books, 2023. | Includes bibliographical references and index.
Identifiers: LCCN 2023009692 | ISBN 9781541675650 (hardcover) | ISBN 9781541675667 (ebook)
Subjects: LCSH: Jordan, Michael, 1963- | Basketball players—United States—Biography. | Basketball—United States—History. | Chicago Bulls (Basketball team)—History. | National Basketball Association—History.
Classification: LCC GV884.J67 S52 2023 | DDC 796.323092 [B]—dc23/eng/20230313
LC record available at https://lccn.loc.gov/2023009692

ISBNs: 9781541675650 (hardcover), 9781541675667 (ebook)

LSC-C

Printing 1, 2023

For Randy Roberts. Thanks for everything.

"You were born where you were born and faced the future that you faced because you were Black and for no other reason. The limits of your ambition were, thus, expected to be set forever. You were born into a society which spelled out with brutal clarity, and in as many ways as possible, that you were a worthless human being. You were not expected to aspire to excellence: you were expected to make peace with mediocrity."

—JAMES BALDWIN, *THE FIRE NEXT TIME*, 1963 (MICHAEL JORDAN'S BIRTHYEAR)

CONTENTS

Preface

THE MYSTIQUE

"Very early I had a personality split. One that was a public persona and one that was private."

—Michael Jordan

Winning his first championship changed Michael Jordan completely and irrevocably. His world split open: he could never again completely satisfy his ambition, just as the public could never get enough of him. The 1991 NBA Finals pitched Jordan into a new realm of fame, creating unprecedented commercial possibilities but also making his life increasingly uncomfortable and lonely. Being on top raised the stakes. Jordan craved success, but once he crossed that threshold he had more to lose than ever. Increasingly, he retreated into himself, knowing that if he surrendered to the demands of celebrity, he would become something he didn't want to be. And yet his reluctance to let the public break the glass wall around him only made basketball fans crave pieces of the Michael Jordan myth even more.

It was just one of the many paradoxes of his life: basketball denied him the freedom he wanted, but it also provided a sanctuary, a brief diversion from the demands of being Michael Jordan, the celebrity. Every game, every appearance on television amplified the clamoring for Jordan to fulfill a hero's obligations. Yet competing on the court was also a way of shutting out the noise—the relentless questions from reporters and photographers, the incessant demands from product reps and producers, and the endless requests from autograph hounds and jock sniffers. The court was the one place in his life that truly belonged to him. And the more famous he became, the more he lived for the game. In the middle of a game, his singular focus on the competition transformed the crowd into a blur of colors. "It's the only place I can get relief from what's happening off the court," he said after winning the 1991 NBA title. "Basketball is my escape, my refuge. It seems that everything else is so . . . complicated."[1]

As he left the court after each game, he could feel the eyes of the crowd fixed on his body, like he was something other than a person—an object of desire. Shielded by a team of security guards, he headed toward the steep steps leading down to the locker room in the bowels of Chicago Stadium. Every night the same ritual took place after the game: hundreds of fans flocked near the stairway just to get within feet of Jordan. Standing near him, grown men beamed like children. Women shouted his name, calling for his attention: *"Michael! Michael!"* Kids stretched out their hands hoping for a high five, while others froze, silently staring in awe at the sight of their idol.

The prying eyes followed him inside the cramped stadium locker room, where a gaggle of reporters would surround his empty cubicle, waiting for him to appear. Whereas most players did not mind answering questions while wearing only a towel, Jordan refused to disrobe in front of the press, even in the confines of a locker room. "I never do that," he insisted. He considered it a matter of dignity. Usually, he dressed in the trainer's room or told the team media director to keep the locker room closed until he had finished putting on a tailored suit. Jordan once said that if a fan only saw him once, he wanted that person to see him as respectable and sophisticated.[2]

When he finally returned to his cubicle, the circle of reporters was still there, crowding Jordan and blocking the doorway, creating a fire hazard. Towering over the correspondents, with tape recorders and microphones extended to his chin, Jordan faced klieg lights and dozens of cameras. Over the course of interviews, reporters squeezed closer together, like passengers on a packed L train, inching close enough to feel Jordan breathe, hanging on his every word.

In his postgame interviews Jordan armored himself, rarely saying anything revealing. He had learned from his father to keep people at arm's length, never letting outsiders get inside his small circle of trust. James Jordan "could talk to anybody," Michael said long after his father died. "He could get along with anybody." James could talk with a stranger for hours and when the conversation ended his new acquaintance could walk away knowing little about him except that he was "a nice gentleman." Michael said that his father "never let people into his life. He never let people see his thoughts. His secrets. I have those traits. I can sit and talk to all the different sponsors, and they know only as much as I want them to know. I am always able to maintain that mystique."[3]

Michael Jordan only let people see what he wanted them to see. It was a conscious choice, influenced as much by his upbringing as by a culture that had turned him into a performance artist. Throughout his career, virtually every aspect of his life was crafted for public consumption. It was as if he occupied a permanent stage where the television cameras never stopped rolling. Everything Jordan did could be seen on tape, played and replayed from every angle. In a way, his life story had become a continuous stream of episodes in an ongoing production, a phenomenon that made it difficult for the public to separate the man from the myth, Michael Jordan from Air Jordan.

In a culture where the most powerful forms of entertainment blurred the lines between reality and fiction, the authentic and inauthentic, the illusion created by television producers and advertisers turned the most famous basketball player in the world into an international idol of personal and collective fantasy. His ubiquitous depiction on celluloid had a cumulative effect, expanding both his fame and the public demand for more and more sensational images of him.

His celebrity was the product of a particular time and place, the country's ideals and innovations, its advancements in television and technology, and a culture in which entertainment was—and remains—the primary value of American life. Yet the pressures of celebrity troubled Jordan, even when he closed his eyes at night. Sometimes vivid nightmares stirred him from sleep. In one version, he robbed a bank. In another dream he abused cocaine. In others he imagined he had become an alcoholic. The terrors all had a common theme, he said: "They're nightmares of something terrible happening to me that would destroy a lot of people's conceptions of me—that's the biggest nightmare I live every day."[4]

Jordan's great fear that he might do something that would tarnish his image and damage his reputation with the public stemmed in large part from the racial conflicts that defined America in the 1980s and 1990s. He realized there was a certain danger to being admired by so many white kids who were not yet "old enough to see color." Jordan believed that if he failed to uphold his standing in society, he would face a punitive backlash from white adults. "Who knows what their parents might say? And they can be the biggest influence in changing me from Michael Jordan the person to Michael Jordan the black guy."[5]

His words revealed an internal struggle that came from living a life of "double consciousness," the life of a famous Black man looking at himself through the eyes of white crowds. Despite his wealth and fame, Jordan recognized he was one misstep away from being reminded that he was not just an American but a Black man living in America. That personal strife, tightly intertwined with the country's racial traumas, shaped the way he fashioned himself.[6]

For all that sportswriters have written about Jordan, the centrality of race—and white America's tenuous acceptance of Black heroes—has been overlooked in his story. During Jordan's career with the Chicago Bulls, journalists, most of them white men, tended to diminish the importance of race in his life. For example, in his otherwise insightful biography, *Playing for Keeps*, David Halberstam says little about how race shaped Jordan's rise or how it framed the way Americans viewed him. Halberstam suggested that because Jordan came of age in the post–civil rights era, after the dissolution of de jure segregation, "precious little had been denied him because of race." Although there's a kernel of truth to that version of history—Jordan had faced fewer overt racial barriers than the generation that grew up during the years of Jim Crow—writers like Halberstam have ignored how his racial consciousness and the country's social conflicts influenced the making of Michael Jordan into an American hero.[7]

Jordan knew what fans wanted from him. They demanded a Black star who could smile and reassure them that all was right in the world. What mattered most, perhaps as much as basketball talent, was the perception of his character. That would be Jordan's trademark. And protecting it meant maintaining a mystique whenever he stepped into the spotlight. The Michael Jordan that America came to know—the character who appeared on-screen—performed for the cameras as well as any actor. He fully understood, as Gay Talese once wrote of another immortal ballplayer, that the sports hero must always play the part and preserve the myth.[8]

In his ascendance as an NBA champion, Jordan became the most famous American in the world. Yet he remained mysterious. But that is the way Jordan designed it. He understood that the less real he seemed, that the more he buried his politics and his past battles with racism, the more likable he would appear to people living under the illusion that the nation had solved its racial dilemmas. If Americans focused on his remarkable feats and good deeds, on the scenes and stories presented in the press, then he wouldn't have to reveal himself and race wouldn't matter. His universal popularity depended upon America's comfort with a world where spectacle supplants truth and people consume deceptions like water out of a willingness to believe comfortable lies about themselves and their country.

Jumpman tells the intertwined stories of Michael Jordan's rise in American culture and how he won his first championship during the 1990–1991 season. It examines how he came to be seen as an emblem of the country's racial progress and how the pressures of being a national symbol changed him. This is a story about basketball's place in America, which inevitably makes it a story about race. Black players—especially Jordan, Earvin "Magic" Johnson, Isiah Thomas, and Charles Barkley—redefined the sport. They not only changed the way the game was played but also reoriented the business of basketball around the cult of personality. Although I am interested in Jordan's life and career, this book is not a biography. Rather, it explores how the NBA and Nike, publicists and producers, reporters, and fans molded a heroic role for Jordan that transformed him into a myth. In short, *Jumpman* is about the making and meaning of Michael Jordan.

The origins of this book can be traced to my youth, growing up in the suburbs north of Chicago, a sports-crazed city that worshipped Michael Jordan. During the late eighties and nineties, no city was as closely associated with a single individual as Chicago was with Jordan. Back then, he seemed invincible, a fearless legend who couldn't miss. Fans admired him for his brilliant artistry, his grace and power, his incredible skill and indomitable will. He was charming, radiating the kind of warmth that made everyone feel welcome. Chicagoans felt like they knew him, like he could be their friend. He was endlessly praised for transcending race, as if a Black basketball player wielded a supernatural ability to make Chicago's racial troubles vanish. People found something meaningful about white fans accepting him as the hometown hero, as a representative of the entire city. "Jordan made us . . . feel better about ourselves and our city," wrote *Washington Post* columnist Michael Wilbon, a Chicago native. "This is a bolder, yet more tolerant place because he brought various peoples and cultures together—if only for two hours at a time—which is something segregated Chicago had always resisted."[9]

Wilbon's sentiment reflected a popular belief that Jordan's heroism was based on his ability to unify people across different races and ethnicities. His admirers viewed him as a powerful cultural figure who eclipsed America's social divisions. Others saw him as something less noble, as a symbol of a country obsessed with winning and the accumulation of wealth, a nation that had individualized the idea of success and celebrated ambition for its own sake.

As the public demands for him to be something more than a basketball player grew, Jordan was forced to reckon with the social and political implications of his lofty platform. He may have been a singular individual, but his accomplishments never belonged solely to him, free of expectation or scrutiny. His rise to become the most recognizable Black athlete in America took place in the context of a painful history of struggle and suffering by a people long denied the power and prosperity he enjoyed. Coming from a community that desperately needed champions—not just on the court—meant carrying the aspirations of Black America, a heavy burden that weighed on Jordan like an imperial crown.

Jordan carried that load during his pursuit of a championship amid internal discord among the Bulls, a time when his coach, Phil Jackson, and a league of rivals tested his ambition and resolve. Before the 1990–1991 season, he rarely confronted the consequences of his aspirations or achievements. But between those two years, the threads that spun his mystique came unraveled.

Jordan wanted to define himself on his own terms, unbound by anything or anyone. He needed to break free. The Jumpman lived to fly.

Chapter One

THE HERO BUSINESS

"We're in the collective business of selling heroes."

—NBA COMMISSIONER DAVID STERN, 1984

In 1987, Don Hewitt, the creator and executive producer of *60 Minutes*, realized that Michael Jordan was the perfect subject for a profile. A longtime sports fan, Hewitt had grown fascinated by Jordan's athletic prowess and sudden fame. He wondered how Jordan, "an instant millionaire," a twenty-four-year-old basketball player who had never won an NBA championship, had become the most famous endorser in sports. The *60 Minutes* segment demonstrated how television would expand Jordan's reach into Middle America and help define the mythic hero who came to dominate the national imagination in the years to come.[1]

In an interview with Diane Sawyer, *60 Minutes* introduced Jordan as a basketball prodigy, a humble and dedicated star who represented the virtues of the NBA—and the financial interests of several companies, including Chevrolet, Nike, and Coca-Cola. During the show audiences watched him take off from the free-throw line, his tongue wagging out from his mouth as he levitated in slow motion before thrusting the ball through the basket. Then CBS showed

By the end of the 1980s, Michael Jordan had become "America's favorite athlete," the biggest star in the NBA's hero business. Credit: Steve Lipofsky/Lipofskyphoto.com

footage of a young Black boy imitating his moves on the blacktop, wearing a pair of Air Jordans. "Kids know," Sawyer said, "that Jordan plays for the same reason they do: he loves it."[2]

Sawyer explained that Jordan was unique among NBA players. This was not just because of his immense talent but because he was the only one who had a "love of the game" clause written into his contract. Under the NBA's collective bargaining agreement, a standard player contract could be voided if a player got injured participating in an unsanctioned basketball game or athletic event. Yet Jordan insisted on a clause that gave him the freedom to play basketball anytime, anywhere. "There was no way I could live with that kind of restriction," he said. "I needed to play."[3]

By the time CBS recorded the interview, in the middle of Jordan's third professional season, he had already emerged as "the most prolific scoring guard in NBA history," finishing the year with the fifth-highest scoring average ever achieved—37.1 points per game. He became the first NBA player to reach three thousand points in a season since Wilt Chamberlain did it in 1962–1963. Although he had missed most of the previous season with a broken foot, once he was cleared to return, he came back with a vengeance, determined to prove that no one could stop him. Chicagoans marveled as he exceeded thirty points in all but fifteen of the Bulls' games, scored forty or more points in thirty-seven contests, and scored at least fifty points eight times.[4]

Yet, for all of Jordan's fireworks, the Bulls remained mediocre, and critics blamed him for the team's poor 40–42 record. Jordan dominated the ball, taking nearly a third of the team's shots and stoking resentment among his teammates. Nonetheless, he maintained that the best way for the Bulls to win was for him to do everything he could to score.

Even so, Jordan remained the biggest draw in the NBA. "Everybody," Diane Sawyer said, "wants to see the player who's pretty much a team by himself." During the interview, Jordan appeared anodyne and accessible, completely charming, comfortable answering questions about any subject—his family, fame, dating, even race. When Sawyer asked him about being a Black basketball star, Jordan insisted that talent mattered more than race, demonstrating his faith in competition and meritocracy. Jordan said that he aspired to be seen not as a Black man but as an individual unburdened by his skin color. "When [people] think of Michael Jordan," he said, "I don't want them to think that he's black or white. I want them to think of him as a person." Throughout his career, Jordan repeated this standard line, as if he had rehearsed it in front of a mirror. That Jordan did not want the public to think of him as Black revealed his desire to cross over into the mainstream where white America defined commercial success. It also revealed a yearning to separate himself from the criticisms and consequences that came with being a famous Black athlete.[5]

Listening to him, viewers realized he was not just selling sneakers and sodas. He was endorsing an ideal vision of America, perpetuating the myth that race no longer mattered. During his career with the Bulls, Jordan virtually never revealed any frustration or anger about the persistence of racism in America or his personal struggles with discrimination. He left his private pain in the past—or so it seemed on camera. It was an intentional choice that allowed him to achieve widespread acceptance from an audience that wanted to believe that race and politics should be separate from sports. Avoiding any meaningful discussion about race meant no one really knew Jordan's true thoughts and feelings. That silence, however, revealed an unreconciled conflict between his lived experience in Black America and how he wanted white America to see him. Seeking respect and recognition in both worlds, Jordan couldn't escape his dilemma: the need to make race important and illusory at the same time.[6]

In his drive for success, Jordan focused more on individual advancement than collective social goals, recasting what it meant to be a Black hero in a country that liked to think of itself as colorblind. In the 1980s, his emergence as a crossover phenomenon carried personal and political repercussions. By the end of the decade, he had achieved virtually every professional dream he ever imagined—save winning an NBA championship. But his commercial success off the court left him grappling with the conflict between his need to be liked and his need to be himself. Becoming a crossover hero could sometimes feel triumphant, an important breakthrough for a young Black man who defied the odds, but there were limits to his liberation. For Jordan, whatever racial progress his achievements signified, living a life of notoriety came with a cost.

David Falk could not have been more pleased with Jordan's appearance on *60 Minutes*. One of the most influential figures in professional sports, Falk, the man who orchestrated the packaging, marketing, and corporate synergy behind America's greatest pitchman, called the CBS profile "our 10-minute Michael Jordan commercial." Television, Falk understood, created mutual benefits for Jordan and his sponsors: it both helped Jordan sell products and made him more famous. Most important, the medium helped make him what no Black man had ever been before—"America's favorite athlete."[7]

Looking out the windows that stretched across an entire wall of his eighteenth-story office in Arlington, Virginia, Falk could see the Kennedy Center, Lincoln Memorial, Washington Monument, and the expanse of marble and greenery that made up the nation's capital. From his vantage point, a few blocks away from the White House, Falk positioned himself within reach of the nation's power brokers, a long way from his father's Long Island butcher shop. His ascendance began in 1974, when he joined ProServ, a sports management firm founded by Donald Dell, best known for representing some of the biggest tennis stars in the world, including Stan Smith, Jimmy Connors, and Arthur Ashe. At that time the agency included very few clients from professional basketball. As an industrious junior partner, Falk recognized that he would have to carve out a niche for himself and began signing professional basketball players. Before he negotiated Jordan's contract with Nike, most of the major endorsement deals went to tennis players and golfers, athletes in individual sports who enjoyed an international following. Unlike basketball players, they were "self-contained business enterprises," Falk explained, "separate from the governing bodies of the sport." In contrast, corporate America defined professional basketball players as representatives of teams, limited by regional geography. In tennis and golf, Falk said, "the mystique is the individual, whereas no matter how great Bill Russell or Bob Cousy was, it was the Celtic dynasty—it was always institutional. Michael changed all that. Single-handed."[8]

In 1984, when Jordan and his parents interviewed sports management firms, there were very few Black agents representing professional athletes. If a Black athlete wanted access to corporate America, he often found it with a white agent like Falk or Donald Dell. A perception existed among professional athletes that Black agents lacked the experience and the contacts to help them manage their careers. ProServ, however, had a remarkable track record representing Black athletes, perhaps none more important than Arthur Ashe. In the late 1960s, Dell, a liberal tennis star who had worked in the Johnson administration's Office of Economic Opportunity, began helping Ashe acquire endorsement contracts with the racquet company Head, Catalina sportswear, Coca-Cola, and Philip Morris. Much of Ashe's marketing success, however, depended on affluent tennis fans and overseas consumers, not Middle America. Over time, though, he and Dell became close friends who could talk frankly about the racism Ashe encountered in a lily-white sport and the challenges he faced chipping away at the hardened racial barriers in corporate America—barriers that Jordan would face as well.[9]

When Jordan and his parents met Dell and Falk in Chapel Hill, they counted on Dean Smith, Jordan's coach at the University of North Carolina (UNC), to serve as gatekeeper. Smith vetted every agent who wanted to speak to one of his players. There was no one the Jordans trusted more than Coach Smith, and if he trusted Donald Dell, then they would be willing to meet with him. Before Jordan, Smith had directed numerous UNC players to ProServ, including James Worthy. During an hour-and-a-half presentation, the attorneys from ProServ explained that they did more than negotiate contracts. They would manage Jordan's accounting, investments, and scheduling. After Jordan signed with ProServ, Falk became his main representative—his attorney, as he liked to say—the person who negotiated his endorsement deals.[10]

In 1984, Jordan arrived in Chicago as the third pick in the NBA draft, hailed as a "patriotic treasure" for leading the US team that won a gold medal at the Los Angeles Olympics. A spectacle of American superiority, the '84 Olympics enhanced Jordan's image, transforming the best player on Team USA into a symbol of the country's democratic promise. His breakout moment came at a time when President Ronald Reagan declared that "a new patriotism is spreading across the country." Jordan's Olympic performance fit perfectly into a heightened mood of patriotic fervor and Reagan's vision of what was possible in America. The president espoused an ethos embraced by Jordan: winning was not enough. The American ideal was about defying limits, "going as far as you can go."[11]

Jordan appeared to be the perfect sports star for Reagan's America. Writers depicted him as wholesome, genial, and completely devoted to family, making him even more appealing to fans and sponsors. Here was a young Black southerner, the grandson of sharecroppers, raised by Christian parents from Wilmington, North Carolina, his father an Air Force veteran, his mother the moral compass of the family, fulfilling the American Dream. Jordan would "come to *represent* America," David Breskin wrote in a *GQ* profile, "as in we may not make cars or televisions too well, but we turn out a helluva Michael Jordan."[12]

Following Jordan's spectacular performance at the Olympics, Falk believed that his client had gained invaluable international exposure and would "come to be seen as an All-American hero." But convincing the executives on Madison Avenue that Jordan could be the country's most popular pitchman was about as easy as selling Tar Heel T-shirts on the Duke campus. At the time, very few Black faces from the NBA appeared in national advertising campaigns. In fact, only 5 percent of the league's 280 players appeared in television or print ads. "There was a general feeling lurking beneath the surface that black team-sport athletes were not marketable," recalled David Falk. "Not so much by the people, the consuming populace, but by the people who were making the decisions to put them on television."[13]

Racist perceptions of NBA players made it very difficult for them to secure endorsement deals. Advertising representatives were convinced that reports of widespread drug use among rich Black players alienated white America. In 1980, *Los Angeles Times* writer Chris Cobbs published a damaging story incriminating nearly the entire league. Although he acknowledged there was no way to know exactly how many NBA players used cocaine, after interviewing team officials, he estimated that as many as 75 percent of the league's players used illegal drugs—almost the exact same percentage as the NBA's Black athletes. At the same time that critics complained the NBA was "too Black" for white fans, they bemoaned that the sport had become an undisciplined playground game of overpaid showboats who came from "unstable families in inner-city ghettoes."[14]

If Jordan was going to break through as an endorser, he would have to defy stereotypes, much like Julius Erving had done during the late seventies and early eighties. Jordan admired Erving for becoming the "first basketball player to combine dramatic athletic ability on the court with a clean, positive image off the court that connected with corporate America." A model of propriety and self-control, Erving internalized his political views, not wanting to alienate any group and offering Jordan a template for marketing products and himself. Erving may have once looked like a Black Panther in sneakers, but in the late seventies he cut his trademark Afro and goatee, cultivating the assuring appearance of a "gentleman" like Sidney Poitier. "I had to go for that corporate business look," he admitted.[15]

Perhaps, Jordan thought, he could change the minds of advertisers by following Erving's example as a Black star whose popularity cut across racial lines. Erving had demonstrated that a Black basketball star had to play by certain rules if he wanted to be accepted by corporate America and a fraternity of white sportswriters. Extolled by reporters as "a heroic role model who cared about family, society, [and] morals," Erving earned endorsement deals with Converse, Coca-Cola, Ford, Crest, Spaulding, and Chapstick, a remarkable sponsorship considering that during Jim Crow Black men were often portrayed in popular culture as cartoonish buffoons with exaggerated facial features and large lips.[16]

Julius Erving may have made the Pro Leather the shoe of choice on the playgrounds, but Converse never built a singular campaign around him the way Nike did for Jordan. Before

Jordan signed with Nike in 1984, the two most influential makers of basketball shoes were Converse and Adidas, though hardly any NBA players became rich from shoe deals. Magic Johnson, Larry Bird, and Julius Erving all wore Converse, but none of them made more than $70,000 endorsing the Pro Leather shoes each year. Converse provided nowhere near the individual marketing attention that Nike delivered for Jordan. At one point all three players appeared together in the same commercial selling the same shoe.[17]

Phil Knight, Nike's founder and CEO, recognized that Converse ruled the domestic basketball market and that Adidas offered a desirable product. After Nike posted its first-ever quarterly loss in 1984, he contemplated cutting spending on basketball altogether. Although more than one hundred NBA players wore Nikes—most of them being paid somewhere between $8,000 and $50,000 each year for doing so—having unrecognizable athletes wearing the swoosh did little for sales. Rob Strasser, a marketing genius with "a gambler's instincts," convinced Knight to embrace a risky business strategy: allow most of those contracts to expire and invest all the company's advertising resources into a single basketball phenom.[18]

Strasser believed that the future of Nike depended on the cult of personality. In 1983, he drafted a memo that became Nike's mission statement: "Individual athletes, even more than teams, will be the heroes; symbols more and more of what real people can't do anymore—risk and win." Nike desperately needed a major win, something that could boost sales and change public perceptions of a cash-strapped company known mostly for selling running shoes. Knight agreed that Nike needed to invest in the "hero business." If Nike could create heroes and attract their fans, he thought, then those fans would become customers. "Nobody roots for a product," he said.[19]

Nike took an enormous chance mortgaging the company's future—committing millions of dollars—to Jordan, especially at a time when most Americans knew little about him. Only serious college basketball fans who had followed him at UNC or had seen him compete during the Olympics knew who he was. But Nike scout John Paul "Sonny" Vaccaro campaigned hard for Jordan. Vaccaro said the kid from UNC had it all: talent, charisma, and a great smile. Best of all, he added, Jordan "could *fly* through the air!" When Strasser asked him if he would bet his job on Jordan, Vaccaro didn't hesitate. "Yes," he answered. "No question. I'd pay him whatever it takes to get him." Strasser trusted Vaccaro completely. He began working with his team at Nike on developing a strategy for signing Jordan and set up a meeting with his agent, David Falk. Soon after striking a deal, Strasser and Falk began contemplating how to make Michael Jordan synonymous with Nike.[20]

Jordan's Nike deal fit into Falk's broader marketing plan for him, one built around American-based companies with global sales. The Nike contract made sense for several reasons. Falk understood that although most companies were reluctant to sign Black athletes as endorsers, a deal with Nike gave Jordan marketing credibility since he was a basketball player selling basketball shoes and athletic apparel. (Similarly, Jordan's second endorsement deal, for a signature basketball with Wilson Sporting Goods, would enhance his authenticity as a spokesman.) Drawing on his experience working with tennis players who had their own lines of equipment and clothing, Falk encouraged Nike to market Jordan as an individual personality, pushing the company to create an exclusive shoe line called Air Jordan. In his mind, the Nike deal was critical because if he could get a shoe company to make his client more visible in American culture, then he could point to the success with Nike as leverage with other companies.[21]

The contract with Nike proved pivotal for securing Jordan's endorsements with three major American brands: Coca-Cola, McDonald's, and Chevrolet. "We wanted to be involved with a limited number of American companies that were prestigious, the fabric of America," Falk said. "So, we have Coca-Cola, McDonald's and Chevrolet. Those companies represent what America is all about. They have products used by the masses." Falk convinced corporate representatives that cross-promotion would transfer the value of Jordan's endorsements from one company to another. McDonald's and Coca-Cola would not have to spend as much money on marketing Jordan, he argued, because Nike had already produced commercials featuring him.[22]

But it wasn't easy for Falk to convince corporate executives that Jordan could enhance their brands. "Outside of the shoe business," Falk said, "there was virtually no interest in Michael Jordan in 1984." That year, however, there were growing signs that Black stars were entering the mainstream in unprecedented ways. Black crossovers who appealed to white audiences shaped every aspect of the entertainment industry—television, movies, music, and sports. Vanessa Williams broke the color line at the Miss America pageant, becoming the first Black winner and representing a new standard of beauty—one that was not white. Eddie Murphy, "the hottest actor in Hollywood," starred in *Beverly Hills Cop*, the highest-grossing film of the year. Murphy's popularity, noted a *New York Times* writer, made him "a historic figure, America's newest and perhaps biggest black superstar." Michael Jackson, the King of Pop, won a record eight Grammy Awards for his *Thriller* album. The "Jackson phenomenon" shattered records for album sales, concert attendance, and endorsement deals, including an unprecedented $5 million sponsorship with Pepsi. And the *Cosby Show* debuted as the top-rated program on television, lauded for humanizing a Black family on-screen. White viewers praised the show as "more American" because it avoided storylines that dealt with racism and the political realities of the times. That powerful message indicated that many white people would accept Black folks as *American* if they ceased talking about race.[23]

It was a bargain Jordan accepted. When Falk spoke to sponsors, he insisted that Jordan could project "an All-American image," a euphemism that had once meant white. But in the mid-1980s, sponsors and sportswriters cast Jordan as "America's player," a hero who had moved "beyond race." Indeed, writers rarely mentioned his race, framing his ascendance as a great American story, not a great *Black* American story. "There's something very American about him," observed conservative political commentator Shelby Steele. "He seems to have a good business sense. He's very refined. He's the kind of figure who goes down easy with most of America."[24]

Jordan's position as an all-American role model took on greater importance after June 1986, when the national conversation around the War on Drugs—and the NBA's role in fighting it—intensified in the aftermath of Len Bias's death. Just two days after the Boston Celtics made Bias the second pick in the NBA draft, the collegiate star from the University of Maryland died from a cocaine overdose. Although cocaine remained a popular recreational drug among white professionals, socialites, and celebrities, Bias's death and the growing news coverage of the inner cities' alleged crack epidemic fueled a moral panic about Black criminality. It hardly seemed to matter that erroneous reports circulated throughout newsrooms that Bias, a modest young man from a tight-knit, middle-class family, had succumbed to crack—"the demon drug"—when in fact he had snorted powdered cocaine.[25]

The death of a talented Black basketball player who drew comparisons to Michael Jordan created greater urgency for escalating the War on Drugs, a movement that also shaped the politics of the NBA. In October, Congress passed the Anti-Drug Abuse Act. The law prescribed mandatory minimum sentences for the possession and distribution of cocaine; it also mandated far more severe punishments for offenses involving crack, a significant difference that created enormous disparities in prison sentences between white and Black offenders. Furthermore, it increased police surveillance in urban Black neighborhoods. Although the NBA had already instituted "a reasonable cause" drug testing policy in 1983, after the death of Bias politicians and editorialists pressured the league to implement mandatory drug testing for all players, a proposal that Jordan supported even though his union did not. "Just saying no to drugs isn't enough," he said in 1987. "You have to live it. That's why I favor mandatory drug testing in the NBA."[26]

Jordan joined the Reagan administration's "Just Say No" campaign, repeating a simple slogan that did not require him to discuss how the War on Drugs had become a war on Black America or how countless kids in the inner cities grew up in neighborhoods where saying no meant risking their lives to gang violence. He didn't have to know the issues. All he had to do was smile and offer simple platitudes. Visiting schools and hospitals, he wore "Say No!" T-shirts and delivered speeches about the dangers of drugs, telling audiences about how he distanced himself from perilous teammates. He recounted a story from his rookie season, during a preseason trip to Peoria, when he entered a hotel suite and found "practically the whole team" drunk, stoned, and coked up. Jordan turned around and walked out of the room. Knowing right from wrong, he just said, *No*. His message of self-restraint and personal responsibility, popular among conservative Americans, helped Jordan define himself in the public imagination as a hero worthy of admiration—the antithesis of the stereotypical Black baller succumbing to the "all-American drug."[27]

It seemed that everybody loved Michael Jordan and what he represented. Falk recognized before anyone else Jordan's potential for fulfilling an American ideal. After Jordan's appearance on *60 Minutes*, Falk told *Sports Illustrated*, "If you were to create a media athlete and star . . . spectacular talent, midsized, well-spoken, attractive, accessible, old-time values, wholesome, clean, natural, not too goody two-shoes, with a little bit of deviltry in him—you'd invent Michael. He's the first modern crossover in team sports. We think he transcends race."[28]

Jordan was not the first Black athlete praised for transcending race. Ambitious and entrepreneurial, O. J. Simpson created the paradigm for the crossover athlete coveted on Madison Avenue. Simpson consciously sought white approval and corporate acceptance, demonstrating disdain toward anything that seemed too political. In the late 1960s, when he first emerged as a national football star at the University of Southern California, he rejected the Black Power movement and dismissed the debate around Black athletes boycotting the 1968 Olympics in protest against racism. While the "revolt of the Black athlete" disrupted the sports world, Simpson acted as a counterrevolutionary, suppressing within himself any expression of Black rage.[29]

His breakthrough as a corporate spokesman occurred because he presented himself as a "good Negro," an advertisement for a colorblind America. Simpson's fans found him charming, affable, and unthreatening. Before he played a single game in the National Football League, he signed endorsement deals with Chevrolet and RC Cola. In 1975, when Hertz built a national advertising campaign around him, the rental car company's consumer surveys indicated that people perceived Simpson as "colorless." A Hertz advertising executive later explained, "People thought of O. J. Simpson as O. J. Simpson, not O. J. Simpson, the black athlete." White America's imprimatur filled Simpson with pride. "My biggest accomplishment," he said in 1969, "is that people look at me as a man first, not a black man."[30]

Twenty years later, Jordan echoed Simpson's colorblind rhetoric. "Sometimes I think I'm looked upon as not just as a black person, but as a person," he said. "And I think that's totally new ground for us—and for society. I'm happy to be a pioneer. When I say, 'Don't think of me as white or black,' all I'm saying is: View me as a person." Jordan aimed to define his place in America more as an individual than as an ambassador for his race. Maintaining his esteemed reputation across racial lines, venerated for being articulate, wholesome, and intelligent, required that he defy the fallacy that Black men did not possess those traits. Thus, the narratives about Jordan transcending race reflected a larger myth: that once he conquered the country's racial barriers, he became liberated from his skin color, which made him more American and more heroic.[31]

Some white people believed that embracing Jordan meant they didn't see skin color. Under this line of thinking, they hardly even noticed race or cared about racial differences anymore. But identifying someone's race was not the problem. The problem with colorblindness—denying the existence of race—was that it allowed people to deny the persistence of racism. By the early 1980s, surveys indicated that 90 percent of whites believed that Black and white children should attend the same schools, 71 percent opposed segregated neighborhoods, and 80 percent said that they would support a Black candidate for president—profound signs that white Americans supported racial equality. But the reality was that white Americans' love affair with Jordan and other Black celebrities did little to erase stereotypes of Black people. In 1989, an ABC/*Washington Post* survey indicated that three-quarters of white people believed it was "common sense," not racial prejudice, to avoid Black neighborhoods. A year later, a survey conducted by the National Opinion Research Center at the University of Chicago revealed that most white people believed that Black folks were more likely to be lazy, less intelligent, less patriotic, and more violent than white people, belying the notion that colorblindness had washed over the country.[32]

In Jordan's America, colorblindness meant different things to different people. Liberals linked colorblindness to racial equality and legal protections against the institutionalization of white supremacy, while conservatives viewed it as a means of promoting meritocratic values and rolling back the advancements of the civil rights movement. Focusing on race, conservatives argued, robbed people of their individuality and gave unnecessary advantages to particular groups—especially Black Americans. Opposing affirmative action, in 1986, President Ronald Reagan declared, "We want a colorblind society—a society that in the words of Dr. King judges people not by the color of their skin but by the content of their character." Distorting King's message, Reagan did not mention the fact that the slain civil rights leader devoted his life to fighting against white supremacy or that he advocated for affirmative action programs.[33]

Yet for many Americans, Black and white alike, colorblindness offered a meaningful aspiration that all people should strive toward, including Jordan. He told a *Chicago Tribune* writer that his parents raised him to be colorblind. "I never see you for the color," he said. "I don't look at you as black or white, just as a person." He also said that he had not encountered racial barriers in his professional career, a comforting notion for white fans who appreciated that he did not harbor racial resentment. His popularity, together with Magic Johnson's, proved to NBA commissioner David Stern that the league had resolved its racial dilemma. Although the racial composition of the NBA had not changed much since the mid-1970s, no one complained that the league was "too

Black" anymore. It seemed that the real trouble for white critics was not so much that there were too many Black players but that the NBA lacked the *right kind* of Black players. In 1990, when a reporter asked Stern if racism made it difficult for the NBA to attract white fans, he replied, "It's a dead issue; our fans grow up colorblind."[34]

Corporate executives agreed with Stern. "The public, especially young people, is colorblind in terms of its athletic heroes," said David Green, a senior vice president with McDonald's. In the late 1980s, Jordan's sponsors—McDonald's, Coca-Cola, and Chevrolet—repeatedly relayed this message in his commercials. In Chevy's Chicagoland promotions, seen across the city and its surrounding suburbs, two young friends, one white, one Black, encounter their hero. In one spot, the boys meet at Chicago Stadium, where they race to their seats, smiling widely, knowing they will see Jordan play. Chevy was not selling a specific car in the ad. Rather, the main theme is that Jordan, like Chevrolet, represents "the heartbeat of America." In another commercial, the boys meet Jordan at night on a city street before he drives away in his shiny red Blazer. Similarly, McDonald's told the story of Jordan joining an integrated group of kids at a local franchise. Surrounded by children, Jordan appeared approachable and friendly, the kind of hero parents could trust with their kids. For Coca-Cola, Jordan played the good neighbor, delivering a six-pack of soda to three friends playing in a tree house. Wearing his white-and-red Air Jordans, he comes running out of his mother's home, cradling the cans like a basketball. While his real mother, Deloris, cheers him from her front-porch rocking chair, Jordan leaps into the air, stretching toward the top of the tree house and delivering Coca-Cola to three ecstatic boys.[35]

In each of the commercials, children bond around Jordan. Watched together, the ads communicate a simple message that he had already expressed in numerous interviews: "I don't believe in race. I believe in friendship." Jordan did not just move American products. He sold a story of racial integration, linking corporations to democratic ideals. If white Americans once saw O. J. Simpson as a Black role model for erasing racism, Jordan followed in his footsteps. For years Blacks athletes had enjoyed commercial endorsements, but none before Jordan were truly marketed as a galvanizing force for racial unity.[36]

His commercials—and NBA broadcasts—projected a kind of "virtual integration," where Black athletes like Jordan became the imaginary playmates of white fans. Television created an artificial experience, giving white Americans the feeling of having meaningful contact with Black people without having social interactions with them in real life. The medium brought Jordan into millions of American living rooms, turning him into someone people believed they really knew. Reflecting on the fabricated images of Black people on television, Harvard historian Henry Louis Gates Jr. wrote, "When American society could not successfully achieve the social reformation it sought in the '60s through the Great Society, television solved the problem simply by inventing symbols of that transformation in the '80s."[37]

Much of Jordan's appeal derived from the fact that he seemed to really be like the innocent, joyful guy he played on television. "He's told us over the past few years to drink Coke, wolf Big Macs, drive Chevrolets, wear Nikes, apply Johnson products, sport Guy Laroche watches, bounce Wilson basketballs, don Bigsby & Karuthers suits, not drive drunk, stay off drugs, work hard, be happy and listen to our parents," David Breskin wrote in 1989. "People are not only awed by Michael Jordan, they *like* him. They believe him."[38]

Jordan's ability to cross over without coming off as phony or unnatural made him popular. He knew how to adapt to an audience. With "his Barry White bass voice alternately starring at power lunches and slurring street jive in the locker room," Curry Kirkpatrick wrote, Jordan "seemed totally secure in either world." Covering Jordan later in his career, Skip Bayless made a similar observation: Jordan frequently used profanity and slang in the privacy of the locker room, but when the cameras were rolling, he "invented his own news-conference language" that people of all ages, races, and backgrounds could understand. Regardless of the setting, he knew how to connect with people, how to earn their acceptance. "Somehow," Breskin wrote, "he manages to be both the downest brother and the whitest bread at the same time."[39]

By 1990, Michael Jordan had become a ubiquitous figure. His name could be found in a hundred daily newspapers and his face appeared virtually everywhere: on television, T-shirts, trading cards, billboards, posters, advertisements, and magazine covers. Most important, he had become a national symbol, a bridge between white America and Black America, evoking the nation's past and its promise for a better future. Writing for *Esquire*, Black novelist John Edgar Wideman suggested that for some people, Jordan "is proof that there are no rules about race, no limits to what a black man can accomplish in our society. Or maybe he's the exception that proves the rule, the absence of rules." American desires for a Black star who could transcend the country's complex racial history helped transform Jordan into a national hero. For the celebrants who claimed that the Bulls star made "us rise above our obsession with race," Jordan provided a reprieve from the troubles of the world.[40]

Soon, though, he would discover that escaping the country's racial dilemma was about as easy as slipping out of a straitjacket.

Chapter Two

THE SPIKE AND MIKE SHOW

"Granny, before I let anyone take those shoes, they'll have
to kill me."

—Michael Eugene Thomas, freshman at Meade Senior
High School and proud owner of Air Jordans, 1989

"Only when black athletes or entertainers get big visibility
do they have to be the moral conscience of America. The
Nike commercials Michael Jordan and I do have never gotten anyone killed."

—Spike Lee, 1990

Toting a ball under his arm as he stood next to the most famous
athlete in the world, Mars Blackmon, a scrawny, wisecracking
motormouth break-dancer, stole the show. A product of eighties urban culture and the imagination of movie director Spike
Lee, Blackmon appeared in a grainy black-and-white Nike commercial sporting a Brooklyn bike cap, thick black-rimmed Cazal
specks, a dangling nameplate around his neck, a tank top, and his
pride and joy—fresh Air Jordan sneakers.

With the enthusiasm of a carnival barker, he announces, "Yo! Mars Blackmon here with my main man Michael Jordan." As Lee's cinematic alter ego from his comedy *She's Gotta Have It*, Blackmon is obsessed with his Air Jordans. In the movie, he fetishizes the shoes, refusing to remove them even when he makes love.

In the television spot, Blackmon, Jordan's biggest fan, wants to know the secret to his game. "What makes you the best player in the universe?" he asks. "Is it the vicious dunks?"

Jordan deadpans, "No, Mars."

Creeping behind Jordan, Blackmon wants to know "Is it the haircut?"

"No, Mars."

Thrusting a sneaker—the Air Jordan V—into the camera for a close-up, Blackmon asks *the question*: "Is it the shoes?"

Smirking, Jordan replies again, "No, Mars."

Blackmon insists, repeatedly, "Money, it's gotta be the shoes!"[1]

It's the classic double act: Jordan, the tall, stoic straight man, Lee, the diminutive, animated comic foil. The first installment of "The Spike and Mike Show" appeared on television in February 1988. Lacking all the usual commercial conventions, the spots had no voice-over announcer, no jingle, not so much as a clip of Jordan's athleticism. Before Lee and Jim Riswold—the irreverent creative director for the Wieden and Kennedy ad agency—made the ads, Nike's spots had basically amounted to highlight reels of Jordan dunking. As a result, most fans recognized Jordan the athlete but knew little about his personality. These commercials, however, humanized him in a way that basketball games and ESPN highlights could not.

The Spike and Mike Show did much more than that, though. The groundbreaking ads fused together elements of Hollywood and hip-hop, resulting in commercials that were as absorbing as

MTV videos. Signaling a watershed convergence for the worlds of sports, entertainment, and marketing, the campaign marked the beginning of a new age, in which Nike ceased being just a shoe company and became, in the words of Phil Knight, "a marketing organization." Nike's creative team no longer built commercials around the shoes themselves; instead, they merchandised athletes as characters who starred in their own television series, including Bo Jackson's "Bo Knows" campaign and "Mr. [David] Robinson's Neighborhood."[2]

For Nike, what mattered most was creating a story that audiences could follow from episode to episode, an approach that turned advertising into entertainment. Jordan's commercials with Spike Lee may have been short, David Halberstam observed in *Playing for Keeps*, "but there were so many of them and they were done with such talent and charm that they formed an ongoing story. Their cumulative effect was to create a figure who had the power and force and charisma of a major movie star."[3]

In the late 1980s and early 1990s, images of Mars Blackmon and his main man pervaded American culture. They could be seen on television, billboards, and posters. The success of the campaign—measured in the incredible sales of Air Jordans—carried the Chicago Bulls star beyond the boundaries of basketball, moving him into an orbit of celebrity that no other player had ever reached. "Nike has done such a job promoting me that I've turned into a dream," Jordan said. "In some ways it's taken me away from the game and turned me into an entertainer. To a lot of people, I'm just a person who stars in commercials."[4]

There were some critics, however, who linked the spots to flashes of violence in the inner cities. Reporters and cultural commentators started talking about a new crisis: Black teenagers seemed to be mugging and killing each other over expensive sneakers and sportswear. "In Chicago and other cities, including

Detroit, New York, and Los Angeles, such incidents," reported the *New York Times*, "underscore the degree to which street crime and violence are now endemic to life in the inner city, but also serve as a perverse measure of the hottest local fashion trend."[5]

Parents and educators debated who was responsible for "the sneaker killings." The fact that these stories were presented as news convinced much of the public that the crisis was real and that someone needed to stop it. But who exactly was responsible? Was it the companies that made and promoted the products? Was it the celebrity endorsers who hawked the shoes on television? Was it society itself, whose values had become too materialistic? Or was it politicians, whose failed policies ignored the deteriorating conditions of America's inner cities?

For the *New York Post*'s Phil Mushnick, a cynical crusader disillusioned with the greed and hypocrisy of professional sports, Jordan and Lee were the culprits. The sports world's "self-appointed watchdog," Mushnick earned a reputation for "always being in a rage." In many ways, he modeled himself after Dick Young, once known as the dean of sportswriters, a pugnacious curmudgeon whose confrontational style and reactionary politics inspired the scorn of critics. Mushnick fashioned himself as a blue-collar sports fan sitting on a bar stool, a populist voicing the outrage of Middle America. Comparing the Nike spokesmen to drug dealers who exploited poor Black youth, he fumed, "They're both working off a copy of the same marketing plan." Why didn't Jordan and Lee tell "these kids to stop killing each other?" Because Nike "bought their silence."[6]

Mushnick's polemics about Jordan, Lee, and inner-city violence appealed to the tabloid's readership, who relished sensational stories about crime and celebrity. The popularity of the *Post*, argued journalist Harold Evans, hinged on "a typology of the lurid," the urban fantasy the paper fleshed out over the course of each edition, playing on people's fears and desires, prejudices and dreams. The *Post*'s "circus layout," loud sans-serif headlines, and emotive wording were designed to "jostle, distract, and entertain, to say to the reader, Move on, read this, look at that." Facts mattered less than "scoops"—stories cobbled out of anecdotes and rumors. And the sports section relied upon opinionated columnists who fueled debates.[7]

Preaching from his soapbox, Mushnick claimed that the sneaker crimes had morphed into an epidemic. "It's happening every day, everywhere," he claimed without evidence. "Almost daily, cops in Los Angeles file reports on kids murdered for their sneakers." But these crimes were not just a "societal problem." In his view, Jordan and Lee encouraged a depraved indulgence, driving Black teens to kill for shoes they could not afford. For Mushnick, the solution was obvious: Nike had to stop running the ads. Otherwise, Jordan and Lee were accessories to murder, no better than the gang leaders and drug lords who rampaged through the inner cities. "It's murder, gentlemen. No rhyme, no reason, just murder. For sneakers. For jackets. Get it, Spike?"[8]

Mushnick's columns infused race into a crime story that Middle America knew very little about. But attaching Jordan's name to reports about inner-city violence sold newspapers and magazines. In 1990, the national hysteria around the sneaker murders was filtered through the lens of sensational headlines—*Guns Don't Kill People, Air Jordans Do!* Those stories created a simple narrative: Black kids killed other Black kids for shoes worn by the great Black hero.

For the first time in his career, people were starting to question Jordan's integrity and his influence upon Black youth, demanding that he account for the sneaker murders. The public scrutiny would force him to confront his own role in the nation's racial divide. Despite all the praise he had received for transcending race, this episode sparked Jordan's realization that he could never really evade the burden of representing Black America.

When the Air Jordans debuted in 1985, Nike executives didn't expect the shoes would become a cultural phenomenon. In fact, when Jordan signed his first contract with Nike, the company stipulated that if it did not sell $3 million worth of the shoes within three years, then Nike could cancel the endorsement deal. In fact, Nike sold more than $100 million worth of Air Jordans in the first year alone. By 1986, Jordan and Nike had become so closely linked—almost synonymous—that his teammate Orlando Woolridge suggested the company be renamed "Mikey."[9]

But just a year later, Jordan was beginning to question his relationship with the company. In 1987, Nike invested heavily into the new Air Max, "the everyman's sneaker with a plastic air cushion visibly embedded in the sole." While the Air Max became the centerpiece of Nike's promotions, sales of Jordan's $100 basketball shoes slowed and some company executives grew reluctant to spend more ad money on the Air Jordan line. Concerned, Jordan met with Rob Strasser and Peter Moore—his biggest company allies—in May of 1987 to discuss his future with Nike. Strasser told Jordan that he wanted to take him "where no sportsman has gone before . . . out of the realm of colored sneakers and into style." Strasser envisioned making "Michael Jordan a label," creating a line of products that fused sportswear and casualwear. Doing so meant scrapping the juvenile wings logo and creating one of the most recognizable emblems in the world: the Jumpman, a silhouette of Jordan dunking with his hand raised skyward, his legs spread like scissors. That logo, Moore believed, would become as indelible as Ralph Lauren's polo player.[10]

Phil Knight remained dubious about risking millions to make a basketball star his own brand. Later that year, tensions over the direction of the company pushed Strasser and Moore to leave Nike and start their own consulting firm. Without their involvement, Jordan feared that his line would not grow beyond the marketing formula that Nike had already established. He began contemplating the idea of forming his own apparel company, but Strasser and Moore encouraged him to stay with Nike.

In 1988, David Falk began negotiating a new endorsement deal with the company since Jordan's contract was set to expire at the end of the year. During one tense meeting, Knight said, "Michael Jordan without Nike won't mean anything." Insulted, Jordan stormed out of the office. In his mind, Knight, the self-proclaimed "Branch Rickey of advertising," neither respected him nor appreciated the enormous value he provided.[11]

That year Jordan proved that Nike wouldn't mean as much without him. He enjoyed his best season to date, winning every major individual NBA honor. Before Jordan, no player had ever won both the Most Valuable Player award and the Defensive Player of the Year award in the same season. In February, he thrilled the hometown crowd at Chicago Stadium when he won the Slam Dunk Contest and the All-Star Game's MVP award. In just his fourth season, the twenty-four-year-old leader in scoring and steals had established himself as a dominant force on both ends of the court. Although he had not yet made the Bulls a championship contender, many of his competitors considered him the best player in the NBA. Early in the season, Magic Johnson said, "Everybody always says it's me and Larry [Bird]. Really, it's Mike and everybody else."[12]

The first installment of the Spike and Mike commercials appeared on television during the All-Star Game. The idea for pairing Mars Blackmon with Jordan began two years earlier when Jim

Riswold watched the trailer for *She's Gotta Have It* with Wieden and Kennedy producer Bill Davenport. Seeing Blackmon wear his unlaced Air Jordans while he made love to his girlfriend inspired Riswold to write a thirty-second spot called "Hang Time." Riswold recognized that Lee had created a movie with a built-in commercial. Now, he wanted to develop a continuing storyline that brought together Mars and his basketball idol.

Riswold called Lee in Brooklyn and made a pitch: Nike wants to pay you $50,000 to direct black-and-white commercials in a national campaign starring Mars Blackmon and Michael Jordan. After maxing out his credit cards to make his first film for $175,000, the struggling young director couldn't believe his luck. Initially, Lee thought a friend was playing a prank on him, but once Riswold explained the offer was legitimate he asked just one question: "Do I get to work with Michael Jordan?"[13]

In the early shoots, Jordan appeared a bit stiff and uncertain, uncomfortable acting out an entirely new persona. Gradually, though, under Lee's direction, he developed into a great straight man, smirking and rolling his eyes at just the right moment. The brilliance of the cinematic ads was that Jordan did not have to play the lead. Rhapsodizing about the shoes, Mars radiated enough energy on camera that Jordan could just play it cool. "The commercials were the perfect counterpart for his other incarnation, Jordan the total predator, the warrior who went out three or four nights a week and simply destroyed enemy teams," Halberstam wrote. "Opposing teams got the killer, and the fans watching the Nike commercials got the charmer, a man of humor and intelligence, someone everyone seemed to like."[14]

The commercials were a hit. In 1989, when Nike finished the year leading the footwear market with a 26 percent share, Knight and Jordan resolved their differences and the company announced that it had re-signed the basketball star to a seven-year deal that guaranteed him $18 million plus a 5 percent royalty on the net wholesale price of every pair of Air Jordans. The ads made Lee a household name, though in the minds of many fans he *was* Mars Blackmon. At times it irritated Lee that people confused him with the character instead of recognizing him as an innovative director, producer, and writer.[15]

Looking back on the commercials, Riswold thought the spots worked primarily because Mars conveyed incredible enthusiasm for Jordan and his shoes. But, surprisingly, Riswold also said that the commercials struck a chord with Middle America because race did not seem to play a role in the story. Given Lee's outspoken racial politics and the fact that the Mars Blackmon character was a Black break-dancer, a figure born out of hip-hop, this may seem a strange conclusion. Yet in Riswold's mind, Jordan's presence erased any notion that this was a *Black* commercial. Like so many white people, Riswold "did not think of Jordan as black." He believed that if the ads accentuated Jordan's charm and wit, then Americans would forget about his race.[16]

Unlike Jordan, Lee was well-known as a prominent race man, a powerful voice speaking for Black America. His politics, however, made some Nike executives nervous about his role as a spokesman for the company. Critics suggested that Lee might tarnish Jordan's pure reputation. In his column for the *Orange County Register*, Mark Whicker wrote, "Jordan can pick his own friends, of course, but you wonder if he sees life through the same eyes as Lee, the most successful racist in America."[17]

Yet Jordan never voiced solidarity with Lee's politics. And although Lee criticized Black celebrities who had "a vicious crossover mentality," he never publicly challenged Jordan for standing on neutral political ground. Jordan valued their friendship, but people close to him felt he should break his relationship with Lee for the sake of his brand. Jordan wouldn't hear it, though, and assured Lee that as long as he was with Nike, Lee would be too.[18]

Spike Lee may have owed Michael Jordan, but Jordan owed him, too. In his 1989 movie, *Do the Right Thing*, Lee built a storyline glamorizing the Air Jordans as a kind of trophy that defined the person who wore them. During a scene outside a row of Brooklyn brownstones, one of the film's most memorable characters, Buggin' Out, a militant antagonist played by the half-Black, half-Italian Giancarlo Esposito, becomes outraged when Clifton, a white cyclist wearing a green Boston Celtics T-shirt, accidentally steps on Buggin' Out's white shoe, leaving a black scuff across the toe.

"Yo!" Buggin' Out shouts hysterically as Clifton walks away, oblivious to his crime. Incensed, he runs down the block and confronts the only Larry Bird fan in Bed-Stuy. "You almost knocked me down. The word is 'Excuse me.'" Clifton apologizes, but Buggin' Out is unmoved. The commotion attracts a small crowd of Black youths on the sidewalk.

"Not only did you knock me down, you stepped on my new white Air Jordans that I just bought."

Stunned that anyone could be so upset over smudged shoes, Clifton, a lame white dude, replies, "Are you serious?"

"Yes, I'm serious! I'll fuck you up quick two times! Who told you to step on my sneakers?"

Buggin' Out's neighborhood friends fully understood what the Air Jordans meant to him. The shoes made a statement about who he was, affording him—and so many others who wore them—a measure of prestige. Wearing the shoes meant he was cool. At a time when many frustrated Black Americans could not solve their social and economic problems, they sought escape by acquiring "wealth signals," commodities that impressed others. Signaling works when strangers recognize the value of the product, and its scarcity makes imitation difficult; that was certainly true of Air Jordans. For inner-city youths who felt invisible, unseen in a society that rarely recognized the individuality of Black men, those shoes made people notice them.[19]

During Buggin' Out's exchange with Clifton, the Black crowd reminds him that he paid more than $100 for shoes that might as well be worthless now that Clifton has ruined them. "Damn," Buggin' Out says, "my brand new Jordans. You should buy me another pair!" Clifton ignores him and retreats from the crowd into his brownstone. Later, Buggin' Out appears on-screen with one foot perched on a fire hydrant, carefully polishing his soiled shoe with a toothbrush, a relatable ritual for anyone who owned Air Jordans.

That scene emphasized that Air Jordans weren't just shoes for playing basketball. Lightweight and versatile, basketball shoes became fashionable in large part because the hip-hop generation turned them into "status symbols, a carrier of cool for an audience that was concerned first and foremost with how a shoe looked, not how it performed on the court." Wearing Air Jordans on stage and on the streets, hip-hop artists became performers of conspicuous consumption, models for urban youth who aspired to be as much like them as like Michael Jordan. In 1985, LL Cool J, a rising star in the rap game, rocked a pair of Air Jordans on the back cover of his debut album. Two years later, Heavy D, one of the most influential rappers of the eighties, donned Jordans on the front cover of his album *Chunky but Funky*. In the late eighties, Easy-E, Ice-T, and the rap duo Kid 'N Play all sported Air Jordans on their album covers. And in 1990 Will Smith, a young rapper turned actor, modeled the Air Jordan V in multiple episodes and in the opening credits of his new hit show *The Fresh Prince of Bel Air*.[20]

These and other images of hip-hop artists promoted an aspirational lifestyle that closely linked sneaker culture with young Black men, even though they were not the only ones wearing expensive basketball shoes. Many white middle-class consumers—Nike's core market—took their fashion cues from Black Americans. Nike executives acknowledged that Black youth set the style trends for white kids in the suburbs. In fact, the company reported that 87 percent of its products—shoes, apparel, and accessories—were sold to white customers. Inspired by crossover stars like Jordan, white people adopted Black aesthetics in the form of clothes and sneakers, although in doing so they rarely learned anything significant about the real experiences of Black people. By the early 1990s, thanks largely to Jordan, Black and white customers associated Nike with "status, glamour, competitive edge, and the myriad intricacies of cool," Donald Katz wrote in *Sports Illustrated*.[21]

Jordan's success as an endorser came at a moment when the idea of the American Dream intertwined with a culture of heedless materialism. Pundits argued that Nike's advertising, built around the slogan "Just Do It," inspired self-indulgence and self-gratification, powerful trends in American life. During the 1980s, millions of Americans relied on multiple credit cards to purchase products they could not really afford. Increasingly, for young people infatuated with material possessions and luxury brands, shopping offered a source of entertainment, a means of acquiring pleasure. Suburban malls became "cathedrals of consumption," gathering sites for people armed with plastic and an urge for instant gratification. Of course, conspicuous consumption was nothing new in America. But in the 1980s, when cable television expanded the imprint of advertising, "images, signs, and signifiers" took on greater significance. In the age of the Yuppie, noted writer Tom Wolfe, labels mattered, especially to young urban professionals who defined themselves by "the perfection of their possessions":

Rolex watches, Gucci briefcases, Burberry trench coats, BMW sedans, and, yes, Air Jordans.[22]

When the Jordan shoes hit the stores in 1985, Nike's market researchers discovered that white people loved them. "Not only have Air Jordans become popular on city playgrounds," reported *Los Angeles Times* writer Randy Harvey, "they are also the best-selling shoes in the suburban shopping malls. The people who have been really making the cash registers ring are the Yuppies." And yet a certain segment of white people associated Air Jordans with urban criminality. When Harvey asked NBA spokesman Terry Lyons if he had purchased a pair, Lyons replied that he could never wear them on the way to his New York City office. "I'm afraid they'd be taken away from me on the way to work by some kid with a gun."[23]

For a moment, Rick Telander thought, Michael Jordan looked like he might cry. In 1990, the senior writer from *Sports Illustrated* approached Jordan before practice and told him about the murder of a fifteen-year-old Black boy named Michael Eugene Thomas. About a year earlier, the ninth grader from Anne Arundel, Maryland, had paid $115.50 for a pair of Air Jordans. The young fan worshipped the Bulls star and the shoes embroidered with his silhouette. Every night he took his sneakers out of a black shoebox and polished them proudly. But about two weeks after he bought the Air Jordans, schoolchildren found him barefoot in the woods, strangled, face down in a puddle. Shortly thereafter, police charged his seventeen-year-old "basketball buddy" James David Martin with first-degree murder.[24]

Jordan sighed. He didn't know what to say. Sitting in a private room at the team's suburban practice facility in Deerfield, Illinois, he struggled to process an incomprehensible and heinous crime. "I can't believe it," he said. "Choked to death. By his friend." Jordan asked Telander if he knew about similar crimes. Unfortunately, Telander explained, he had read numerous accounts like this one. In his jarring cover story, he wrote about the "frightening outbreak of crimes among poor black kids" assaulting and sometimes killing each other for sneakers and Starter jackets. After collecting stories from Chicago newspapers and *Sports Illustrated*'s national news bureau, Telander concluded that the crimes were not new but "the pace of the carnage [had] quickened."[25]

In Chicago, where Telander lived, the city papers devoted copious amounts of ink covering two phenomena: the ascendance of Jordan and a rising wave of violent crime. Between 1989 and 1990, Chicago's murder rate climbed 14.5 percent. City aldermen decried a "murder epidemic" that afflicted Chicago's youth. One survey found that 74 percent of Chicago school students had witnessed a murder, shooting, stabbing, or robbery and nearly half of them had been victims themselves. For middle-class Americans far removed from the country's urban centers, cities resembled lawless war zones. "Violent crime," *Newsweek* reported, "much of it drug-related, is on the rise in virtually every city in America. Inner city neighborhoods are disintegrating in an escalating cycle of mayhem."[26]

Increasingly in the 1980s, in Chicago and other cities, white reporters treated violent transgressions like spectacles, embellishing an image of a Black underclass that produced roving hordes of violent juvenile delinquents. "When the sun sets on Chicago's West Side, the armies of the night come out to play," Paul Weingarten wrote for the *Tribune*. "People in the neighborhoods retreat into their homes—or if they're brave to their porches—and wait. Out in the night, a new order takes shape. It is an alien world, strange and incomprehensible. A world where junior-high kids carry shotguns, and no one ventures out unarmed."[27]

THE SPIKE AND MIKE SHOW

The alarm over sneaker crimes reflected a growing anxiety over "juvenile superpredators—radically impulsive, brutally remorseless youngsters, including ever more pre-teenage boys, who murder, assault, rape, rob, burglarize, deal deadly drugs, join gun-toting gangs, and create serious communal disorders." Columnists accused apparel companies of encouraging "violent lifestyles by directing advertising campaigns toward black urban teens." Without any evidence, they suggested that such marketing was an effective strategy because basketball was "the sport of choice among urban drug dealers." Like Mushnick, John Leo, a conservative writer for *U.S. News & World Report*, argued that Nike exploited impoverished inner-city Black youth who could not afford Air Jordans. Some of them legitimately worked and saved for the shoes, Leo wrote, but others acquired them illegally or paid for them using drug money. Using coded language, Leo suggested that Black people were more susceptible than white people to advertising that emboldened them to commit crimes. "The line 'Just Do It' means one thing to the middle-class, and something else to people in the ghetto," he said. "To the middle-class, it means get in shape, whereas in the ghetto it means, 'Don't have any moral compunction—just go out and do whatever you have to do in your predicament.' There's an immoral message imbedded in there."[28]

Liz Dolan, Nike's director of public relations, combatted charges of exploitation by arguing that sneaker crimes were not a result of advertising. Rather, the root of the problem stemmed from income inequality and a growing sense of "hopelessness" in the inner cities. Furthermore, she told Telander, Nike's endorsers were excellent role models. Who was a better example for children than Michael Jordan? "What's baffling to us," she said, "is how easily people accept the assumption that black youth is an unruly mob that will do anything to get its hands on what it wants.

They'll say, 'Show a black kid something he wants, and he'll kill for it.' I think it's racist hysteria."[29]

In response to Mushnick, Spike Lee wrote an op-ed in the *National*, a short-lived daily sports paper. Lee suspected that the *New York Post* writer who started the furor against him and Jordan had "a hidden agenda" couched in "thinly veiled racism." He wanted to know why Mushnick, who had never given so much attention to poor Black kids before, suddenly became interested in their plight now. Further, Lee maintained his commercials with Jordan were not exclusively directed toward Black youth. Car theft was a major urban crime, too—millions of cars were stolen or looted annually—but no one called for Jordan to stop doing Chevy commercials.[30]

Unlike Lee, Jordan never said that the attacks on him stemmed from racism, but he clearly felt that he was targeted in a way that white athletes were not. "It's kind of ironic that the press builds people like me up to be a role model and then blames us for the unfortunate crimes kids are committing," he said. "Kids commit crimes to get NFL jackets, cars, jewelry, and many other things. But nobody is criticizing people who promote those products. I also don't hear anybody knocking other sports stars like Larry Bird and Joe Montana, who also endorse their brand of shoes and other sporting goods."[31]

Implicitly, Jordan suggested that blaming him for sneaker crimes was unfair because reporters failed to provide precise numbers when writing of murders involving products bearing his name. *How many teenagers were killed for wearing expensive sneakers? And how many of them wore Air Jordans? Did anybody know?* In interviews with police officers, Telander tried to answer those questions and received varying answers. The Atlanta police estimated that over a period of four months they encountered more than fifty mugging cases involving sportswear. A Chicago police sergeant estimated there were fifty incidents involving jackets and about a dozen shoe crimes each month. Richard Lapchick, director for the Center of Sport in Society at Northeastern University, argued that reports about sneaker murders were grossly exaggerated. A month after Telander published his story, Lapchick told an Associated Press writer that since 1983 there were only *nine* documented murders involving sneakers.[32]

Yet Telander's four-thousand-word cover story, bolstered by television news reports, gave the impression that "an unconscionable number of killings have actually occurred over status-symbol sneakers, pro or college team jackets, and major league baseball caps." In the second week of May 1990, when *Sports Illustrated*'s subscribers opened their mailboxes, they found the most provocative cover of the year: an illustration of an armed Black man pointing a revolver into the back of another man wearing a satin Starter jacket as the gunman snatched the victim's Air Jordans. Telander's story posed an important question: What could explain the violence over expensive shoes and jackets? Dr. Elijah Anderson, a distinguished sociologist at the University of Pennsylvania, suggested that the crimes were linked to larger forces of racial inequality. "The uneducated, inner-city kids don't have a sense of opportunity," he said. "They feel the system is closed off to them. And yet they're bombarded with the same cultural apparatus that the white middle class is. They don't have the means to attain the things offered, and yet they have the same desires. So, they value those 'emblems,' these symbols of supposed success. The gold, the shoes, the drug dealer's outfit—those things all belie the real situation, but it's a symbolic display that seems to say that things are all right."[33]

The narratives produced about sneaker killings perpetuated the myth of Black-on-Black crime, a trope rooted in the idea that Black Americans were or are inherently more violent than white people. Studies have shown that most violent crimes occur between people who live near one another, which in a residentially segregated country meant most violent acts were intraracial. And yet no one ever used the phrase "white-on-white crime." Instead, news reports about sneaker murders pathologized Black youth as criminals who valued "pieces of rubber and plastic held together by shoelaces . . . more than human life." Phil Mushnick insisted, "The only kids dying for the kind of outrageously expensive junk these influential Afro-American role models are pushing are black kids." But was that true? Did Mushnick or other writers ever investigate whether sneaker crimes occurred in the suburbs? Or did they just assume that sneaker crimes only took place in urban neighborhoods? According to Mushnick's logic, Spike Lee wrote, "Poor whites won't kill for a pair of Jordans, but poor blacks will."[34]

In response to *Sports Illustrated*'s cover story, Chicago journalists and fans defended Jordan. *Chicago Sun-Times* columnist Raymond Coffey wrote, "What is really senseless here is any suggestion that Michael Jordan has blood on his hands for selling shoes on TV. The people responsible for killing people are the people who kill people." Joseph H. Brown, a Black man who grew up on the South Side of Chicago during the sixties, agreed. In a letter to *Sports Illustrated*, Brown wrote, "None of this is Jordan's fault. He is not responsible for the moral decay in our inner cities . . . The moral revival that is needed to stop this madness must be carried out by families, churches, schools, and community organizations, not by a slam-dunking hoopster."[35]

Telander did not blame Jordan for the sneaker crimes, even if the magazine cover implicated the Nike pitchman. In fact, Telander portrayed Jordan as a sympathetic figure suffering from a devastating loss, saddened that Black boys he had never met were killed simply because they wore his shoes. In a sense, then,

Jordan grieved with the nation; America's tragedy was his tragedy, and he mourned as deeply as the real victims' families. If previously he had believed that being an example of self-help and self-empowerment would help inner city kids, Jordan now recognized that he could not rescue them. "I thought I'd be helping out others and everything would be positive," he told Telander. "I thought people would try to emulate the good things I do. They'd try to achieve to be better. Nothing bad."[36]

In so many instances, observed *Chicago Tribune* columnist Bob Greene, Jordan appeared completely confident answering questions about various matters outside of basketball. Yet these crimes perplexed and distressed him. What could he do about it? "I don't have the answer," he said. "If a parent in a high-crime neighborhood sees his son or daughter going out the door with your brand of shoes on, and the parent is scared," Greene asked, "what can you possibly say, knowing that?"

"I would tell the parents to tell their kids: 'Please give it up.'"

"Give up the clothing? If the child is being robbed?"

"Yes, give it up. The jacket, the shoes—give it up." Then Jordan said something without thinking through the implications. "They should tell the kids, I will buy them a replacement." Not Nike, he insisted, but Jordan himself. *He* would replace the stolen shoes.

It seemed unrealistic that Jordan could provide insurance to every kid who bought his shoes, but he conceived of his own power in financial terms. He could not imagine joining community activists in the fight against inner-city crime or urban poverty. The only movement he belonged to was the one that hyped the products with his name on them.

And yet the crime stories attached to his name weighed on Jordan, exposing his vulnerability in a way that little else did. He simply couldn't make sense of the awful violence in America's cities. "It just makes me so sad," he said. "The whole thing.

Everything is changing." Jordan didn't have the answers to the sneaker murders. And he quickly realized that nothing good came from talking about it. Burying his feelings helped bury the story.[37]

Less than a month after *Sports Illustrated*'s sensational cover story "Your Sneakers or Your Life" hit the newsstands, Bob Greene returned his attention to Jordan's performance on the court and what he meant to the city. One of the nation's most widely read syndicated columnists, Greene, a white, middle-aged writer known for inserting himself into his stories and dwelling "in nostalgia and sentimentality," had become fascinated by Jordan. Although Greene was not a sportswriter, he was an unabashed hero worshipper. He knew that writing about Jordan would be good for his career and draw even more readers to his column. So, he started attending Bulls games regularly and began interviewing Jordan, tossing softball questions that never really challenged the man or the myth.[38]

Two years before he published *Hang Time: Days and Dreams with Michael Jordan*, a hagiographic account that emphasized "a growing friendship" between the author and the basketball star, Greene gushed over Jordan in his columns. Romanticizing Jordan's place in sports and Chicago, Greene became a flack for the Bulls' star, one of many journalists who wrote uncritically about Jordan at that time. Previously, he had positioned himself as "Chicago's social conscience," writing about battered children, crime, and urban poverty. Burned out from writing too many tragic stories, he told readers that he found a renewed sense of hope and optimism watching the way Jordan touched the lives of countless children at Chicago Stadium. At a time when critics asked whether the Nike spokesman shouldered some responsibility for the endangered youth caught in the crossfire over his sneakers,

Greene's columns reminded the country that Jordan remained a source of goodness for the nation's children.[39]

In Greene's wonderland, Chicago Stadium became a shelter from the relentless cruelty of society. Writing for a credulous audience, he advised readers to embrace the virtues of Jordan, urging them to find a way to see the Bulls star in person before it was too late. "Pay close attention, because you're never going to see anything like this again."[40]

Chapter Three

SWEET HOME, CHICAGO

"It's not hard to please the public. All you have to do is to remember that we were all born children, that we all die children, and that in between times we are children."

—PATRICK "PADDY" T. HARMON, FOUNDER
AND BUILDER OF CHICAGO STADIUM

The camera follows Michael Jordan as he drives around Chicago Stadium in his new Chevy Blazer, capturing his fond gaze at the massive gray barn, a warehouse filled with memories. Watching him slowly cruise the West Side streets in a local commercial produced in the early nineties, Chicagoland viewers couldn't see the decaying public housing projects or the barren parking lots surrounding the stadium. In a scripted television spot, Jordan expresses affection for his adopted city and its residents, who embrace him as one of their own. Reminiscing about the crumbling arena, an aging relic from the Jazz Age, Jordan says from behind the wheel, "I love that old building. You know, to me, that's home."[1]

"This place," he told a reporter, "is full of history." Since 1929, the "Madhouse on Madison" fulfilled the fantasies of Chicago's children and the adults who wanted to be children again. For decades crowds flocked to 1800 West Madison Street to see the circus, but now the greatest show in Chicago was an acrobatic basketball player who could soar without a trapeze. Built for grand spectacles, the stadium hosted some of the city's biggest sporting events, concerts, and political rallies. Long before Jordan, the most famous athletes who performed there were boxers and hockey players—husky brawlers and bold sluggers, the kind of hardy men celebrated in Carl Sandburg's "City of the Big Shoulders," an industrial hub of steel mills and stockyards that had largely vanished by the time Jordan arrived in the mid-1980s.[2]

On game nights a carnival atmosphere enveloped the stadium, "a stone citadel rising from the middle of a field of cars." The streets howled with a cacophony of noise—rumbling buses carrying excited fans, taxi drivers laying on the horn, and impatient cops blowing whistles, urging drivers to keep their cars moving. In the stalled traffic snaking around the arena, "squads of shills and barkers," most of them young Black men, maneuvered between cars driven mostly by white people afraid to roll down the windows. In 1990, when John Edgar Wideman took a cab to the stadium, he noticed Black people mixing "into the crowd—vendors, scalpers, guys in sneakers and silky sweat suits doing whatever they're out there doing," he wrote. Most of them were just trying to make a buck hawking peanuts and T-shirts.[3]

For the poor Black men living near Chicago Stadium, in a desolate neighborhood lined with currency exchanges and liquor stores, one of the best ways to make money on game nights involved parking cars. In the age of Jordan, the stadium had become a regular destination for affluent white people who would have never visited the area otherwise. Suburbanites heard all sorts of stories about fans being robbed or carjacked after a game. Not even the presence of dozens of uniformed cops could prevent grand larceny. So, when an anxious, white-knuckled driver navigated unfamiliar streets, seeing a parking attendant wave cars into unpaved lots with signs that read "Safe Parking," he might wonder just how safe the lots really were.[4]

Some kids from the neighborhood got in on the parking action, too, offering to watch people's cars on side streets, for a price. If a driver refused to pay them a few dollars in exchange for protecting the car, he might return later that night to find his windows smashed or his radio stolen. Most of the kids, though, were not interested in breaking into cars and wanted nothing more than a little pocket money. In *There Are No Children Here*, a searing chronicle of two young Black brothers growing up in the West Side projects, Alex Kotlowitz recounts a 1988 story in which a white cop grabbed one of the boys by the jacket collar, tossed him into a puddle of water, and said, "Little punk, you ain't supposed to be working here. These white people don't have any money to give no niggers."[5]

The overflowing police presence on game nights made residents living two blocks from the stadium in Henry Horner Homes, one of the city's least habitable public housing projects, ask why the cops swarmed the neighborhood when the Bulls played but provided little protection against gang violence that terrorized their community. Why, they asked, "does it take all these white people, these outsiders, to flood the area with police? Why is it only on stadium nights the area is well lit?" Growing up in deteriorating red brick buildings, Henry Horner's Black youngsters learned to live without—without security; without heat during cold winter nights; without telephones; without working elevators; without a grocery or a pharmacy nearby; and without a public library where they could escape into a storybook that took them away from the "graveyard," a nickname given to the projects by a young boy.[6]

For children habitually awakened in the middle of the night by piercing screams and crackling gunfire, an evening at Chicago

Stadium offered a fleeting reprieve from a dangerous world. Repeatedly, however, the kids learned from police and the arena's gatekeepers that Chicago Stadium was not for them. In the hours before a game, Black boys canvassed the streets searching for generous basketball fans with extra tickets. Finding a ticket was like winning the lottery. But even if they got their hands on tickets, sometimes stadium attendants refused to let them inside the building. One time a gatekeeper took one look at a Black kid and humiliated him by ripping up his ticket. On another occasion, when a youngster presented his standing-room-only ticket, a cruel man responded, "No neighborhood kids allowed."[7]

Most kids never got any closer to Jordan than when they gathered around the high fence that surrounded the players' parking lot on the west side of the stadium. In a familiar ritual that took place during every one of the Bulls' forty-one home games, the crowd of fans grew larger and larger as tip-off neared. Looping their tiny fingers through the chain-link fence, children pressed their bodies against the barricade and craned their necks looking for Jordan. They recognized the different cars that he drove, and when they saw a sleek black Ferrari 512 Testarossa with tinted windows and a license plate that read "M AIR J" approach the gate, they knew it was his.[8]

Draped in an oversized power suit, Jordan stepped out of the car, unfolded his body like a three-part extension ladder, and rose to his feet as a chorus of kids shouted his name. There he stood, sculpted out of the pages of *GQ*, sporting a diamond stud earring and Ray-Ban sunglasses, the embodiment of cool. Surrounded by a squad of security guards wearing bright yellow jackets, Jordan handed the car keys to a valet and disappeared inside the stadium.

Although he did not always acknowledge the youth waving to him outside the parking lot fence, the kids did not seem to mind.

Just seeing him, if only for a fleeting moment, brought them a kind of joy that rarely touched their lives. Even after Jordan vanished, he remained on their minds, a source of inspiration. But when the kids crossed the street and returned to the blacktop courts at Henry Horner Homes, a playground for restless souls, high school dropouts, and aging men who could talk a better game than they could play, the shadow of the projects loomed over their lives like a hulking prison where hoop dreams died.

In the mid-1980s, shortly after Harold Washington became Chicago's first Black mayor, the city fundamentally altered the lives of three young Black Americans, each of whom went on to become important cultural figures who broke racial barriers and represented Black achievement in their own way. First, in January 1984, an emerging television star named Oprah Winfrey took over as host of a local show called *AM Chicago*. Within two years she had her own nationally syndicated eponymous show, and soon she would become one of the richest and most influential people in the world. A few months after Oprah's Chicago debut, Michael Jordan began playing at the stadium, quickly building the city's growing enthusiasm for professional basketball. Finally, in 1985, after graduating from Columbia University, Barack Obama, completely unknown to the city's power brokers, moved from New York to Chicago, where he became a community organizer on the South Side.[9]

When Obama came to Chicago, he knew two facts about his new hometown: it was "America's most segregated city" and "a black man, Harold Washington, was just elected mayor, and white people don't like it." Washington's story reveals how racially polarized the city had become nine months before Jordan debuted with the Bulls. When the charismatic sixty-one-year-old congressman became mayor in 1983, Washington's Democratic supporters viewed his triumph in a three-way primary race and victory over Republican Bernard Epton as an end to the city's "plantation politics." Although African Americans carried Washington to the mayor's office, his success was based on a rainbow coalition of Blacks, Hispanics, and "Lakefront liberals," a movement that inspired Obama's journey to Chicago. Yet that political narrative diminishes the fact that Washington had to overcome widespread racist hysteria perpetuated by white people who feared that a Black mayor born and raised in Bronzeville would ruin the city.[10]

During "Chicago's Ugly Election," Washington's opponents circulated flyers saying that they refused to vote for a "baboon." In white ethnic wards, Republicans campaigned wearing buttons that were completely white—a wordless gesture to white power. Republicans distributed facetious leaflets outlining Washington's "campaign promises," which allegedly included raising "Whitey's Taxes" and replacing CTA buses with Cadillac Eldorados. The racist flyers claimed that Washington would move City Hall to Martin Luther King Drive and relocate government offices to Leon's Rib Basket. The leaflets were so vile, noted the *New Yorker*'s David Remnick, that some "implied that Washington was guilty of child molestation."[11]

After the *Chicago Tribune* endorsed Washington, hate mail flooded the newspaper's offices. In her column, Leanita McClain, a Black member of the *Tribune*'s editorial board, wrote about the paper's decision to publish "a full page of these rantings. But when the mirror was presented to them, the bigots reveled before it. The page only gave them aid and comfort in knowing their numbers. That is what is wrong with this town; being racist is as respectable and expected as going to church." When Washington visited St. Pascal's Catholic Church on the Northwest Side with former vice president Walter Mondale, a riot nearly erupted as a jeering white mob confronted him, shouting, "Nigger Die!"[12]

Throughout the eighties, Chicago remained a crucible of America's racial divisions, a battleground between Black advancement and white backlash. "In neighborhood meetings and political gatherings," Thomas Byrne Edsall reported in 1989, "working-class whites say their lives are dominated by fears of black gangs, black crime, drugs sold by blacks, and by the threat of declining property values, owing to black migration into these neighborhoods."[13]

Those fears shaped the perceptions of white Chicagoans who bumped shoulders with Black men throughout the city—on busy streets in the Loop, in packed L trains and crowded elevators. The city's image had become closely associated with widely circulated news stories about Black men committing violent offenses against white people. One study of Chicago's television newscasts "found that the majority of perpetrators portrayed in the news were black or persons of color, while the majority of victims were white." The crime coverage in the local newspapers was not much better. In 1990, *Chicago Magazine* reported that while white people represented 30 percent of the city's hate-crime victims, nearly two-thirds of hate crimes were committed against Black people; yet those stories rarely received any attention from newsrooms staffed almost entirely with white reporters.[14]

Perhaps unsurprisingly those same newspapers celebrated Jordan as the beau ideal of Black Chicago and the city's preeminent hero. He fit a particular type of Black athlete celebrated by white locals. "We are a town of limited celebrity and there is always one 'model Negro,'" observed Aaron Freeman, a Black actor and Second City performer. First, Ernie Banks, an amiable, soft-spoken ballplayer, broke the color line with the Chicago Cubs in 1953; in the coming years, "Mr. Cub" became the star

of the team. Then, during the late 1960s, Gale Sayers, an electrifying running back, joined the Chicago Bears. After Sayers
published a memoir detailing his friendship with Brian Piccolo, a
white teammate stricken with terminal cancer, ABC produced a
moving film—*Brian's Song*—a story about interracial brotherhood
forged through football. Between 1975 and 1987, Walter Payton,
a dynamic athlete, perhaps the greatest running back of all time,
carried the Bears offense. "Sweetness," as he was known, earned
a reputation throughout the city for his kindness and generosity
to fans. Similarly, Chicago's sports fans revered Jordan because he
seemed wholesome and completely unthreatening to white people.
There were no illusions about him joining Jesse Jackson or other
civil rights activists in the fight for affordable housing or equal
employment opportunities.[15]

Chicago's racial politics shaped the mystique of Michael Jordan. His detachment from the city, including his choice to live
in the affluent North Shore suburbs, helped insulate him from
any association with Chicago's Black community. The distance
between his home and work turned him into a commuter separated from the city's growing "politics of resentment taking hold
on both sides of the color line." By the time he joined the Bulls,
Black folks had grown increasingly resentful about all the broken
promises of the civil rights era. At the same time, white people
had become deeply resentful because they believed that too many
Black residents refused to stop complaining about racism despite
the legislative victories of the civil rights movement and the election of a Black mayor. The city's entrenched racial resentments
explain a great deal about Jordan's refusal to become entangled
in the political debates and protests taking place outside Chicago
Stadium.[16]

Throughout his career, and especially after 1987, when Harold Washington died of a sudden heart attack and Walter Payton

retired, Jordan filled a void, not just as a redemptive Black hero but as *the* face of the city. In Chicago, people of all races celebrated him as an emblem of the Great American City, an imaginary place unified by a Black sports hero who had the power to extinguish racial conflicts. "For those of us who lived in Chicago," Barack Obama reflected, "Michael and the Bulls brought a constant, wonderful diversion to our lives. But [they] also brought the city together, a city that in the past had been known for its ethnic and racial divisions."[17]

Yet not everyone bought the idea that Jordan could heal Chicago's deep racial wounds. In the eighties, Bulls fans earned a reputation for being yuppies, "shouting, cheering wanna-be white basketball players" with attractive wives and deep pockets. Those fans, local historian Douglas Bukowski wrote in the *Tribune*, visited Chicago Stadium to watch Jordan play basketball and left wondering why all Black people could not be more like him. Even at a time when Chicago remained one of the most segregated American cities, there were white basketball fans who romanticized the modern NBA as a manifestation of the hard-fought victories of the civil rights movement. And that made Jordan even more important as a Black hero for white America.[18]

For the Chicago faithful who witnessed the apotheosis of Jordan as "America's only living man-god," a figure whose name and likeness spanned the oceans, watching him compete for two hours at the stadium awakened something in the human spirit. Throughout his career, Jordan's idolaters deified him, comparing the artistry of "basketball's high priest" to a mystical experience that converted fans into followers. Going to a Bulls game reminded Arthur Droge, a professor at the University of Chicago Divinity School, of attending church. In an age of declining religious affiliation, Chicagoans—and Americans throughout the country—searched for meaning beyond themselves, gravitating toward an athlete who seemed to walk on air, a man who called himself "Black Jesus." As a symbol, Jordan evoked religious connotations, noted cultural critic Neal Gabler. The Jumpman logo—a silhouette of Jordan splaying his arms and legs as he rises for a dunk—"looked suspiciously like an athletic crucifix," transforming his image into a totem, an object infused with tribal significance.[19]

From the very first moment Jordan donned a Bulls uniform, local fans and writers christened him the savior of Chicago, projecting worshipful ideals onto him. In 1984, when Jordan played his first home game, resulting in a sixteen-point victory over the Washington Bullets, local sportswriter Jim O'Donnell wrote, "They should have hung a halo atop Chicago Stadium Friday night because this was no basketball game. It was a revival meeting. Step aside Elmer Gantry. Shut down Billy Sunday. The Bulls have been saved." Even though the Bulls' star rookie only made 31 percent of his shots that night, no one denied "that the celestial Mr. Jordan had alleviated the spiritual malaise plaguing the team for the past three years."[20]

Michael Jordan performed inexplicable deeds, defying the boundaries of ordinary human life. He seemed to play without limits, expanding the court's vertical space, levitating above the rim. Jordan possessed a rare ability to make a spectacular play that people had never seen before, a move so original that it defied the imagination. Attacking opponents with relentless fury, he unleashed a vengeance against anyone who dared to stand between him and the basket. In the blink of an eye, he could accelerate, leap into the air, and somehow conceive of a way to contort his body into a balletic form, finishing an improbable move of unmatched power and grace. Jordan, observed journalist Ralph Wiley, knew "what was humanly possible. And then he would go on to expand the envelope of that possibility."[21]

"The Prophet of Possibility" made Chicago Stadium his very own house of worship, delivering a performance that kept his flock coming back for more.[22]

Ask any Bulls fan who visited Michael's house during the 1990s and they will tell you that they experienced a rush of adrenaline pulsating through their veins when the stadium lights went out right before tip-off. Chicagoans lived for an event that connected them to a citywide congregation that venerated an idol—a man Larry Bird once described as "God disguised as Michael Jordan." Before every game, Chicago Stadium darkened like a cave, completely blacked out. Suddenly, more than eighteen thousand people erupted in "a low guttural roar, like a hurricane or the rumble of a great train," Ralph Wiley wrote. The stadium speakers cranked to an earsplitting pitch, amplifying the sound of "an echo-drenched synthesizer riff and a roof-raising guitar solo."[23]

The team's theme music—the Alan Parsons Project instrumental "Sirius"—reverberated throughout the arena as a spotlight circled the stands. It was as if the music and the lights plugged the entire stadium into an electrical socket, thought Cheryl Raye-Stout, a local radio reporter. Bouncing on the balls of their feet, clapping, and shouting, the crowd roared as they anticipated the spotlight illuminating the greatest entertainer on Earth. Then Ray Clay's familiar voice boomed from the public address speakers, "Aaaand now, the starting lineup for your Chicago Bulls!"[24]

Virtually every kid who grew up in Chicago during the Jordan era could mimic Clay's introduction of the Bulls' starting lineup. The team's PA announcer became Chicago famous for the way he introduced the players like they were Roman gladiators preparing for battle. Strangers stopped him on the street or at the grocery store and asked him to deliver the most famous introduction in American sports. One by one, always in the same order, Clay called the starting players onto the court: Horace Grant, Scottie Pippen, Bill Cartwright, John Paxson, and Michael Jordan.

Tim Hallam, the Bulls' director of media relations, explained that a confluence of factors gradually made the Bulls' introduction increasingly popular: "an old building that was very, very loud; a fired-up fan base starved for a great basketball team; and one of the most exciting, marketable athletes ever in Michael Jordan." Without Jordan the introduction to the starting lineup may not have become a Chicago tradition. But *everything* Jordan did seemed special, worthy of celebration.

He made the Madhouse on Madison the noisiest arena in the NBA. The deafening noise from the boisterous crowd grew louder and louder with each introduction. The thunderous sound at Chicago Stadium reached 130 decibels—louder than a propeller plane taking off or a racing subway train. Rick Telander likened the sound to a machine gun being fired next to his ear. "The hair on your arms would rise and stand straight up," he recalled. Unlike Los Angeles, where some Lakers fans showed up fashionably late to the Forum, the Bulls' introduction, a spectacle unlike any other in the NBA, inspired Chicagoans to find their seats well before the lights faded and the music began. No one wanted to miss Ray Clay's voice rising above Parsons's guitar solo, trumpeting, "Frrrooom NORTH Carolina, at guard, 6-6, Michael Jordan!"[25]

By the time Clay called Jordan's name, the noise in the stadium had grown so tumultuous that whatever he said after "Carolina" could not be heard. Trotting onto the polished hardwood court, Jordan could feel the heat of the spotlight warming his body. He admitted that sometimes, before the most important games, he became so moved by the boisterous crowd that tears filled his eyes.[26]

Chapter Four

RAGING BULL

"What makes him a great player is his impatience with defeat. It's also the quality that dismisses any talk of his being
a prima donna. No one who's ever seen Jordan disgusted
with himself or his teammates on an off night can question this impulse. His face contorts, he shakes his head, he
screams at the referee, he scolds his teammates, but, most
often and most important, he looks inward and tries to raise
his game another notch. If, at some point, the offense fiz-
zles or the chemistry just won't come, then Jordan decides to
take things into his own hands. His efforts, at these times,
take on the crazed determination of a man trying to halt an
avalanche."

—TED COX ON MICHAEL JORDAN, *CHICAGO
MAGAZINE*, FEBRUARY 1, 1989

In the Jordan lore, the central myth is that he was "the most intense competitor on the planet." That theme appears in countless stories told and retold by journalists, coaches, teammates,
friends, and rivals. Perhaps the most infamous yarn is the one
shared with a smile by Buzz Peterson, his close friend and teammate at UNC. One time during a visit with the Peterson clan,
Buzz caught Michael cheating Buzz's mother in a casual card

game of Crazy Eights by hiding an eight card under his leg. Stunned, Peterson said, "Are you really that competitive that you were going to cheat my own mother in cards? You gotta be kidding me."[1]

During his career with the Chicago Bulls, Jordan continued to indulge a penchant for gambling. The wealthiest player on the team had no problem cheating his teammates out of money. One time when the Bulls were still flying commercial, the team landed in Portland and gathered around the airport baggage claim. Waiting for their luggage, Jordan slapped a hundred-dollar bill on the conveyor belt and announced that he would bet any takers that his bag would arrive first. Nine teammates eagerly accepted the wager and began tossing hundred-dollar bills into a pile. Suddenly the first bag dropped out of the mouth of the conveyor. Sure enough, it was Jordan's. He laughed and collected nine hundred dollars. His teammates had no idea that he had bribed the baggage handler with fifty dollars before arranging the whole ruse.[2]

For many fans, that story only made Jordan seem more admirable—he was the kind of competitor who would do anything to win, even when there was little or nothing at stake. Writing for *ESPN The Magazine*, Bill Simmons opined, "If I owned the Bulls and found out my franchise guy—the dude cashing seven-figure checks every two weeks, the dude responsible for filling my stadium eight months per season, the dude who would make or break my dream of holding the Larry O'Brien [NBA championship] trophy—was bribing baggage handlers just to win a few hundred bucks, well, the news would warm my heart. That's what alpha dogs do. They compete, they dominate, they don't know when to quit."[3]

The celebration of Jordan as the Most Competitive Man on Earth reveals as much about America as it does about him. Throughout US history, people have competed for just about everything: land, jobs, housing, elections, status, and their beliefs. In a diverse nation with few safety nets, competition—between groups and individuals—became highly valued. Living in the "land of opportunity," Americans have long believed that ambition and initiative reward the most relentless competitors not just in sports but in everyday life. That's why Nike's slogan, "Just Do It," resonated so much with Americans during the late 1980s and 1990s. Success, Americans were told, was the result of productive individuals who shouldered the responsibility for their own advancement. Those who failed lacked the grit and talent to make it. In the last quarter of the twentieth century, that culture of hyperindividualism and hero worship produced a society that increasingly glorified winners like Michael Jordan.

His competitive impulse made it virtually impossible for him to satisfy his desire for perfection. Jordan's urge to dominate everyone, even in practice, turned him into a cruel bully who relentlessly tested his teammates. People who watched him up close described Jordan's competitiveness in violent terms. "He wants to cut your throat out and then show it to you," said former Bulls coach Doug Collins. "He's Hannibal Lecter," commented Bob Ryan, the *Boston Globe*'s featured basketball columnist. Chicago Bulls owner Jerry Reinsdorf once told Jordan that he reminded him of Jake LaMotta, the brawling Italian American middleweight champion, a fighter immortalized on-screen by Robert DeNiro's brilliant performance in *Raging Bull*. The real LaMotta gloried in his fanatical ability to withstand pain. And with LaMotta, Reinsdorf said, the only way anyone could stop Jordan was if somebody killed him.[4]

LaMotta's life story offers a cautionary tale about an egotistical man tortured by his zealous desire to succeed. If Reinsdorf identified similar characteristics in Jordan, perhaps it was because the basketball star unleashed malevolence against teammates who failed to live up to his expectations. Tex Winter, the Chicago Bulls' longtime, silver-haired assistant coach, believed Jordan's vicious insults toward his teammates alienated them. Jordan's ferocity and fits of anger, more than his supreme talent, made it difficult for them to crack his hardened outer shell. And for Jordan it made contending for a championship feel like an arduous solitary pursuit.[5]

"The fire in me," Jordan explained, began with his family. Throughout his life "people added wood to that fire," especially his father, James. When he was a boy, "Pops" poured the foundation of his basketball career when he built a backyard court with two baskets on a patch of dirt behind the family's split-level home in Wilmington, North Carolina. On that dusty court, the story goes, Michael developed a rivalry with his brother, Larry. Like many younger brothers, he measured himself against the talents of an older sibling. What fueled him more than those heated battles against Larry, though, was the validation he sought from his father. Michael genuinely believed that Pops favored his brother. "I always felt I was fighting Larry for my father's attention," he admitted.[6]

Looking back on his childhood, Jordan acknowledged that his father ignited in him a burning desire to prove his self-worth. Growing up he watched Pops work on cars with Larry, but he felt out of place in the garage. He has often repeated a story about the time his father asked him to retrieve a wrench from a toolbox. When Jordan had no idea which one Pops wanted, James grew irritated by his son's mechanical ignorance and said, "Get back in the house with your mom, boy. You're never going to be anything. Just go back with your mom."[7]

You're never going to be anything. Those blistering words exacerbated his insecurities. Out of this vulnerable adolescent moment, Jordan's boyhood began dissolving and he began forming his manhood—not in his father's garage but on the playing field. He won his father's affection playing sports, forging a bond over his accomplishments on the court. In the process, basketball ceased being a game for boys; instead, it became his crucible of manhood, an inextinguishable pursuit of conquests, and a lifelong retort to his father.

This coming-of-age story, told by Jordan, serves a larger purpose for understanding the central myth of his crossover from the ordinary to the extraordinary. It's the classic tale of the hero confronting his childhood fears—fears of humiliation and anonymity. The story humanizes him and softens the sharp edges around his monomaniacal ambitions. It casts the making of a hero born out of personal pain. In that darkness, Jordan found the light, a path to salvation.

Yet that story overshadows how larger social forces sparked Jordan's drive to succeed. In the late 1970s, as a teenager growing up in Wilmington, a southern port city grappling with the consequences of court-ordered school desegregation, Jordan experienced racism that made his blood boil. The episodes inflicted anguish upon a young Black boy coming to terms with his heritage and the history of racism in America. Looking back, Jordan distinctly remembered rebelling against bigotry during the ninth grade after watching *Roots*, an award-winning miniseries about the forced voyage of African people who were transplanted, abused, and mistreated as property in America. After watching the series, he began confronting racism at school. Several times, he said, hostile white kids antagonized him, hurling the most degrading racial epithets. Jordan recalled, "I retaliated, in some ways violently." Rage threatened to overwhelm him. Fighting back with his fists, he refused to let anyone denigrate him with *that word*—the one that cruel white folks cut time and time again to tell Black people that they were inferior—a lie infused with a violent history against his ancestors.[8]

Harnessing his anger and channeling it into something productive meant disproving any notion of weakness or inferiority. In a formative period of his life, he conceived of the playing field as the great equalizer. He came to believe that success in sports would lift him out of Wilmington. On the basketball court, no one could tell him that he wasn't good enough or that he didn't belong. He would prove that he was the best. Young Michael made up his mind that achievement would define him—not the color of his skin. Basketball would become the battleground for crushing the great white lie into dust.

No amount of pain could prevent Michael Jordan from competing. The basis for that legend formed during his rivalry with the Detroit Pistons. In the 1990 Eastern Conference Finals, the Pistons, despised in every American city but Detroit, smothered Jordan every time he attacked the basket. Repeatedly, Jordan absorbed body blows that wrenched his back, shoulders, and legs. The collisions left him feeling numb, like he'd been crushed in a car wreck. But no matter how many times the Pistons knocked him down, he kept rising for another round of abuse. Witnessing his suffering, America rooted for him and the redemption of a sport corrupted by a team of ruffians.

Jordan loathed the NBA's defending champions. Detroit had knocked Chicago out of the playoffs the previous two seasons, and they did it by pounding Jordan into submission. Chuck Daly, the Pistons' head coach, refused to let him dictate the game. Two years earlier, after Jordan burned the Pistons for fifty-nine points, Daly and his assistant coaches devised the famous "Jordan Rules," a suffocating defense designed to prevent him from beating them single-handedly. In short, the rules could be reduced to three principles: *No layups. No dunks. Nothing easy.*[9]

Daly believed that Jordan's hypercompetitiveness and his singular focus on scoring made him somewhat predictable. Facing intense defensive pressure, Daly predicted that Jordan would try to beat the Pistons all by himself. For all his immense scoring talent, Jordan had a weakness: tunnel vision blinded him from seeing open teammates. So, Daly enticed him into a series of traps. He instructed the Pistons to funnel Jordan into a clog of bodies whenever he initiated his drive, forcing him to shoot over a wall of arms.[10]

On the precipice of Game Seven in the 1990 Eastern Conference Finals, Jordan stood one victory away from advancing to the NBA championship and fulfilling his dream. But inside the Bulls' dressing room at the Palace of Auburn Hills, shortly before the game, Scottie Pippen, an emerging twenty-four-year-old All-Star forward, could barely keep his eyes open. Jordan's wingman told team trainer Mark Pfeil that he couldn't see clearly. The searing pain felt like someone had taken an ice pick to his head. He blinked rapidly but the throbbing migraine seemed to get worse. When Pfeil asked Pippen if he could play, Jordan interrupted and answered, "Hell, yes, he can play. Start him. Let him play blind."[11]

Jordan demanded unwavering devotion from his teammates, especially since the Bulls were about to play the most important game in the history of the franchise. Somehow, Pippen dragged himself around the court for forty-two minutes, but it was the worst game of his career. He could barely distinguish his teammates from the Pistons. He attempted ten shots and made only one, scoring just two points. Sitting on the bench during a long break, he pressed an ice pack against the back of his head, but it couldn't relieve the throbbing. Everyone on the team could see Pippen struggling, and without him—and without starting guard John Paxson, hobbled by a sprained ankle—there was no way the Bulls could beat the Pistons on their home floor. In the end, not even Jordan could rescue the team from a blowout.

After the Pistons routed the Bulls 93–74, Pippen broke down and cried in the locker room. He couldn't help but feel like he had let everyone down. The "migraine game" would haunt him for years. In Chicago, fans questioned his fortitude, calling him "soft." Diminishing his pain, sportswriters doubted whether he even had a migraine or if a headache could prevent a true pro basketball player from performing. Pippen's harshest critics included Michael Jordan. According to *Chicago Tribune* reporter Sam Smith, after losing the series to the Pistons, "Jordan told management that he wouldn't mind seeing Pippen traded." Pippen was unreliable, Jordan thought. In short, Smith wrote, "Jordan had sized him up as a loser."[12]

Yet the agony of the migraine frightened Pippen far more than Jordan realized. For days, Pippen's headache persisted. "I was afraid I was dying," he admitted, a gut-wrenching revelation considering that his sixty-nine-year-old father had passed away less than a month earlier, during the Eastern Conference Semifinals. After missing the fourth game of that series against the Philadelphia 76ers so he could attend his father's funeral, Pippen, still grieving, returned to work carrying the painful loss in his chest. When he rejoined the team, Phil Jackson recognized the sadness in his face, a child in mourning. Acknowledging his anguish, the Bulls' head coach asked the team to form a circle of love around Pippen in the locker room, reminding the men that a team was like a family. Then, Jackson, the son of Pentecostal ministers, lead the group in the Lord's Prayer, a gesture that clearly moved Pippen.[13]

After the loss to the Pistons, Jackson defended Pippen. He had no doubt that his "suffering was real." Yet watching the Pistons vanquish the Bulls, Jackson wondered how he could revitalize a team whose faith had completely collapsed. He could see that the players had lost trust in one another. That season, his first as head coach, the Bulls won a franchise-record fifty-seven games, but no one in the locker room cared after the Pistons flattened them. Jackson had failed to lead the Bulls further than his predecessor, Doug Collins, and he fully understood that he had to win *now*. "I knew it was either win or be gone," he said.[14]

The Bulls had reached a "crisis point," Jackson thought, one made worse when general manager Jerry Krause stormed into the locker room, his jowly face beet red, berating the players. "This will never happen again!" he shouted. "We will not allow this to happen again. You guys should have won tonight." Then, Krause, known inside the organization for reminding players that he was the boss, slammed the door and stormed out of a room teeming with resentment.[15]

No one detested Krause more than Jordan. The Bulls star often complained that Krause, a contentious, disheveled man built like Alfred Hitchcock, had not done enough to surround him with more talent. In fact, that season the Bulls had one of the lowest-paid rosters in the league—nearly $1 million under the NBA's salary cap—enough money to acquire a veteran player who might have helped them beat the Pistons. And yet Krause had made no moves before the trade deadline.[16]

Jordan had lost patience with Krause and everyone around him. Losing infuriated him. He couldn't stand being embarrassed. Each loss pained him, like a deep cut that never healed. He grumbled about carrying inferior players who did not know how to win. After Game Seven, he stood before his teammates in the center of the locker room and delivered a fervid speech, choking back tears, vowing that he would never swallow defeat like this again. Stacey King, a rookie forward, recalled, "It was almost like a religious thing. He had a glow to him." His message struck the room like a "lightning bolt."[17]

Afterward, Jordan showered, dressed, and spoke to reporters. Then he headed for the team bus, his somber eyes downcast, looking like he had just left a cemetery. Standing near the stadium entrance, Pistons general manager Jack McCloskey spotted him across the Palace parking lot. He approached Jordan and offered words of encouragement.

"Mr. McCloskey," Jordan asked, "are we ever going to get past the Pistons? Are we ever going to win?"

"Michael," he answered, "your time is coming, and it's coming very soon."[18]

Jordan boarded the bus. Completely depleted, he slumped into a seat near the back next to his father, as tears streamed down his cheeks.

The Pistons, Phil Jackson said, "punished us. We got blasted. But the Monday after that debacle the guys showed up for work."

Two days after losing Game Seven of the 1990 Eastern Conference Finals, around 7:30 a.m., virtually the entire team began training at the Bulls practice facility in Deerfield, an affluent North Shore suburb. When the players returned to Chicago, some guys began talking about their travel plans for the summer, but Michael Jordan urged them to get back into the gym immediately. It didn't matter how exhausted they felt after an arduous season. Resting wasn't an option, not for him, not for anyone. For years he questioned whether his teammates shared his commitment, but their presence in the weight room that day signaled that they were determined to compete for a championship.[19]

Yet Jordan preferred training alone, separate from his teammates. Early in his career he avoided lifting weights, fearing that added bulk would make him less explosive. Jordan had tried working with a weight trainer once but injured his back and hesitated to do it again. However, after the Pistons battered him during the 1990 Conference Finals, Jordan concluded that he had to get stronger.

When he told reporters that he needed to harden his body, a young physical trainer in Chicago named Tim Grover read about it in a local newspaper. Three years earlier, during America's growing fitness craze, Grover, a former benchwarmer on the University of Illinois at Chicago basketball team, wrote a master's thesis about conditioning basketball players. Working at a local health club, he dreamed of becoming a personal trainer for the pros. He wrote letters to every player on the Chicago Bulls except Jordan, assuming the team's biggest star already had a private trainer. Reading about Jordan's growing frustrations, though, Grover was convinced he could help him. So, he contacted the Bulls' team doctor, John Hefferon, a family friend who connected him with Jordan.[20]

Hefferon and the Bulls' team trainer Mark Pfeil arranged for Grover to meet Jordan at his home. Grover arrived well prepared, laying out a detailed plan focused on making him more durable, stronger but not slower. He explained the importance of strengthening Jordan's core and avoiding nagging injuries that plagued basketball players—groin pulls and ankle sprains. Grover told him that every physical change they made to his body would affect the way he played and that this training would require adjustments. Undoubtedly, adding weight would alter his balance and his shot. Basketball is a muscle-memory sport and Jordan would be disrupting his body's memory. "Your timing will be off, and you'll be missing your jump shot, and you'll be furious," Grover said, but "you're just going to have to trust me when I tell you that eventually it will all come back."[21]

Gradually, they would add muscle mass to Jordan's body, taking him from about 195 pounds to 215 pounds over the course of three or four years. "If we try and bulk you up too quickly, your game will suffer and you'll lose something," Grover explained. He also warned Jordan that if they began working together, the first few months could be painful and bewildering.

Jordan listened intently without saying a word. He doubted Grover's plan would work and that lifting weights would alter his shot. Grover persisted: "I'll give you a thirty-day schedule detailing exactly what we're going to do, how it's going to affect your body, your game, your overall strength. I'll tell you how you're going to feel so you can adjust to the changes we're going to make. We'll plan what you'll eat, when you'll eat it, when you'll sleep. We'll look at every detail, leaving nothing to chance. You'll see how everything works together."[22]

Finally, Jordan agreed and told him to spare no expense building a home gym. Then, he added, "You better keep up. You better keep up."[23]

Grover was as obsessed about the process as Jordan—that's what made them such a great match. From the very beginning, Jordan made clear he wasn't interested in gimmicks or shortcuts. No matter how grueling the program became, no matter how much his muscles burned, he exerted himself beyond any expectations Grover set. When they began training, Grover's warning came true: for a brief time that summer Jordan could not find his shooting rhythm. But that only gave Grover more credibility, deepening Jordan's trust.

Jordan required absolute loyalty from Grover, which meant he could not discuss what they did with management or the press. This training program gave him an advantage over his competition, he thought. He guarded it like it was the secret formula to Coca-Cola. Ultimately, the partnership paid off. By the time training camp began for the 1990–1991 season, Jordan had already grown bigger and stronger, especially in his shoulders and arms. Now, on the precipice of a new season, he had reforged his body like a sword, sharpened out of a desire to turn his body into an unstoppable weapon.

In early October, on the eve of training camp, Jordan met with Phil Jackson in the head coach's office. For several weeks Jackson had tried to reach him by phone, but he could not locate the globe-trotting star. Jordan had spent the off-season pumping iron with Grover, hitting the links, and traveling to Europe for a Nike promotional tour. Two years before the Barcelona Olympics, Jordan toured the capital of Catalonia, making highly publicized appearances at the offices of Olympic officials, Nike, and the Associated Club of Basketball. In August, shortly after the Gulf War began, he performed basketball exhibitions in front of a few thousand American soldiers, young men and women who appreciated the diversion from the escalating conflict in the Middle East.[24]

Jordan did not want to tour Europe. He preferred staying home and playing golf, but Nike rep Sonny Vaccaro convinced him that a hastily planned excursion would help him escape a developing political controversy that threatened his reputation as much as the stories about the so-called sneaker murders. Earlier that summer, Jesse Jackson and his lieutenant Rev. Tyrone Crider—the leaders of Operation PUSH, a Chicago-based civil rights organization—encouraged Black Americans to boycott Nike products, claiming that the shoe company exploited young Black consumers and failed to hire Black executives. Jackson pointed out that Nike had no Black members on its board of directors and no Black vice presidents. The footwear company did not consult Black ad agencies or spend one advertising dollar on Black Entertainment Television or in *Ebony* magazine. In other words, he charged, Nike's relationship with the Black community was exclusively transactional.[25]

Jackson, a former presidential candidate who admired and knew Jordan, said Operation PUSH was not targeting Nike's Black spokesmen, though he expected them to use their influence to change the company's culture. As a crossover star, Jordan enjoyed an unprecedented platform, but he retreated from using it for any social or political cause. Jackson called Jordan, trying to recruit him to the movement, but Jordan refused, saying that racial problems permeated corporate America and that it was unfair to target Nike exclusively. Protective of the Jordan brand, Nike execs did not want their most famous endorser answering questions about the boycott on television. On August 15, Jordan released a short press statement, opposing PUSH's boycott, and then flew to Europe.

The leaders of PUSH misjudged the public's appetite for a Nike boycott. A Gallup poll found that Chicagoans supported Nike over PUSH by a three-to-one margin, though nearly half of Black people interviewed said they did not know enough about the campaign to express an opinion. Throughout the summer PUSH activists, some ironically wearing Nike shoes, protested outside of Chicago's Foot Locker stores. The trouble for PUSH, however, was that most Black youths did not view Nike as a racist or discriminatory company. Rather, they viewed Nike through the eyes of its most prominent Black endorsers—Jordan, Bo Jackson, and David Robinson. No other brand in America was so closely associated with Black representatives. The boycott, therefore, failed to put a dent in Nike's bottom line. By the time Jordan returned to the States, the controversy had faded from the news. Reporters stopped asking him questions about the boycott and crimes associated with his shoes. It turned out that a summer vacation overseas solved Jordan's public relations problem.[26]

Phil Jackson's summer was far more peaceful than Jordan's. Outside his sprawling ranch on the banks of Flathead Lake in western Montana, he meditated in the wilderness, visualizing a team in harmony. When he was a boy, Jackson had vacationed with his family in a cabin on the Flathead River, forty miles upstream. Every summer since 1973, when he bought the lakefront property with bonus money he earned as a player on the New York Knicks championship team, he returned to a land he considered sacred. A sparkling blue gem located at the base of rugged mountain ranges and lush forests, the quiet lake became Jackson's sanctuary, a site for rejuvenation after another long, draining season. Returning to his roots in Montana made him feel whole. It provided a remedy for his striving life, a break from the demands of the circus world of professional basketball and the constant pressure to succeed.[27]

At Flathead Lake, Jackson "realized that anger was the Bulls' real enemy, not the Detroit Pistons." In the team's losses he recognized an alarming pattern: the players' frustration turned into blame. When the Pistons rattled the Bulls, Jackson's team lost all concentration. The core problem, he thought, was that Jordan didn't trust his teammates or a head coach who had only spent one year leading the team.[28]

How could Jackson convince Jordan to change? How could he build a championship team around a basketball prodigy and integrate his exceptional talents into a system that did not marginalize players Jordan deemed mere mortals? He knew that Jordan loved challenges, and nothing fueled him more than his ambition to win the championship. So, after returning to Chicago, instead of dictating what he wanted from him, Jackson asked Jordan to reimagine his relationship with his teammates on and off the court. He told Jordan that the ball served as a spotlight and when it was in his hands the spotlight shined brightest on him. But Jordan needed to share the spotlight with his teammates, or they would never grow.[29]

Jackson explained that the Bulls had played Jordan's way for six seasons and the team had never reached the NBA Finals. In fact, since the NBA instituted the twenty-four-second shot clock in 1954, only one NBA team had won the title with the league's leading scorer—and that was when the Milwaukee Bucks did it with Kareem Abdul-Jabbar in 1971. It was time for the Bulls to try a new approach, one that reduced the team's dependence on Jordan. The deeper the Bulls advanced into the playoffs, Jackson explained, the more likely they were going to face the Pistons, a formidable defensive team that had proved it could focus its entire attention on stopping him. Too often, during crunch time, the Bulls ran what assistant coach Johnny Bach called the "Archangel Offense." That's what happened when the Bulls gave MJ the ball and said, "Save us, Michael."[30]

Jordan's talent posed a paradox for Jackson. "Michael Jordan is a coach's dream and a coach's nightmare," he said. Jordan did not need to play within an offensive system to dominate. He could score at will. But for every incredible play he made, Jackson said, he "defies the rules of the game. Like when the double team comes at him, instead of passing the ball, he *beats* the double team." In some circumstances, that could be good for the Bulls, but it also created poor outcomes for the team because it prevented the other players from developing their own identities on offense.[31]

Jackson knew that Jordan could embrace an offense where the players shared the ball. As an All-American at UNC, Jordan thrived in Dean Smith's motion offense. Smith called it "a passing game," a free-form arrangement with no predetermined cuts and no set pattern. Players read the defense and reacted to it. Similarly, when Jordan played on the US Olympic team, Indiana University coach Bob Knight ran a motion offense. However, when he first came to the Bulls, coach Kevin Loughery turned the offense over to him, giving Jordan complete freedom with the ball. Early in his pro career, Jordan never developed confidence in his teammates. In virtually every scoring situation, he believed that he had a better chance of making a shot than anyone else on the team. And that may well have been true. But playing each game, possession by possession, eventually wore Jordan down by the end of the season.

During the 1989–1990 season, Jackson's first as a head coach in the NBA, he installed the triple-post offense, or "the triangle offense," as the players called it, a continuous motion arrangement based on the involvement of all five players. He learned the offense from his assistant Fred "Tex" Winter, who refined it as head coach at Kansas State University in the 1950s after his mentor Sam Barry taught it to him as a player at the University of Southern California. Winter had encouraged Jackson's predecessor, Doug Collins, to read his textbook, *The Triple-Post Offense*. Yet Collins argued that the triple-post offense was better suited for the college game than the pros. He preferred to run dozens of different set plays through Jordan. Collins installed so many of them throughout the season that the team began calling the offense "a play a day."[32]

In March 1989, Collins moved Jordan from shooting guard to point guard, a strategy designed to keep the ball in his hands. The responsibilities of the two positions were very different: the point guard's primary job was to advance the ball up court and direct the offense; the shooting guard's main task, as the position indicates, was to score. The upside of having Jordan run the offense in the middle of the court was that it became difficult for defenses to trap him, giving his teammates more open space when opponents tilted too much toward him. If Jordan was the greatest weapon on offense, then it made sense to him and Collins that they should just eliminate the process where someone else started with the ball while Jordan fought through traffic to receive a pass. Playing point guard allowed Jordan to see the whole floor and forced him to think about his teammates. In some respects, the experiment seemed to work. That season Jordan averaged 32.5

points—the best in the NBA—and 8 assists, good for tenth in the league. During one stretch, he finished with seven consecutive triple-doubles—an impressive feat that the NBA had not witnessed since Wilt Chamberlain completed nine straight in 1968.[33]

Yet carrying the load as the team's primary distributor *and* scorer exhausted him. Between the time Jordan took over as point guard and the end of the season, the Bulls finished with a modest 13–11 record. Although the team advanced to the Eastern Conference Finals against the Pistons, Chuck Daly's players believed defending *Jordan the point guard* was easier than guarding *Jordan the shooting guard* because his teammates had not yet developed into serious scoring threats.

Jackson, then Collins's assistant coach, never liked the idea of making Jordan the point guard. "The problem with making Jordan the point guard, as I saw it, was that it didn't address the real problem: the fact that the prevalent style of offense reinforced a self-centered approach to the game," Jackson observed. He deplored the way that "inner-city playground basketball" had infiltrated the NBA after the merger with the American Basketball Association (ABA) in 1976, expressing an anxiousness that many white observers held about the way Black players had altered the game's style and purported values. Although he knew that Jordan's basketball heroes, Julius Erving and David Thompson, made the sport more entertaining, Jackson also thought the individualized expression that they brought from the ABA to the NBA diminished professional basketball. He lamented the way players, empowered by the financial benefits of free agency and television stardom, glorified individual achievement and material excess.[34]

Jackson's complaints about playground basketball revealed an underlying prejudice that dated back to his playing days. In the seventies, when he was still a tall, gangly reserve for the New York Knicks, Jackson traced the rapid "disintegration" of the NBA "into a one-on-one sport" to the predominance of Black players "who had a strong compulsion to succeed as individuals." Jackson maintained that white players were more often "willing to work collectively" than Black players, a baseless claim rooted in stereotypes. He recognized that many Black players from the inner city grew up in anonymity, dreaming of becoming "the superstar of their neighborhood." Competing against Black players, Jackson came to believe that many of them preferred playing in one-on-one situations because basketball gave them a space where they could assert their manhood and demonstrate their "raw ego power."[35]

Long before he became the Bulls' head coach, he concluded that the best teams were those that integrated individual talent and "group consciousness into one functional unit." "As far as I am concerned," he reflected in 1975, "the only way to win consistently in the NBA is to have several selfless players who are willing to do things even when the spotlight's on somebody else." Crucially, his interest in adopting Winter's offense, an egalitarian system that offered each player a vital role, stemmed from his experience playing for the Knicks during the late 1960s and 1970s.[36]

From Jackson's perspective, one shared by several sportswriters, the old Knicks, a racially integrated unit known for being unselfish, represented the essence of team basketball. "In a game of individuals," New York Times writer Lawrence Shainberg wrote in 1970, the Knicks "are a community." The 1970 NBA championship team seemed special, a model of how the game *should* be played. Those Knicks, a balanced group featuring Walt Frazier, Willis Reed, Dave DeBusschere, Dick Barnett, and Bill Bradley, embraced the idea that everyone should pass the ball and everyone should shoot. "When the 'back door' works, when the defense collapses like a net in the direction of the ball, when the movement without the ball finds its groove," Shainberg wrote, "the Knicks became a metaphor for all the visions of social interaction in which men don't just sacrifice themselves to the group but actually get their kicks from what they do together."[37]

Three years earlier, when Jackson came to the Knicks as a second-round draft choice from the University of North Dakota, Coach Red Holzman told him that if he wanted to play, he needed to accept an unremarkable role: rebounding, setting screens, and shutting down his man. An unrefined offensive player, Jackson learned "how to move the ball and how to move himself without it," noted biographer Roland Lazenby. Standing six feet, eight inches, Jackson, "a stick figure constructed entirely of straight lines and right angles," looked like a "human coat hanger" with bony square shoulders. Gradually, "Action Jackson" molded himself into a scrappy defensive player, a windmill of arms and elbows. His teammate Bill Bradley recalled, "I had to play against him every day in practice and it was murderous. He would bang you and bang you and bang you all the time—not dirty, just very physical—and he had those long arms. It was like being guarded by a spider. After practicing against him, playing games against other defenders was a vast relief."[38]

The experience of being a substitute who often watched the game from the bench helped Jackson the coach imagine how he could involve all the players. In Tex Winter's triple-post offense he discovered a cooperative system that reminded him of the way his teams with the Knicks empowered every player on the floor. Instead of static isolation plays and predetermined sets called by the coach on the sideline, the triple-post offense depended on spacing, cutting, and frequent passing—a more democratic arrangement that gave the players greater responsibility for making decisions on the court. The "sideline triangle," as Winter described it, began when three players on one side of the floor formed a triangle—a center on the block, a forward on the wing, and a guard in the corner. From there, the player with the ball made an "automatic"—a pass based entirely on defensive alignments. The basic idea was to orchestrate constant movement that would lure the defense out of position and create a mismatch, an improved scoring angle, or an open shot.[39]

The triangle offense appealed to Jackson for several reasons: all five players on the court were interchangeable and necessary for the system to work; anyone could occupy the post, even a guard like Jordan; the constant passing and cutting allowed less skilled players to get open shots without having to dribble; and, most importantly, it made every player an offensive threat, which made Jordan even more dangerous. If the defense had to account for all five offensive players, Jackson reasoned, then that would spring Jordan free from traps and double-teams.

Regardless of talent, everybody on the team had something to learn within the triangle offense. Mastering all the components—footwork, spacing, and terminology—created a shared experience for the players. Yet the Bulls players resisted the complicated system, complaining that it was arcane. Many of them found it completely foreign to the way they had played throughout their careers. During an interview with a *Sports Illustrated* writer, John Paxson tried explaining something Jackson had said during practice. "It went something like this," Paxson recalled. "Phil said he wanted 'reverse action off the blind pig [a defender the Bulls try to catch in a backdoor cut], to triangle on the weak side, with a two-pass to the top of the key, to a pass down the gut.'" Paxson paused, confusing himself and the writer. Exasperated, he said, "Look, maybe you should just go read Tex's book."[40]

In a way, Jackson's leadership—and his implementation of the triangle offense—reflected the management approach of a post-industrial society that valued knowledge production, creativity, and systematic innovation. Jackson rejected the idea that authority flowed in one direction—from top to bottom. He preferred the art of persuasion more than commands. Compared to the coaches of the industrial age, the ones who stood on the sidelines for an entire game, barking instructions like a drill sergeant and killing the creativity of players, Jackson often sat on the bench, legs crossed, giving his players the space to work out a problem on the court. He conceived of a team not as a hierarchical pyramid but as an interdependent network of collaborators. That paradigm could be seen in the triangle offense, a basketball laboratory where the players, like postindustrial workers, employed special skills in positions that were less rigidly defined. Jackson believed an effective coach spurned micromanagement in favor of decentralized decision-making. If the players were going to master the triangle offense, he thought, then "they would have to have the confidence to make decisions on their own. That would never happen if they were constantly searching for direction from me. I wanted them to *dis*connect themselves from me, so they could connect with their teammates—and the game."[41]

The greatest challenge for Jackson was blending two clashing philosophies about how the Bulls should play. Reconciling the views of two stubborn, opinionated men—Tex Winter and Michael Jordan—proved difficult. In his fifth decade of coaching, Winter could be brutally honest and critical. He thought of himself as a pedagogue, and he took every opportunity to teach, even if it meant correcting Jordan in practice. The self-proclaimed "old-fashioned basketball coach" rejected the idea that the game should be a test for a single player's ventures. Jordan was "competitive to a fault," Winter said. "He wants to come out and dominate every practice session. He gets into the one-on-one situation too much . . . I think we would be a better team and he would be a more effective player if he didn't try to score every time he touched the basketball."[42]

Jordan dismissed Winter's objections. He sneered, "What's Tex ever won, anyway?" The game had evolved since Winter began teaching the triangle, Jordan said. The modern players were more athletic and explosive. And, in his mind, the game rewarded those who could generate their own shot: "The players today can do things they couldn't do twenty years ago. The game isn't played any more like Tex Winter taught it." Winter's concepts, he argued, "don't work against bigger, faster players who jump higher." Yet Winter maintained that when Jordan operated by his own rules, his teammates did not always know how to play the game.[43]

In Jackson's first year as head coach, the team struggled mastering "that triangle stuff," as Jordan called it. It was a season of learning and unlearning, setbacks and growth. Mostly Jordan played within the system, but when he became impatient with his teammates, he would just put his head down and improvise. Assistant Coach Johnny Bach, an old Navy vet and father of a California state trooper, favored Jordan's gun-slinging boldness more than Winter. During close games, when the team huddled near the bench, Winter would often draw the triangle on his whiteboard, exhorting the players to stick with his offense, but Bach would pull Jordan aside and say, "Fuck the triangle. Just take the ball and score. Get everyone else to clear out."[44]

On the eve of training camp, when Jordan sat down with Jackson, he hoped that his head coach would tell him that he was scrapping the triangle. Instead, Jackson told him that his commitment to the system had only deepened. Jordan feared that meant taking the ball out of his hands and giving up control. He met Jackson's plan with skepticism. "He's the coach and I'll follow his scheme," Jordan told reporters. "But I don't plan to change my style of ball because I've been successful. I'm sure everything will be fine as long as we win. But if we start losing, I'm going to start shooting."[45]

Before the 1990–1991 season began, Phil Jackson informed Michael Jordan that the Bulls would run the triangle offense, a system that would require Jordan to pass the ball more to his teammates. Jordan didn't like the idea and made his feelings known. Jackson said, "Well, at least now he's been warned. He knows, and we're going to stick with this. We'll see what he does." Credit: AP Images

Chapter Five

BOBOS AND WARRIORS

"All my life I had to carry myself as a minister's son."

—Phil Jackson

In 1989, when Jerry Krause introduced reporters to the next head coach of the Chicago Bulls, Phil Jackson, a man who once described himself as a "long-haired, pot-smoking hippie," looked nothing like the unshorn rebel who once questioned the importance of basketball. Since those turbulent years of the late sixties and early seventies, the forty-three-year-old coach had traded his denim overalls and lumberjack flannels for tailored suits designed by Bigsby & Kruthers, one of Chicago's best-known haberdashers.[1]

He had come a long way from the small towns of the Great Plains, following his parents, itinerant Pentecostal preachers, across rural Montana and North Dakota. When the former Knicks forward arrived in New York City in 1967, he embarked on a new journey, contemplating his future in basketball and the possibility of becoming a minister. But at the height of the Vietnam War, Jackson immersed himself in the counterculture, protesting almost everything his parents had taught him. In his search for identity, he crisscrossed the country on monthlong motorcycle rides; he studied psychology, Buddhism, and Native American philosophy; he joined peace demonstrations and made friends in the forested hills of Woodstock. Like so many young Americans seeking an alternative to what they viewed as a polluted, corrupt world, he sought refuge, experimenting with meditation, mind-altering drugs, and "a variety of sexual partners," all of which he divulged in his provocative 1975 memoir, *Maverick*.[2]

That book cast a long shadow over his coaching career. For years Jackson believed that his bohemian image—born out of his politics and his quest for autonomy—prevented him from securing a head-coaching job in the NBA. He regretted writing *Maverick* because the stories he shared hurt people close to him. His second wife, June, despised the book, insisting that it misrepresented the man he had become. In 1989, a reporter from the *Chicago Sun-Times* asked him about the memoir. "I'd just as soon not talk about that book," Jackson said, and then he proceeded to talk about that book. "I liked it. It's a unique book. I've been flattered by the people who liked *Maverick* for what it represented. As a personal history of myself, I'm not particularly fond of all the things I disclosed. Maybe I was too open, but I was a very open person at age 29."[3]

There was a time when Jackson had all but given up on coaching in the NBA. After an eleven-year career with the Knicks, his journey as a coach began when he joined the New Jersey Nets as a player and assistant to Kevin Loughery. For three seasons he served as an assistant coach before leaving basketball altogether for one year. Then he returned to New Jersey as color commentator for one season of Nets games. Jackson left broadcasting to become head coach of the Albany Patroons in the Continental Basketball Association (CBA), a minor league where young pros showcased their talents in the hopes of being discovered by the

NBA. In 1984, he led the Patroons to the CBA championship and the following season the league named him coach of the year. Jackson's coaching record impressed Jerry Krause. Scavenging every corner of the country for overlooked prospects, Krause turned to Jackson for scouting reports on CBA players. Soon, he began calling him regularly, serving as Jackson's only lifeline to the NBA.[4]

Krause did not care about Jackson's reputation as a free spirit. What mattered, he thought, was that Jackson knew the game and knew how to coach. He was inquisitive and related well to players. Convinced that Jackson could help the Bulls, Krause tried persuading head coach Stan Albeck to hire him as an assistant, but when Jackson arrived for an interview wearing flip-flops, chino slacks, and a feathered straw hat, an aesthetic influenced by his summer coaching gig in Puerto Rico, Albeck determined that they were not a good fit. "Stan was a little afraid of Phil," Krause said. "Phil had a long beard. He was an intellectual. He'd been an activist. I think Stan might have thought he was a revolutionary."[5]

After returning to the CBA for two more seasons, Jackson became disillusioned with an organization that had become a revolving door for players looking for a better deal, whether it was in the NBA or Europe. Feeling underpaid and unappreciated, in 1987 he quit without any prospects, not knowing where he might land. Paying his dues in the CBA hardly paid the bills. And he doubted that the NBA would ever call him. So, the father of five contemplated an entirely new path. He began reading a self-help manual for job hunters, titled *What Color Is Your Parachute?*. A placement test indicated he was best suited for four different careers: homemaker, trail guide, counselor, and lawyer.[6]

Without basketball, he struggled to find purpose and provide for his family. Twisting in the wind, Jackson applied for unemployment. Then one day in September, while he waited for his first insurance check, the phone rang. It was Jerry Krause calling to see if he was still interested in working as an assistant coach with the Bulls. By that time, Krause had replaced Albeck with Doug Collins, who agreed that Jackson should interview. Before Jackson flew to Chicago, Krause told him to shave his beard and don his best suit. The GM also suggested that he wear his two championship rings from the Knicks, conspicuous symbols of a winner. That idea made Jackson a little uncomfortable. It contradicted his more modest instincts, but he showed up sharply dressed with a neatly trimmed mustache, sporting the rings, and got the job. "It was time to conform," Jackson said.[7]

He arrived in Chicago at a pivotal moment for the franchise. A few months earlier Krause had drafted Scottie Pippen and Horace Grant. Over the next three seasons, as Pippen and Grant developed into major contributors, they grew resentful of the way Collins treated them compared to the way he treated Jordan. Collins roamed the sidelines, his tie loosened, perspiring as much as the players, berating them for their alleged ineptitude. Collins "would come in the locker room at halftime," Pippen recalled, "looking like he played the whole first half. Take his jacket off. Be soaking wet. Screamed at everybody . . . except for Michael." The problem, Pippen thought, was that Collins acted more like Jordan's biggest fan than his coach.[8]

Observing Collins, Krause noticed that some players shrank under the head coach's frequent outbursts. Team owner Jerry Reinsdorf could see it too. Although the Bulls had reached the Eastern Conference Finals in Collins's third year as head coach, Reinsdorf thought that the team was disintegrating under his leadership. Players complained that Collins impulsively yanked them off the floor for the slightest transgressions. He became exceedingly critical of everyone around him, including his assistant coaches. At one point he refused to talk to Jackson, fearing that

Phil was angling for his job. Supposedly, Collins warned Jackson about plotting against him. Another time, he banished Tex Winter from practice, relegating him to sideline observer. "Reinsdorf," Sam Smith reported in the *Chicago Tribune*, "saw a driven, insecure Collins, grasping desperately to succeed while fighting madly not to fail. He saw his coach missing sleep and meals and breaking down in his office over the pressures of the job." That insecurity, and his dependence on Jordan, Reinsdorf calculated, would make the team crash and burn.[9]

And there was something else that bothered Reinsdorf. In a legal pad he scribbled a note about Collins: "Wants to be Mike Ditka." After leading the Chicago Bears to win the Super Bowl in 1986, Ditka, a raging, egotistical martinet, became one of the most popular figures in the city, appearing in numerous local television commercials. His notoriety made an impression on Collins, and, Reinsdorf thought, "he was driven to duplicate it." Like the head coach of the Bears, Collins became increasingly confrontational with management, arguing with Krause over strategy, personnel, and the general manager's presence during practices.[10]

The two Jerrys, as they were known in Chicago, had enough of Collins. When Reinsdorf phoned Michael Jordan to break the news about replacing the head coach, Jordan laughed. There was no way that Reinsdorf would fire Collins after the Bulls had reached the conference finals for the first time in fourteen years. "You don't have the balls," Jordan said and hung up.[11]

Citing "philosophical differences," on July 6, 1989, Reinsdorf abruptly told Collins to empty his office. The popular coach's dismissal stunned the city's fans. Collins had become the "personification of the Madhouse on Madison Street," his frenzied energy reverberating throughout the crowd. Angry Chicagoans penned harsh letters to the local newspapers and Bulls management, blaming Krause even though he was the one who fought

Reinsdorf to hire Collins in the first place. "I got tremendous heat," Krause recalled. "It was like I'd killed Christ."[12]

Immediately, rumors circulated over the airwaves of Chicago's sports talk radio shows that Jordan had pressured management to fire Collins, but the Bulls star vehemently denied it. Although they clashed occasionally, Jordan was not the reason Reinsdorf fired Collins. Yet some of his teammates speculated about Jordan's involvement. "Michael plays a big part in everything that goes on with the Bulls," Horace Grant said. "Who knows?"[13]

Reinsdorf and Krause agreed there was only one serious candidate for the job: Phil Jackson. They appreciated the way he communicated with the players. He treated them with dignity, seeing each man as an individual with different needs, strengths, and weaknesses. Compared to Collins, Jackson displayed greater poise on the sidelines, a calming influence that reminded Jordan of Dean Smith. "Phil doesn't usually raise his voice," Jordan said. He listened carefully, thought about his words, and looked for opportunities to challenge the players. The previous season, when Jackson was still an assistant coach, he approached Jordan with advice about how he could better help the team. Jordan respected him for talking to him directly, something few people did because of his status. "A lot of coaches have been afraid to do that with me," Jordan said. "They were afraid it would ruin their relationship with me."[14]

Jordan recognized the qualities that made Jackson an excellent coach, as did Jerry Reinsdorf. Before the Bulls owner hired him, he called one of Jackson's old teammates from the New York Knicks, Bill Bradley, then a United States senator. A Brooklyn native, Reinsdorf grew up idolizing Bradley and the Knicks. When he bought the Bulls in 1985, he said, "The New York Knicks of the Red Holzman era epitomized the way basketball should be played. Total unselfish basketball. That's going to be Chicago

Bulls basketball." When Reinsdorf phoned Bradley, he wanted to know whether Jackson shared Holzman's coaching philosophy. Would he be able to work with a dominant personality like Jordan? Jackson, Bradley answered, "thinks group, but he always sees individuals. He's not going to be a drill sergeant trying to force everyone into the same mold. He has a real appreciation—and respect—for individuality."[15]

Jackson's ability to reconcile individual freedom and collective action within a community made him the ideal coach for Michael Jordan. His unique perspective was rooted in a journey of self-discovery, a lifelong search for fulfillment on and off the court. When he became the Bulls' head coach, Jackson shaped the team culture around the philosophical trinity that had guided much of his adult life: Christianity, Zen Buddhism, and the teachings of the Lakota Sioux. In the coming years, he blended these disparate influences into his coaching methods, fashioning himself a New Age philosopher, a basketball guru fusing the values of competitive team sports with his own spiritual code. Yet, Jackson's odyssey was built as much around a deep urge for winning as any spiritual impulse. And more than anything, that competitive urge earned him Jordan's respect.

Being a coach reminded Jackson of being a minister. "When you're a basketball coach you're a little like a minister in that you do a lot of preaching," he explained. "A coach has to be a combination of teacher, a boss, and a friend. At times you have to be a person concerned about the welfare of the individuals under your care. Other times you need to be ready to give advice, not only in basketball but things with regard to one's personal life."[16]

The minister's son learned the game playing basketball on a backyard court built by his father. Playing sports was one of the few secular activities that Charles Jackson allowed. Phil remembered his father as an austere but compassionate man who did "everything by the Book" and expected his boys to do the same. Charles attended as many of Phil's games as an itinerant preacher could, but his wife, Elizabeth, "a striking, charismatic woman" and the former captain of her high school basketball team, never saw her son play. Intensely devoted to preparing for Christ's resurrection, Elizabeth drilled her children on the scriptures, requiring they memorize the King James Bible and warning that the rapture was imminent. Perhaps Elizabeth's unwillingness to watch Phil play basketball was her way of telling him that there was no higher act than worship, nothing more important than preparing "spiritually for His arrival because it might come at any moment."[17]

Born in Deer Lodge, Montana, Jackson spent most of his childhood in Williston, North Dakota, a small, sports-crazed town, where the rhythms of the church and the high school basketball team dictated his life. On Sundays his family attended service twice, once in the morning when Charles preached and later in the evening when Elizabeth delivered her own hellfire and brimstone sermon. Twice during each week the family organized evening church events, but when Phil joined the high school team he avoided Friday night services. In some ways, the household functioned daily like a regimented basketball team: meals occurred at eight, twelve, and six, "and if you were late," Jackson recalled, "you just went without eating." Every morning before breakfast, the family read devotionals, and after supper, they memorized passages from the Bible "as a way to keep evil thoughts from creeping in."[18]

Jackson grew up cloistered away in a tightly wound household that suppressed individuality and emotional expression. His parents forbade him to dance or watch television. He could sing hymns in the church choir or play music in the school band, but he could not listen to rock 'n' roll records, certainly none performed by Elvis Presley, another young rebel raised in the Pentecostal church. Jackson could read textbooks or encyclopedias, but he could not indulge in the fantasies of comic books or pulp fiction. And his parents allowed only one magazine in the house: *Reader's Digest*. Library books offered him an escape from the repressive grip of his parents. Literature, along with sports, helped him imagine the possibilities of a life outside his home. He grew into a voracious reader, checking out stacks of library books two or three times each week, searching—*always searching*—for answers to questions that could not be found in any Bible.[19]

The shy, insecure preacher's kid came of age under great scrutiny from the adults in the church. He felt constant pressure to live up to his parents' moral standards and avoid their judgmental thinking. He struggled, too, seeking the Holy Spirit. He prayed for hours and hours, but he never felt "the gift of tongues" awaken his soul. The Pentecostal rituals involved people humming, wailing, and throwing themselves on the floor, emotional reveries that made no sense to him and marked him an outsider in the eyes of people who did not belong to the Assemblies of God. Children mocked him as a "Holy Roller," refusing to befriend the awkward preacher's kid who wore a crisp white shirt to school every day.[20]

Belonging to the Assemblies of God made it difficult for him to fully connect with people outside the church. It created a yearning for shared secular experiences and a community free of moral judgment. Basketball helped the skinny, bespectacled boy with remarkably long arms and rare athletic gifts find his self-confidence and a place where he truly belonged. By the time he was seventeen years old, he had grown to six feet, eight inches, capturing the attention of college scouts. His arms were so long that he could sit in the middle rear seat of a car and open both front doors simultaneously. Starring on the high school team as a junior and senior, he relished being part of a group that didn't care about his religion. Phil's brother Chuck speculated that the Jackson boys played ball "because it was one of the few things open to them and because it allowed them some degree of normality: It was the only time when they were allowed to do what other kids were doing."[21]

Basketball provided Jackson with a means of differentiating himself. His mother had encouraged her three sons in their aspirations, telling them they could achieve anything they wanted. Competing against an older brother in one-on-one games drove Phil to prove his self-worth, fueling his competitiveness and his own desires for perfection. Looking back on his youth, Jackson reflected, "Winning was a matter of life and death. As a kid, I often threw temper tantrums when I lost, especially if I was competing against my brothers. Losing made me feel humiliated and worthless, as if I didn't exist."[22]

Yet Jackson proved himself a winner, leading his high school team to a state championship during his senior year. His athletic talent helped him discover a life beyond Williston, earning him a basketball scholarship to the University of North Dakota, where he became a two-time All-American. When he arrived at the Grand Forks campus in the fall of 1963, he embarked on a transformational journey that would fundamentally change his life. Studying a composite major in religion, philosophy, and psychology liberated him from the dogmatic teachings of his parents. He found joy debating classmates and engaging in late-night bull sessions. His life became a constant exercise in introspection, a tugging impulse, as he described it, "to see what doors I could open."[23]

During his freshman year, Jackson considered himself an ardent Goldwater Republican. Given his background, it's not surprising that he identified with conservative senator Barry Goldwater, a self-described frontiersman from Prescott, Arizona, who belonged to a fraternal organization of white men who dressed in Native American regalia. Goldwaterites railed against liberalism, communism, and civil rights legislation. Calling for the complete annihilation of communists, they also advocated for the widespread bombing of North Vietnam. Yet as the Vietnam War escalated, Jackson began questioning both his conservative principles and the government's foreign policy. His girlfriend Maxine, a liberal political science major, challenged him intellectually and encouraged him to become more active on campus. In 1967, during the "Summer of Love," when the counterculture blossomed across America, Phil and Maxine married.[24]

That same summer, a few months after the New York Knicks drafted Jackson, the newlyweds visited Williston. During a church service he became aggravated listening to unsophisticated ministers using poor grammar as they preached. Being a Pentecostal made him feel ashamed, especially after taking a sociology class where he learned that fundamentalists often came from lower socioeconomic and educational backgrounds. In New York, Jackson began cultivating a public persona, presenting himself as a philosopher—a public mask that he inhabited years later as the coach of the Chicago Bulls. In the midst of his own spiritual crisis and the fracturing of America, he filled the void by becoming, in his words, "Phil Jackson, the intellectual, the hippie, the social thinker and political activist."[25]

Fully absorbed in the ideals of the counterculture, Jackson explored a life without restraints. Engaging with his generation meant questioning conformity and embracing dissent. In 1968, during the Democratic National Convention, he joined thousands of antiwar protesters in Chicago, a confrontation that erupted into a full-fledged police riot. Two summers later, when he returned to North Dakota as a longhaired, pot-smoking counselor in the American Legion's youth program, Jackson organized group discussions around protest and avoiding the draft. His protests extended beyond the war: he marched on Earth Day and resigned from the Elks when they refused to admit Black members. In 1972, he joined Athletes for George McGovern, demonstrating his belief that NBA players should use their platform for disseminating political messages. During Knicks games, in the nosebleed section of Madison Square Garden, Jackson became a kind of folk hero of "Woodstock Nation."[26]

Yet he struggled to reconcile his intellectual pursuits and his competitive instincts. After his first season with the Knicks, Jackson experienced disenchantment with life in the NBA. In *Maverick*, he wrote, "I also discovered that being a professional athlete provided me with no great thrill." There were times when he thought pro basketball was "nothing more than a primal struggle for dominance." Jackson appeared an exemplar of a new breed in sports: the radical jock. For most people who identified with the counterculture, sports were "hopelessly bourgeois, counterrevolutionary, more opium for the masses." But during the "Athletic Revolution" of the late 1960s and 1970s, "jock liberationists" viewed sports differently. Sports, they argued, reflected the broader society, being "prone to the same bigotry, biases, and blind spots." Furthermore, athletes who turned into activists, as Jackson did, imagined sports becoming more democratic and empowering.[27]

Yet whatever doubts he once had about basketball's import, Jackson could never deny his competitive nature. "I must be competitive," the Bulls coach said more than twenty years after writing *Maverick*. For a man who preached that there was more to life than basketball, he nonetheless built his life around the game. As the counterculture dissolved into the mainstream and the urgency of protest faded over the years, political action became less important to him than belonging to a community. The truth was that Jackson was never all that radical. He may have protested the war and experimented with recreational drugs, as so many others of his generation did, but he never dropped out or turned his back on the sports establishment. For him, the legacy of the sixties remained the comfort he found in the unity and brotherhood of basketball.[28]

It smelled like marijuana, Will Perdue thought. When the pale seven-foot backup center from Vanderbilt University entered the Bulls' facility before a team practice during the 1989–1990 season, he noticed a strong, herbaceous odor. The sight on the court stunned him: Phil Jackson was marching around the gym waving a smudge stick of sagebrush. When Perdue asked Jackson what he was doing, the head coach explained that he was "scaring away evil spirits." Jackson had learned the practice of smudging from the Lakota Sioux, who performed this sacred ceremony as a spiritual cleansing—the smoke a rising prayer to the Great Spirit, an invocation for protecting the tribe from the forces of darkness.[29]

Ever since he was a boy living on the Great Plains, the Sioux fascinated him. He first encountered Native Americans when he visited his maternal grandfather in Wolf Point, Montana, a hamlet on the banks of the Missouri River at the edge of the Fort Peck Indian Reservation. Grandfather Funk, as Jackson called him, ran a boardinghouse near the reservation. He told young Phil that he should avoid any contact with Native Americans. "They were supposed to be dirty and weren't to be trusted and they had no concept of civilization," Jackson recalled. In his sixth-grade class in Williston, two Native American children attended the same school that he did. The preacher's kid noticed the way that white children treated them as inferior outsiders—foreigners trying to assimilate into a culture that often denied their humanity. Jackson read countless library books about the history of the American West and Native American heritage, imagining a violent frontier past filled with "noble warriors" who fought to defend sacred land from gun-toting cowboys. "When I was a kid growing up, I never liked the cowboys," he said. "I knew the Indians and I liked the Indians."[30]

In the summer of 1973, when Jackson and two of his teammates from the Knicks—Bill Bradley and Willis Reed—organized a basketball clinic for the Oglala Sioux at the Pine Ridge Reservation, his connection to Native Americans deepened. A few months earlier, Oglala tribe members and activists in the American Indian Movement (AIM) had seized the town of Wounded Knee, South Dakota—the site of an 1890 massacre of three hundred Native men, women, and children at the hands of US cavalry. For seventy-one days, in an armed confrontation between AIM protestors and federal agents, activists occupied Wounded Knee and demanded the federal government honor unfulfilled treaties with Native Americans. After tense negotiations that freed several Oglala hostages, they reached an agreement that the federal government would investigate the Bureau of Indian Affairs and the ruinous conditions on the reservation. In the aftermath of the violent confrontation, Jackson hoped that his basketball clinics would provide the Sioux children a healthy diversion from a traumatic experience.[31]

Teaching basketball to the Lakota Sioux shaped Jackson's worldview and his coaching methods. He became particularly focused on the Lakota's "warrior heritage." In Lakota culture, he wrote in his 1995 memoir, *Sacred Hoops*, "a warrior didn't try to stand out from his fellow band members; he strove to act bravely and honorably, to help the group in whatever way he could to accomplish its mission." It was a message he hoped would resonate with his players, especially Michael Jordan. Presenting himself as intimately knowledgeable and empathetic to Native American experiences, Jackson instilled in his team the idea that a basketball season could serve as a spiritual journey—a communal experience of peaceful aggression based on bonding rituals and a shared purpose. He conceived of the Bulls in the image of the Lakota: "a band of warriors" pursuing "a sacred quest."[32]

Jackson incorporated a variety of Native American practices into the culture of the team. The Bulls started and ended each practice session standing in a circle, forming their own sacred hoop, a unifying ring symbolizing how they would all grow and develop as one. "In Native American culture," Jackson explained, "the unifying power of the circle was so meaningful that whole nations were conceived as a series of interconnected rings (or hoops). The tepee was a ring, as were the campfire, the village, and the layout of the nation itself—circles within circles, having no beginning or end."[33]

During training drills, Jackson conditioned the team using "the Indian file," a term rooted in the idea that Native American warriors marched single file into battle with each tribesman walking in the footsteps of the man in front of him. Jackson's drill, one commonly used in team sports, consisted of players lining up single file and jogging around the perimeter of the court until he blew the whistle, calling for the man at the end of the line to sprint to the front. When that player reached the front of the line, he set the team's pace until Jackson blew the whistle again for another man to sprint from the back to the front. Jackson liked the drill because he believed that it taught the player at the front of the line to be mindful of those behind him.[34]

Although Jackson was often characterized by sportswriters as an authority on Native American history, his adoption of Indian

rituals served his interests more than it preserved tribal knowledge. Appropriating Native American traditions helped him cul-
tivate a marketable public persona: the basketball whisperer, the
wise white sage who taught Jordan how to win. "Swift Eagle" (the
name given to Jackson by Edgar Red Cloud at Pine Ridge) decorated the team's practice facility with tribal artifacts: drums, ar-
rows, feathers, a painting of Lakota war leader Crazy Horse, and
photos of white buffalo—the most sacred of animals, according
to the Sioux, "a symbol of prosperity and good fortune." Jackson
believed that surrounding his team with Native American objects,
burning sage, and banging a drum during a losing streak would
help prepare his team for "battle." Yet in removing tribal totems
from their original contexts as Lakota members interpreted them,
Jackson employed Native relics in superficial ways that aligned
only with his needs as a coach.[35]

His cultivation of the Bulls as Lakota warriors was inspired in
part by Hollywood, particularly *The Mystic Warrior*, a controversial television miniseries based on Ruth Beebe Hill's epic novel
Hanta Yo. Broadcast by ABC in 1984, the television production
is a sweeping fictional saga of the Lakota Sioux during the early
nineteenth century told through the eyes of a young, virtuous
warrior who survives numerous trials and ultimately becomes the
chief of his tribe. Although some members of the Lakota Sioux
praised the series, critics lamented that it "fit a white culture's fan-
tastic notion of tribal people and their way of life." Writing in the
Los Angeles Times, Gerald Vizenor, a professor of Native American
literature at UC Berkeley, opined, "*The Mystic Warrior* proves to be
a simplistic buckskin melodrama in the Hollywood tradition of
racism and stereotype."[36]

Jackson heard these criticisms but nonetheless selectively ap-
propriated aspects of Lakota culture from the film. Showing
clips to his players, he emphasized how Lakota warriors made

"personal sacrifices for the good of the group." It mattered little that his friends at Pine Ridge disapproved of *The Mystic Warrior*'s misrepresentations. Although he long believed he was honoring Native American culture, for him, the real power of the Lakota's experiences rested in inspiring his team.[37]

Jackson had been "playing Indian" since boyhood, and as coach of the Bulls he posed for an NBA photographer wearing a gray suit and a Native American headdress, a performative act that trivialized the brutal history of Indian colonization. The historical persecution of Native tribes could not be separated from the warbonnet Jackson wore. Native people shed blood in defense of their life, land, and liberty wearing the sacred warbonnet on the battlefield. Yet as a white man, Jackson claimed to identify with Native Americans—a people who suffered racial genocide—without also inhabiting the destructive material conditions and psychological scars produced by that violent history. Unlike Native people, Jackson had the privilege of wearing and removing the headdress like a costume and avoiding the discrimination indigenous people endured for embracing that same regalia.[38]

Jackson personified a group of New Age followers who mixed Native American traditions with Zen Buddhism and other therapeutic philosophies. During his spiritual evolution, he fabricated his own beliefs as a "Zen Christian." He remained uncomfortable with the intolerant religion of his childhood, though he still believed Christianity could inspire compassion for others. Gradually, Jackson gravitated toward what he described as the intersection between Zen Buddhism's principle of awareness and Christianity's tenets of grace and love. "I use the term 'Zen Christian' to describe my personal beliefs, because I still like to think of the Christian precepts I learned as a child as the basis of how I live," he explained. "Do unto others as you would have them do unto you—what I call the dispensation of grace, the idea that love is an all-conquering force. The Zen part is living in the moment—that brings the *now* into Christianity, which most of the time is focused on heaven and hell. A combination of the two makes sense to me, because I think practice is what Christ was doing when he stepped away from his disciples and became one with the Father."[39]

In the mid-1970s, his older brother Joe, equally skeptical about their parents' fundamentalism, introduced him to the East Asian philosophy of Zen Buddhism, which teaches that enlightenment can be discovered when a person realizes that one is already enlightened. After reading Japanese monk Shunryu Suzuki's *Zen Mind, Beginner's Mind*, one of the most influential books on Zen in the West, Phil began meditating beside Flathead Lake. What appealed to him about Zen was its emphasis on clearing a busy mind from tainted thoughts centered on the self. "All self-centered thoughts limit our vast mind," Suzuki taught. "When we have no thought of achievement, no thought of self, we are true beginners. Then we can really learn something."[40]

Perhaps the best way of understanding Jackson's spiritual syncretism is to think of him as a Bobo, a term *New York Times* columnist David Brooks coined to describe the sensibilities of bourgeois bohemians who merged the rebellious antiestablishment values of the 1960s counterculture with the competitiveness of 1980s entrepreneurs. Bobos aimed to change institutions in ways that aligned with their own ethos. That was Jackson. What united Bobos was their commitment to reconciling the conflicting values between "worldly success and inner virtue," the central tension of Jackson's coaching career.[41]

Bobos like Jackson rejected institutionalized religion and embraced a personal spirituality that allowed them to dabble in multiple faiths. The seeds of his spiritual ethic can be traced to his native Montana, a place that long cherished freedom, independence, and resisting authorities who told people how to lead their lives. It's apparent, too, in the way that he and other folks from Montana described their relationship to the land; the soil beneath their feet gave them an identity, a past, and a future, a timeless bond that made Montanans "suspicious of change and anything that would alter the landscape or character of the beloved place." Returning to Montana every summer—his roots—made Jackson feel more connected to nature. His favorite time at Flathead Lake occurred after Labor Day, when all the vacationers—the polluting outsiders with RVs and speedboats—left town. "The lake is quiet then," Jackson observed, "and it's a good time to think."[42]

Bobos toiled with monastic self-discipline because they viewed work as an intellectual and spiritual exercise. And Jackson the coach was no different. "Creating a successful team," he wrote, was in itself "a spiritual act." He conceived of the game as a spiritual journey where the players—"modern-day warriors"—discovered opportunities to transcend themselves for the good of the tribe. Sharing lessons about Lakota warriors or meditating as a team before practice served a larger purpose. All that "spiritual stuff," Jackson explained, "brings an act of community to us."[43]

Yet he also understood that the players would only embrace his approach if they could see how his spiritual practices could help them win. Jackson recognized that they came from different backgrounds and had different belief systems—and that meant he could not impose his views on them. Nonetheless, he believed that group meditation would help the players become more aware of their own thoughts and their relationships with teammates. Meditation had helped him quiet his own mind as a player and enhance his focus. Pro basketball players, Jackson observed, had been critiqued their entire lives—by scouts, coaches, teammates, writers, and fans. And under the most intense competition, a player's mind could race out of control. Practicing a form of Zen meditation—*zazen*—taught Jackson how to concentrate on the present, living in the moment rather than fixating on thoughts about the past or future, a useful exercise for a coach.[44]

Michael Jordan, however, resisted "that Zen stuff." The first time Jackson told the players that he wanted them to meditate as a team, Jordan thought his coach had to be kidding. During the session, Jordan peeked through one eye and glanced around the gym to see if his teammates were meditating. And to his surprise, many of them were in fact practicing mindfulness. Although Jordan maintained he did not need meditation to become a better basketball player, he acknowledged that Jackson helped him remain calm in the cauldron. Jackson taught him how "to find a quiet center within" himself, a crucial lesson in Jordan's journey.[45]

Jordan appreciated that Jackson's visualization techniques were intended to help the players find clarity. Jackson "didn't force-feed us, he just provided options," Jordan recalled. "He presented the thoughts intelligently. You could say there was some wisdom in his approach. He would appear to direct a thought or idea to the entire team, but usually the message was meant for an individual player. If you were that player, you got the message even though it was delivered to the entire group. That was one of Phil's gifts, his ability to talk to us individually within the collective."[46]

From the moment Jackson became head coach of the Bulls, he told Jordan that he would treat him like any other player. If Jordan made a mistake during practice, Jackson wouldn't hesitate to correct him. Jordan accepted constructive criticism, knowing it would help the rest of the team see that he did not occupy a venerated place in the mind of the head coach, an important difference from his time playing under Doug Collins. He commended Jackson for holding him accountable and maintaining the highest standards of excellence for everyone on the team.[47]

The more time Jackson spent around Jordan, the sharper his instincts became for protecting him from the outside forces that threatened the team's bond. He realized that Jordan needed a quiet space, a sanctuary that he could trust would not be broken. So, Jackson erected a curtain around the Bulls' practice court, blocking the view of prying reporters and photographers. He made it clear that anyone who did not belong in the team's inner circle was an outsider—and that included Jerry Krause.[48]

But the creation of Jackson's sacred hoop further exacerbated the growing tension between Krause and Jordan, two men striving to define themselves in opposition to one another.

Standing next to Bulls GM Jerry Krause during a press conference in 1988, Jordan smiled widely after signing a contract extension with the team. It was one of the rare occasions where Jordan and Krause could be seen sharing a moment of joy together. Credit: AP Images

Chapter Six

CRUMBS

"My dad is buried here. He never lived to see me do what I really wanted to do in life. I want to win real bad here . . . Nobody wants to win here more than I do."

—CHICAGO BULLS GENERAL MANAGER JERRY
KRAUSE, ON THE EVE OF THE 1990–1991 SEASON

Nobody would ever let Jerry Krause forget that he inherited Michael Jordan. Critics argued that without Jordan, the Bulls would be a mediocre team and the general manager would be out of a job. Writers depicted him as jealous of the attention Jordan received for the team's success. And the players just didn't trust him. Krause wanted the players to love him, but they treated him like a punching bag, forever the round-faced kid stuffed into a gym locker. His portly figure made him an easy target. Sometimes the players mooed like cows when he entered the locker room. On one occasion, when Krause left his hat behind on the team bus, he returned to find it at the bottom of the toilet.[1]

No one mocked Krause more than Jordan, who thought the GM was an inept loser standing in the way of a championship. He believed Krause suffered from a pathological need to prove he mattered more than the players and that he had failed to build a championship roster as a result. Jordan attacked him the same way he played: mercilessly and with exacting precision. Needling Krause constantly, Jordan called him "Crumbs," a reference to the donut flakes that supposedly covered his shirt.[2]

Jordan's distorted view of Krause revealed not just a hunger for victory but a craving for confrontation. He possessed a virtual compulsion to prove his own greatness, and his entire sense of self was tethered to his place in the NBA. Of course, the same could be said of Krause, but Jordan's ego, his sense of self-importance, was derived from being the best at *everything* he did. Dominating others, whether it was on the basketball court or in a high-stakes game of cards, fed his ego and reinforced his own idealized version of himself as a powerful man. And if anyone threatened his exalted position, then that person became the enemy. That's why he hoarded slights, real and imagined, inventing reasons to bear a grudge against anyone who doubted or challenged him, whether it was an opposing player, a teammate, a coach, or an executive like Krause.

The origin of the feud with Krause can be traced to Jordan's second year with the Bulls. During the third game of the 1985–1986 season, he broke a bone in his left foot. No one knew how long it would take for his foot to heal, and the Bulls' doctors advised Reinsdorf and Krause not to let him play until it had completely healed. The injury would end up sidelining him for sixty-four games, virtually the entire season, nearly driving Jordan mad in the process.

Eager to return to the team, Jordan became increasingly frustrated wearing a cast on his foot. Eventually, he convinced the two Jerrys that the best way for him to get his mind and body right was for him to rehab in Chapel Hill, where he could also work on completing his bachelor's degree. But Jordan wasn't just hitting the books. Krause soon found out that MJ was playing full-court pickup games on campus. He erupted and told Jordan that he couldn't keep playing in Chapel Hill, fearing that the young star was risking his career and the future of the franchise.[3]

In March 1986, when Jordan returned to Chicago, he declared himself fit enough to rejoin the Bulls. Yet orthopedists warned Reinsdorf that Jordan had a 10 percent chance of breaking the bone in his foot again if he returned to the court too soon. The doctors explained that although Jordan did not feel any pain in his foot, he could break the bone again without warning. After team doctor John Hefferon reviewed a CAT scan that indicated enough improvement for Jordan to return, Reinsdorf finally caved but limited the number of minutes Jordan could play. Exasperated, Jordan urged Reinsdorf to let him loose, but Reinsdorf worried about the risk involved.[4]

"If you had a terrible headache, and I gave you a bottle of pills, and nine of the pills would cure you, and one of the pills would kill you, would you take a pill?" Reinsdorf asked.

Jordan famously replied, "'Depends on how fucking bad the headache is."[5]

He became convinced that Reinsdorf capped his minutes for another reason. Jordan came to believe that the front office had determined it made more sense to lose without him on the court and thereby improve their chances of securing a higher draft pick. In fact, Krause told Jordan that he had no plans to let him play an entire game all year. Losing intentionally completely violated Jordan's competitive values and he did not hesitate to question the motives of the two Jerrys in front of reporters.[6]

The rift between them deepened when Krause insisted that the decision about whether Jordan would play was in Reinsdorf's hands. Jordan never forgot how Krause coldly said, "You're Bulls property now, and we'll tell you what to do." Telling a Black man that management—*white men*—owned him struck Jordan as dehumanizing. Jordan insisted on maintaining control of the one thing that mattered most: his body. He refused to be reduced to a commodity—no one would control him or deprive him of his freedom. Furious, he responded, "I'm not a piece of property. I don't care what they pay me. I'm still a human being."[7]

Jordan's dispute with Krause revealed his drive for independence, but on a deeper level it testified to the growing power of Black players as they challenged the paternalistic white basketball establishment. For years, since the NBA's founding in 1949, the league's corporate owners and executives treated players like chattel, to be used and discarded like pieces of equipment. But in the 1970s, Black players contested the owners' autocratic power in the fight for free agency and higher salaries. Those battles may have won the players greater freedom and mobility, but in his confrontation with Krause, Jordan realized that they had not fully transformed the way management valued or treated them. Expressing his self-worth, Jordan made clear to Krause—and everyone watching—that he would not be manipulated or exploited. For Jordan, standing up to Krause—and Reinsdorf—proved a pivotal moment in his pursuit of self-determination.[8]

Jordan took his frustrations directly to the press, challenging management in a public manner that turned Chicago fans against Krause and Reinsdorf. He criticized the two Jerrys for holding him back and jeopardizing the team's chances of making the playoffs by benching him. In the process, Jordan leveraged his popularity and power, forcing the team's owner and general manager to let him play without restrictions. When he returned to the Bulls, Jordan vented his frustrations in a playoff series against the Boston Celtics, then the best team in the NBA, where he scored sixty-three points in a single game—a playoff record. Seared into his memory, Krause's words fueled him. "I was a piece of meat to him," Jordan said years later. "He felt he could control me, because

No matter what Scottie Pippen did on the basketball court, he would always remain in Jordan's shadow. But during the 1990–1991 season, Pippen played his best season yet, proving to everyone in the NBA that he was a bona-fide all-star. Credit: Steve Lipofsky/Lipofskyphoto.com

I had so much value to him. But he didn't realize that I had value to myself. I was independent, and I understood what I was."[9]

Yet Jordan was not the only player on the Bulls who clashed with Krause. Throughout the 1990–1991 season, Scottie Pippen battled the GM over a new contract. He demanded a raise and when Krause refused, Pippen threatened to sit out. Krause reminded Pippen, as he once told Jordan, that he belonged to the organization and there was nothing he could do about it. Incensed, Pippen began contemplating how he could gain leverage over Krause by withholding his labor—a risky proposition. While Jordan wielded his rage at Krause like a seasoned heavyweight fighter jabbing away at the body, Pippen's raw emotions, rooted in the vulnerabilities of his hardscrabble youth, inspired wild swings that didn't always connect. In his defiance, however, Pippen took on the same fight as Jordan, demanding the kind of autonomy and respect he thought he deserved.

The sting of childhood poverty haunted Scottie Pippen, even as an accomplished, twenty-five-year-old NBA star. The youngest of twelve children born to Preston and Ethel Pippen, he grew up wearing hand-me-downs in a crowded two-room house in Hamburg, Arkansas, a sleepy mill town of about three thousand people. His father labored under dangerous conditions on long shifts at the Georgia-Pacific paper plant cutting logs. Every workday, a strong pulp odor as noxious as rotten eggs followed Preston home from the mill. This large, poor southern family's struggle to survive in what Scottie described as "sort of a racist town" hardened Pippen's resolve to find a way out of Hamburg.

Life grew increasingly bleak after Preston's health declined. When Scottie was in the eighth grade, his father, already ravaged by arthritis, returned home from work and suffered a massive stroke during dinner, leaving him unable to walk or speak. Confined to a wheelchair, he never saw Scottie play professional basketball in person. After the stroke, Scottie said, Preston "could never be the father I needed him to be or show me what is required to be a man—a black man, especially in a white world."[10]

After his father's stroke, Scottie never forgot about the fragility of life. "I've always thought that one injury could wipe all of this away," he said. It was his worst fear: in the blink of an eye, a freak accident could steal his ability to run and jump. His brother Ronnie, a strong, healthy teenager, suffered a debilitating injury when a bullying classmate hit him during gym class, leaving Ethel to care for a paralyzed son and a paralyzed husband. "Everybody told her there wasn't nothing that could be done for them," Scottie recalled. Completely devoted, Ethel carried the burden of the family, caring for Preston and Ronnie—"Fed them, put them to bed, changed their diapers." Watching his mother, Pippen learned another important lesson: no amount of anguish could overwhelm an abiding love for family.[11]

When Pippen signed his rookie contract in 1987, he vowed he would always be the provider his family needed. He built his parents a sprawling ranch that could accommodate wheelchairs, purchased a Cadillac for his mother, and regularly sent money to his siblings. Still, he often wondered how long his good fortune would last. Before signing the contract, he asked his agent Jimmy Sexton how much he would earn if the Bulls released him after one season. "He wanted security," Sexton recalled. "That's what he was most concerned with." Sexton negotiated a six-year deal worth more than $5 million. Four years of Pippen's contract were guaranteed, and the Bulls reserved two option years.[12]

Now, before the 1990–1991 season began, Pippen prepared to play the last year of his guaranteed contract. Determined to prove his value, he had spent the summer training harder than ever, adding ten pounds of muscle, mostly in his upper body. Still, he worried that if he were ever injured, the Bulls would decline the option agreement. During his rookie season in 1987–1988, he had suffered a herniated disc that required back surgery. After a surgeon performed a laminectomy, which involved removing vertebral bone and easing the pressure on Pippen's sciatic nerve, he lay in bed, scared, thinking his career had come to an end. Throughout that season he had complained about pain in his lower back and legs. He struggled sitting in a chair. Sometimes the aches got so bad during his forty-minute commute to Chicago Stadium that he had to get out of the car two or three times. A tingling sensation ran through his leg, making it difficult to feel the gas pedal and the brake.

Pippen's fears that the Bulls would be unwilling to invest in a player with questionable health were stoked by an unsympathetic response during his rookie season. Team trainer Mark Pfeil thought Pippen was a malingerer, "weak and lazy," a demeaning charge for a Black man who had come from nothing, endured incredible hardship, and trained tirelessly to become a professional athlete. Pfeil insisted that all Pippen needed to do was stretch more often, but Scottie feared that the problem was much worse than management recognized.[13]

After making his first All-Star team in 1990, Pippen believed he had leverage for negotiating a long-term guarantee from the Bulls. At a time when the average NBA player earned an annual salary of nearly $1 million, the highest in professional sports, he was scheduled to earn $765,000 during the coming season. Pippen complained that, though he was clearly the second-best player on the team, he was only the fifth-highest paid on the Bulls— behind Michael Jordan, starting center Bill Cartwright, and reserves Stacey King and Dennis Hopson. After the NBA signed a record-breaking four-year $600 million television deal with NBC during the off-season, the league salary cap rose by $2 million; based on the league's collective bargaining agreement with the Players Association, this meant Krause had to spend the revenue on salaries. However, instead of giving Pippen a raise, he signed free agent forward Cliff Levingston, a veteran reserve who would earn more than $2 million during the next two seasons. Making matters worse for Pippen, Krause had selected Croatian star Toni Kukoč in the 1990 NBA draft, raising questions about whether the Bulls planned to replace Pippen altogether. Pippen had also seen how his cohorts from the 1987 draft received new contracts. After one All-Star appearance, the Indiana Pacers extended the contract of Reggie Miller, the eleventh pick in the '87 draft, signing him to a new deal worth more than $3 million a season. Taken six spots ahead of Miller in the draft and having made as many All-Star games, Pippen believed he was worth at least that much.[14]

On the eve of training camp, he spent time with his family in Hamburg, contemplating his next move. He'd had a difficult year, losing his dad and divorcing his first wife, Karen McCollum. Pippen was the father of a toddler and now owed monthly alimony and child support. He felt overwhelmed at times and confessed to *Chicago Sun-Times* writer Lacey Banks that ever since he began playing college ball he had drifted away from church, though he wanted to "walk closer with God." Sam Smith wrote that Pippen could be "somewhat irresponsible," "running with people of questionable character." Years later Pippen admitted that he "messed around a lot" when he was a young pro, enjoying the fruits of his labor. He bought fancy suits, luxury cars, and jewelry. He wore dazzling diamond earrings and a gold "PIP" necklace, though he gained notoriety in Chicago for leaving meager tips at restaurants and nightclubs, earning the nickname "No-tippin' Pippen."[15]

After visiting with his family and friends in Hamburg, Pippen drove his Black Mercedes-Benz SEL, valued around $80,000, east across the plains of Mississippi on US 82. On the first of October, only a few days before training camp began, he planned to meet his agent in Memphis. As Pippen turned north, toward the Tennessee line, he developed a scheme: he would refuse to report to camp and hide out in a Memphis hotel where Krause could not find him. "I just thought I'd sit out a few days and see what they said. Maybe I'd even sit out all of training camp," he explained.[16] He liked the idea of making Krause sweat in front of the Chicago television cameras, trying to explain why he refused to negotiate with his relatively underpaid All-Star forward, a man earning a salary less than 150 other NBA players.

When Pippen had last approached Krause about negotiating a new contract, the GM balked, maintaining that club policy— one that he established—prohibited him from renegotiating with a player who had three years remaining on his contract. Krause routinely made lowball offers to players and their agents and then refused to bargain. Exasperated, agents would inevitably turn to Reinsdorf, who seemed much more reasonable. Reinsdorf would reassure the player and his agent that he would pay more than the "final offer" that Krause had made. Sometimes, Reinsdorf would bring Krause into his office during a negotiation with an agent and instruct him to sit quietly. Repeatedly, the good cop–bad cop routine worked even as agents caught on to the act.

But Pippen was done playing games. He cursed out Krause and told Sexton he didn't want to talk to either Krause or Reinsdorf anymore. "Let them see how many games they win without me," he fumed. Sexton convinced him to call Reinsdorf and tell him that he would not report to camp unless he received an acceptable contract extension. During the call Reinsdorf promised Pippen that he would be fairly compensated in a new deal soon enough, but until then he had to come to camp. Pippen had an obligation to him and the team, Reinsdorf maintained—"You live up to contracts."

Pippen disagreed. He told Reinsdorf that he would not honor a bad contract and then he hung up.

Holding out, Sexton advised, might come at a cost. Nike had just offered Pippen an endorsement deal and if he attracted bad publicity, it might force the shoe company to reconsider. Pippen understood the risks and relented—for now. "All right," he said, "I'm reporting to camp. But they better do something quick."

Jerry Krause loved to remind people that he drafted Scottie Pippen. He never forgot the first time he saw the skinny forward from the University of Central Arkansas playing in an exhibition tournament for NBA prospects on the eve of the 1987 draft. Sitting in the stands in Portsmouth, Virginia, isolated from other league executives and scouts, Krause scooted to the very edge of his seat when he saw a player with arms that "came down to his knees" warming up on the court. "I almost had an orgasm," he recalled.

Elbowing Bulls scout Billy McKinney, the man who had convinced Krause to watch Pippen play in Portsmouth, he exclaimed, "There he is! There he is!"

McKinney turned to Krause and said, "How do *you* know?"

"Look at his arms!" Krause cried, his eyes nearly bulging. "You said he had long arms. They're down to freaking *here*!"[17]

Krause fell head over heels for Pippen. He loved athletic players with long arms and large hands. As he studied Pippen, a surge of adrenaline coursed through his veins. There was no greater thrill than finding a player who could change the fortunes of the team. Krause panicked that another team would steal Pippen before the

Bulls had a chance to draft him. Before the Portsmouth Invitational, the only person in the NBA who knew anything about Pippen was Marty Blake, the league's director of scouting. Blake had urged every general manager and scout to see Pippen play, but only Krause took him seriously. Blake had found the most recent Rookie of the Year—the Pistons' Dennis Rodman—at Southeastern Oklahoma State, another small school that scouts overlooked. When Krause spoke to Blake on the phone, he heard "an edge in Blake's voice" and determined that McKinney should travel to Conway, Arkansas, to see whether Pippen had NBA talent. Impressed with Pippen's performance against Henderson State, McKinney, the only scout in the stands that night, still questioned whether a player competing in a league comparable to "amateur night at the Y" could make it in the NBA. So, he urged Krause to see Pippen for himself.[18]

Like so many scouts in the business, Krause believed his eye for athletic talent was a gift that could not be taught. "It's God-given," he explained. He had built his entire identity around the idea that he could detect better than almost anyone else a man's ability to play ball at the highest level. For the nearly twenty-five years before Reinsdorf hired him as the team's general manager in 1985, Krause had worked year-round scouting basketball and baseball players. He liked to boast that he was the only scout in history who had worked as an executive in the NBA and Major League Baseball. He had evaluated baseball prospects for the Cleveland Indians, Oakland Athletics, Seattle Mariners, and Chicago White Sox; and he had worked in the NBA for the Baltimore Bullets, Phoenix Suns, Los Angeles Lakers, and, of course, Chicago Bulls.[19]

Krause learned scouting from the old-timers who passed down the tricks of the trade. "He liked hearing stories," Mark Vancil wrote in *Chicago* magazine. "Of one scout beating another by

sneaking in the backdoor; of the scout who rubbed his eyelids with onion before entering a prospect's house so the kid's parents would think he was crying at the thought of signing their son." For Krause, "these were not the antics of con men—they were brilliant strokes of artists manipulating paint on a canvas."[20]

Krause treated scouting like a covert operation. In 1969, when Bulls GM Pat Williams employed him as head scout, Williams realized he'd hired a sleuth—a nickname that followed Krause for the rest of his career. "He's a classic," Williams observed, "slinking, suspicious, secretive, talking low and fast, plotting, planning, hiding behind potted plants, wearing disguises." Living out of a suitcase, "like a stalker tracking a starlet," Rick Telander wrote, Krause packed sunglasses, a trench coat, and a wide-brim hat that he could pull over his face—hoping that no one would recognize him in the shadows. Completely paranoid, he tried making himself invisible sitting in the stands. Traveling alone, he made few attempts to make friends with scouts working for other teams. He was never one of the guys who bought a round of drinks after a game, swapping stories. "I'm a loner," Krause once said. "All those years on the road, I stayed to myself and didn't make a lot of friends. I had a job to do."[21]

On Krause's office wall there hung an unattributed quote that captured his furtive credo: "HEAR ALL, SEE ALL, SAY NOTHING." When Johnny Bach, a voracious reader of history, first saw the sign, he could not believe that Krause would broadcast a maxim that had originated with Nazi spymaster Admiral Wilhelm Canaris. "Jerry," Bach said, "that's a very strange slogan for someone who's Jewish . . . to have on his wall." Bach walked away convinced that Krause had no idea that Canaris was the head of German intelligence during World War II. But Krause knew. When Rick Telander inquired about the quote, Krause explained, "We have some Jewish ownership and . . ." his voice trailed off. Then he continued, "People have said that if Canaris had been an American, there never would have been a Second World War. He would have known everything there was to know before it happened."[22]

The grandson of Russian Jewish immigrants, Krause often told reporters that he endured anti-Semitism as a kid growing up in Chicago. His father, Paul Karbofsky, Americanized the family name to Krause when he began boxing as an amateur, a common practice among Jewish fighters trying to assimilate. Struggling to make ends meet, Paul Krause ran a delicatessen and later opened a shoe store in Norwood Park, on the northwest side of the city. According to Jerry, anti-Semites in the neighborhood "burned out Jews," but discrimination didn't prevent his father from pursuing the American dream. He also said that he confronted discrimination at Taft High School as the only Jewish student. Bullies hurled all sorts of epithets at the feisty, pudgy kid—*Sheeny. Kike. Jew bastard.* Fearless, he fought back, just like his father in the ring. "It was the same old thing, a guy called me 'kike,' and I took a swing and the next thing you know we were fighting; I must have got into a dozen fights."[23]

Looking back on those battles, Krause said they were the best thing that ever happened to him because they taught him how to confront discrimination, a valuable lesson he thought helped him as an executive in the NBA. "When a black player says to me, 'You don't know what it's like to be prejudiced against,' I say, Man, try being the only Jew in a school with 2,000 non-Jews." Yet Krause's depiction of Taft High as a "hotbed of anti-Semitism" was a stretch. According to his Jewish classmates, Krause was far from the only Jewish student at Taft and Jews had not been "burned out" of the neighborhood. In fact, Taft had a reputation for being "one of the most progressive high schools in Chicago."[24]

Deeply insecure, Krause desperately wanted people to see him as triumphant, overcoming long odds, not as a stubby nebbish. Narrating his own rags-to-riches story, one that erased his shortcomings, he imagined himself a brilliant executive and fierce negotiator. Long after he built six championship rosters in Chicago, most basketball fans had forgotten that he had failed during his first stint as the Bulls general manager—and Krause preferred it that way. In 1976, shortly after the Phoenix Suns released him from his scouting duties, citing budget constraints, Bulls owner Arthur Wirtz hired him as director of player personnel—a dream job for Krause. Reporters were stunned that Wirtz had hired "little Jerry," a thirty-seven-year-old basketball nut who embellished his scouting resume. "Even if you've never heard of Jerry Krause," Rick Talley wrote in the *Tribune*, "you know him. He's the kid from down the block who comes over to swap baseball cards. He knows every player in every sport and their numbers. He saves rosters and programs and has a transistor radio plugged into one ear while he's watching another game on TV and talking on the phone."[25]

In just three months, however, every Bulls fan would know who Jerry Krause was. Wirtz forced him to resign when Krause offered the head coaching job to DePaul University coach Ray Meyer without consulting ownership. Fuming, Wirtz told Krause that he had no plans to hire a college coach. Krause maintained that he never offered Meyer the job and that the DePaul coach had misunderstood him, but Meyer had already told the university athletic board that he was considering the Bulls' offer. Critical newspaper headlines—"Bulls' Job Was Too Big for Jerry"—tarnished his reputation. Wirtz gave him a choice: resign or accept termination. Krause quit, totally embarrassed, buried in the papers of his hometown. "I'll never forget the feeling I had walking out of the office that day. It was complete humiliation."[26]

In Chicago, the local writers mocked Krause as a ruffled oaf wearing bulky suits with sagging pant cuffs and gravy-stained ties. "In their minds," Ben Joravsky wrote in the *Chicago Reader*, "he was forever the coffee-fetching copyboy at the *American*, the dumpy kid with no athletic talent of his own and a passion for sports that seemed almost pitiful. He didn't have any outside hobbies or interests. He was a loner. His whole life was wrapped up in sports to an extent that seemed peculiar even to a bunch of sportswriters."[27]

After leaving the Bulls, Krause returned to scouting baseball players for the Chicago White Sox. When Jerry Reinsdorf bought the club from Bill Veeck in 1981, he learned that Krause worked relentlessly, cultivating deep knowledge about prospects. Four years later, after Reinsdorf bought the Bulls, he hired Krause as general manager, perplexing nearly everyone who followed the NBA. Nonetheless, Reinsdorf and Krause shared a similar philosophy of building the team through the draft, and two years later, Krause would seize an opportunity that would redefine his career: he would pursue Scottie Pippen.

Krause proceeded as if he were the only one in professional basketball who knew Pippen existed. Like a seasoned poker player hiding an ace up his sleeve, Krause tried concealing his plans. "Jerry was like a cat burglar around me," Pippen recalled. "Everything was done as a big secret. He didn't want anyone to know that he even knew who I was." Before the predraft exhibition games, Krause thought he had uncovered a diamond in the rough, but when Pippen excelled against the best college prospects, his stock climbed. Desperate, Krause tried to convince Jimmy Sexton to take Pippen to Hawaii before the draft, all expenses paid by the Bulls, so that Pippen could avoid interviews with other teams. Of course, Pippen's agent declined the offer.[28]

When Krause gave Doug Collins and his assistants highlight tapes of NBA prospects, all he provided them with was a roster of players with their names, heights, weights, and schools; he offered no background details about them. After reviewing the films, the first thing Collins said to Krause was "Who the hell is Scottie Pippen?" Krause brought Pippen to Chicago so Collins could meet him. During a workout Pippen demonstrated "exceptional fluidity," moving with unusual efficiency, expending less energy than most players with each stride. The Bulls' strength and conditioning coach Al Vermeil set up a "side-to-side drill," a lateral quickness test where Vermeil placed basketballs on the floor near the foul circle. The object was for a player to pick up the balls and dunk as many times as he could within thirty seconds. According to legend, Pippen dunked *fifteen times*—a record performance that left Krause convinced he'd found a future star.[29]

Yet Krause would have never heard of Scottie Pippen in the first place without a high school coach named Donald Wayne. Playing for Wayne on the Hamburg High School team, Pippen had earned All-District honors as a scrawny senior point guard. Although Pippen then was not very tall for a basketball player, standing about six feet, Wayne thought that he might grow and mature as a player. More important, though, he wanted Scottie to have a college education, and since none of the surrounding colleges had recruited him, Wayne decided to intervene. He called his old college coach, Don Dyer, and recommended that he let Pippen try out as a walk-on at the University of Central Arkansas. Dyer took a chance on the shy kid from Hamburg who did not say much beyond "Yes, sir. No, sir." After one season, Pippen proved himself worthy of an athletic scholarship and allowed himself to begin dreaming about a life beyond rural Arkansas. Even before his sophomore year, when Dyer asked the players to fill out an annual "goal card," Pippen wrote, "I would like to be an N.B.A. player."[30]

By his senior year, he had sprouted all the way to six-foot-seven and his confidence in himself on the court had grown, too. For two seasons he had distinguished himself as the best player in the Arkansas Intercollegiate Conference, increasingly driven by the need to prove doubters wrong. He frequently called the assistant coaches at the University of Arkansas, the state's top basketball program, telling them that he wanted to transfer there and that he could outplay anyone on the Razorbacks roster. They ignored him. Years later, long after Pippen had become a regular NBA All-Star, Razorbacks head coach Nolan Richardson admitted overlooking Pippen was the worst mistake of his career.[31]

Krause wouldn't make that same mistake. On the eve of the 1987 draft, at 2:30 a.m., he cut a complicated deal. The Seattle SuperSonics agreed to draft Pippen with the fifth pick—provided that neither Georgetown star Reggie Williams nor UNLV All-American Armon Gilliam were available. Then Seattle would trade Pippen to Chicago in exchange for the Bulls' eighth pick—Virginia center Olden Polynice—and a second rounder. It seemed risky in 1987 to gamble on a player that no NBA executive even knew about just six weeks earlier. If Pippen had not become an All-Star, Krause said, "I'd have been crucified with a dull typewriter." But it turned out to be the best draft night trade any team had ever made.[32]

Michael Jordan wasn't impressed with Krause's management skills, but he couldn't deny that by drafting Pippen and Clemson forward Horace Grant—the ACC Player of the Year—Krause added the two most important teammates who would help Jordan realize his championship dreams. When the GM traded Jordan's bruising bodyguard, forward Charles Oakley, for Knicks center Bill Cartwright—a veteran past his prime—Jordan grumbled, though he later admitted that the move helped the team. What bothered Jordan most was the way Krause exaggerated his own record and took credit for the players' accomplishments. Someday, Jordan predicted, when the fans' memories became a little hazy, Krause would take credit for drafting him, too.[33]

As much as Jordan despised Krause, the truth was that he had constructed a roster that could compete with any team in the NBA. Now, on the precipice of the 1990–1991 season, it was time for Jordan, Pippen, and the rest of the Bulls to make a run against the Detroit Pistons.

Isiah Thomas fueled the Detroit Pistons to consecutive NBA championships in 1989 and 1990. The leader of the "Bad Boys," the Bulls' greatest rival, Thomas became the villain in Jordan's hero story. Credit: AP Images

Chapter Seven

BAD BOYS

"I think as the media, as the public, as the fans say, 'They're Bad Boys,' the Pistons are going to live up to it. That's something they take pride in now, especially with the success they've had being Bad Boys. We've created a monster, and now nobody knows what to do."

—MICHAEL JORDAN, 1989

eating Detroit was all anyone seemed to care about in Chicago. For all that Michael Jordan had accomplished individually, his place among basketball royalty hinged on whether the Bulls could dethrone the Detroit Pistons. Whatever it takes, just beat Detroit.

Defeating the Pistons became a virtual obsession inside the Chicago locker room. Phil Jackson and his assistant coaches spent the off-season reviewing game footage trying to figure out how to crack the winning code. But no matter how many times Jackson toggled the remote—pausing the tape, rewinding it, or watching it in slow motion—the film always revealed an ugly history of defeat and disappointment. "Detroit," Johnny Bach said, "was our albatross."[1]

The Bulls seemed to lose all confidence the moment they stepped onto the Pistons' home court. When the Bulls entered the Palace of Auburn Hills on December 19, 1990, they could not help but remember that they had lost eight consecutive times there. In fact, they had not won a game at the Palace in nearly three years. During the 1990 Eastern Conference Finals, the Bulls averaged 108 points in three games at Chicago Stadium, but in four games at the Palace they only averaged 82 points. Returning to Detroit, the players wondered whether they could escape the sinking feeling of failure on the Pistons' home floor.[2]

In November 1990, during the first few weeks of the regular season, the Bulls struggled with a 5–6 record before breaking out a seven-game winning streak later that month and into early December. By the time they visited the Palace, they had won ten of their last twelve games, though Jordan was not convinced that the team was any better than it had been a year earlier. The real test, he said, would come at the Palace. After a torrid start to the season, when the Pistons won thirteen of their first fifteen games, suddenly the two-time defending champions stumbled, losing seven of eight games in December, the team's worst slump since 1985. Exasperated, reserve forward Mark Aguirre ripped his teammates for losing focus. "We've become nice guys," he said. "What we need to do is get back to being 'Bad Boys.'"[3]

Being the Bad Boys gave the Pistons an identity, one they had built through physical intimidation and an attitude of defiance. The origins of the Bad Boys moniker can be traced to January 16, 1988, when a fistfight erupted between the Pistons and Bulls at Chicago Stadium. In the third quarter Jordan snagged an offensive rebound, pump-faked Rick Mahorn out of his sneakers, and began rising for a dunk. But before Jordan could leap off the floor, Mahorn hooked him around the neck and tossed him onto the hardwood. Immediately, both benches cleared in a melee. Afterward, Jordan told reporters that Mahorn had intentionally tried to hurt him. Sportswriters charged that the Pistons' hard fouls—*love taps*, Mahorn called them—could be categorized "somewhere between assault and criminally negligent homicide."[4]

The Pistons had been involved in brawls before, but when they attacked Jordan, already the crown prince of basketball, they crossed a line. This had made them, in the words of TBS announcer Bob Neal, "the team people love to hate." A few weeks later, CBS produced a halftime segment called "The Bad Boys of Basketball," sensationalizing the danger the Pistons posed to the sport. Instead of letting outsiders define them, point guard Isiah Thomas encouraged his teammates to embrace a sordid persona, adhering to a gladiatorial code: "Take no prisoners, take no shit." Cultivating the Bad Boys identity, he thought, would raise the intensity of his teammates and intimidate opponents. It would give them an edge. "If we're going to be the Bad Boys," he said, "we've got to *act* like the Bad Boys."[5]

The Pistons adopted an unofficial black and silver Bad Boys logo: a cracked skull and crossbones superimposed on an orange basketball. The insignia was embroidered on T-shirts, hoodies, caps, and flags and became popular throughout Michigan. Virtually every basketball fan in the state supported the Bad Boys, though the organization seemed to cater more to the affluent white fans in the suburbs. For example, Coleman Young, Detroit's longtime Black mayor, a cantankerous and combative politician often portrayed by white reporters as a "race-baiting demagogue," argued that moving the Pistons' home arena thirty miles from downtown Detroit to Auburn Hills, a suburb completely cut off from urban mass transit, represented "a hostile act" against Black Detroiters. Although sportswriters liked to romanticize the idea that the Pistons held together a fractured city and the entire metro area, the truth was that no NBA arena was as far removed from the team's namesake city—an overwhelmingly *Black city*—as the Detroit Pistons' stadium. At the same time, the Palace crowd was unmistakably *white* and *suburban*. It is true, however, that the Pistons were not the only professional basketball team that had moved away from downtown. By 1989, eight out of twenty-five NBA teams played outside city limits.[6]

Located along Interstate 75, the Palace, a circular arena that looked like an enormous tan hockey puck, sat in the middle of a massive concrete parking lot. Surrounded by lush forests, private country clubs, and opulent estates belonging to "the Big Three's white-collared gentry," the Palace was promoted as "America's ultimate Basketball Disneyland," an amusement park with 180 luxury suites designed to entertain corporate clients. There was no stadium like it in the NBA. "Every detail was exquisite," reported a writer covering the team. "Hardwood floors, marble counters, ankle-deep carpets, polished brass, miles of glass, spacious rooms, cocktail lounges, a fine restaurant, a preternaturally polite staff, space age electronics, and the best accommodations for watching basketball."[7]

"The House That Isiah Built" glamorized the Pistons and made the franchise one of the most profitable in the NBA. When Thomas came to Detroit in 1981, the Pistons had no tradition or culture of success. The team sorely needed an identity and a clear, unified purpose. Gradually, over the course of the 1980s, as General Manager Jack McCloskey surrounded Thomas with more talent, team owner Bill Davidson recognized that a championship team needed a home that inspired players and fans. "For us to be successful," Thomas told Davidson, "it's got to *mean* something to be a Piston."[8]

Being a Piston meant that they owned what Michael Jordan so desperately wanted—championship trophies. When the Bulls entered the Palace for the first time since losing the 1990 Eastern Conference Finals, they could see two championship banners hanging from the rafters. In their first meeting since that decisive playoff series, the Bad Boys thrashed the Bulls the same way they always did on their home turf, 105–84. Jordan scored thirty-three points, but none of his teammates scored more than nine. Scottie

Pippen played so poorly, making only two of sixteen shots, that Jordan asked him if he had another migraine. "This was a royal ass-kicking," Jordan told reporters. "That's all you can say. We're just gonna take our ass-kicking and go home."[9]

The Bulls seemed rattled. But Jordan wouldn't back down from a good fight. Nothing the Pistons did could shake his tenacity or his unwavering belief in himself—though he still harbored doubts about his teammates and Phil Jackson's coaching methods. Looking ahead at the team's schedule, however, he couldn't wait until the next showdown with the Bad Boys, an embattled team reckoning with a public backlash and the inner turmoil of its biggest star.

Six months earlier, on June 15, 1990, the Pistons celebrated their second consecutive NBA championship after defeating the Portland Trail Blazers in five games, becoming just the third franchise in league history to win back-to-back titles. The next morning, however, ominous newspaper headlines intruded on Detroit's festive moment. The *Washington Post* announced, "8 Die as Detroit Revels in NBA Victory." The *New York Times* reported that in downtown Detroit spontaneous revelry among Pistons fans flooding the streets degenerated into violence and vandalism. "Scores were injured by gunfire, stabbings and fighting . . . numerous instances of looting were reported; cars overturned, and police and emergency vehicles were damaged." The Detroit newspapers reported two dozen people wounded from gunshots and 140 people arrested. *Sports Illustrated* attributed the mayhem—"one of the ugliest episodes in Detroit" since the '67 riots—to "the success of the local professional basketball team."[10]

Television newscasts captured images of the city's poorest neighborhoods and paired them with the imagery of urban unrest. Crackling gunfire could be heard echoing off the crumbling buildings, stripped cars, and weed-strewn parking lots as riot police mobilized like they were going to thwart a mob. At a time when Detroit held a national reputation as a hopeless city of ruins, the night's violence reminded frightened white suburbanites why Bill Davidson had moved the Pistons out of the city in the first place. Mayor Coleman Young protested the sensational media coverage, complaining that reporters ignored the fact that tens of thousands of Detroiters celebrated peacefully and committed no crimes. Furthermore, he explained, of the eight reported deaths, four were the result of a single hit-and-run incident. But those arguments fell on deaf ears.[11]

The Bad Boys soon became synonymous with inner-city violence and Black criminality. Although some writers suggested that it was "wrong to link the Pistons' success with riots in Detroit," other commentators took to describing the players as "thugs and muggers" corrupting the purity of the game. "They've gotten away with murder," grumbled one Western Conference executive. The Bad Boys "should have been handcuffed years ago," said Cleveland's GM Wayne Embry. Undoubtedly, noted Todd Boyd, University of Southern California professor of media studies, a native Detroiter and longtime Pistons fan, the Bad Boys were perceived nationally as a *Black team*, even though Bill Laimbeer, the team's most despised agitator—the Rush Limbaugh of basketball—was white. "Pistonphobia," therefore, was largely rooted in the anxieties of white Americans terrified by everything the Bad Boys represented: an incorrigible group of Black rebels with no respect for rules or order, streetballers rewarded for turning basketball into a blood sport.[12]

Public animosity toward the Pistons became inflamed in the aftermath of the 1987 Eastern Conference Finals. After Game Seven, inside the Boston Garden's visiting team locker room, the Pistons brooded over a devastating loss to the Celtics. Reporters surrounded rookie forward Dennis Rodman and asked him about the challenges of guarding Larry Bird, a three-time winner of the Most Valuable Player award. Rodman told writers, "He ain't God. He ain't the best player in the NBA." The only reason Bird won the MVP trophies, Rodman said, was "because he's white." Immediately, a reporter approached Isiah Thomas, telling him that Rodman had called Bird "an overrated white player." Did Thomas agree with his teammate? "I think Larry is a very, very good basketball player, an exceptional talent," Thomas answered. "But I'd have to agree with Rodman. If he was black, he'd be just another good guy." Thomas chuckled, though no one laughed with him. Some reporters interpreted it as nervous laughter; others thought of it as sarcasm, but none of the writers asked him any follow-up questions about Bird or race in the NBA.[13]

Newspapers throughout the country quoted Thomas, and within days commentators were twisting his words and condemning him as a racist. *New York Post* columnist Dick Young compared him to Louis Farrakhan, the Black Nationalist leader of the Nation of Islam. Another white writer for the *Los Angeles Herald-Examiner* called for a boycott of the Pistons until the team fired Thomas. The Pistons received more than one hundred phone calls from angry season-ticket holders threatening to cancel their commitments. White fans throughout the country demanded the NBA punish Thomas for perpetuating so-called reverse discrimination—an invented term stemming from white American fears that discrimination against them was on the rise.[14]

Thomas tried to defuse the controversy. He spoke to the press and admitted that he made a mistake talking sarcastically with people who did not really know him. He insisted that he was joking—after all, who in their right mind thought *Larry Bird* was just another good player? In an interview with *New York*

Times columnist Ira Berkow, Thomas explained that he was not criticizing Bird personally but trying to draw attention to how white commentators perpetuated stereotypes about Black players. "When Bird makes a great play, it's due to his thinking, and his work habits," he said. That was "not the case for blacks. All we do is run and jump. We never practice or give a thought to how we play."[15]

Thomas pointed to the ways that white writers and broadcasters praised Bird's acumen and ambition, attributes rarely credited to Black players. Instead, commentators perpetuated the myth that Black players were naturally superior athletes. Gesturing toward himself, Magic Johnson, and Michael Jordan as examples, Thomas said, "We're playing only on God-given talent, like we're animals, lions and tigers, who run around in a jungle, while Larry's success is due to his intelligence and hard work." Those dehumanizing stereotypes emphasized innate Black athletic advantages—advantages rationalized by the disproportionate number of Black players in the NBA, whose presence gave the public the impression that they were "watching a different breed of athlete." Many Americans—Black and white alike—who believed in inherent Black athletic superiority subscribed to the survival of the fittest theory, a pseudoscientific fallacy that only the strongest and healthiest Black slaves survived the Middle Passage and their descendants—selectively bred on Southern plantations—benefited athletically.[16]

Since the 1960s, when Black basketball players increasingly appeared on professional teams, members of the sports-industrial complex—athletes, coaches, scouts, team executives, owners, journalists, and doctors—attempted to explain why Black athletes dominated certain sports. These armchair anthropologists speculated that Black athletes benefited from genetic advantages: longer limbs, larger heel bones, bigger thighs, and more fast-twitch muscle fibers that allowed for explosive bursts of speed and greater jumping ability. However, these debates not only lacked scientific evidence, they also failed to account for social conditions and cultural factors that influenced Black American participation in sports. Too many people ignored how historical racial barriers funneled young Black men and women into performative roles as athletes and entertainers.[17]

William Rhoden, a distinguished African American columnist with the *New York Times*, dismissed the debate over Black athletic superiority as an "obsession" among white people. That preoccupation colored the way nostalgic white fans viewed Bird as the "Designated Savior of professional basketball," a "Great White Hope" who could restore the place of white players in a sport that no longer exclusively belonged to them. That fantasy included white sportswriters and fans who celebrated Bird as the best player in history, claiming he overcame "gifts that God didn't give" him. To many observers, he did not look like the "typical" basketball player. His pale, fleshy body lacked muscular definition. The fact that he lumbered down the court and could hardly jump over a shoebox seemed to prove that he played at a disadvantage against Black players. Bird himself perpetuated that very mythology. "I'm not a natural talent like a [Michael] Jordan," he said. "I have to practice and practice and practice." That effort, he thought, allowed him to compensate for his "deficiencies," proving that "a white boy who can't run or jump can play this game."[18]

The fury over Thomas's comments about Bird struck a nerve in white America, producing a public relations nightmare for the NBA. Despite Commissioner David Stern's repeated pronouncements that the league's fans were colorblind, his office orchestrated a spin campaign in the hopes that Thomas could convince the public he was not a "troublemaker" harboring resentment against white people. In Los Angeles, where the Celtics prepared for the

NBA Finals against the Lakers, Thomas joined Bird in front of a packed pressroom to plead his case. Bird insisted that Thomas's remarks did not offend him and that people should move on, as he did. Here was the Great White Hope rescuing the Black Bad Boy from the mob. "He saved my career," Thomas said a year later. "The same [reporters] who voted that I was the most charitable guy in the NBA for the J. Walter Kennedy Award are the same people now that wanted to lynch me."[19]

The backlash against Thomas deepened public contempt for the Pistons and transformed the team's biggest star into a despised villain. When Thomas first came to the NBA, he carried the reputation of a Boy Scout, admired as one of the most likable and accessible stars in professional basketball. Writers often described him as charming, intelligent, and articulate—adjectives used to package Black athletes as nonthreatening. Thomas was "a sweet-faced handsome man with doe eyes; a soft, thoughtful voice; and a fluorescent grin," noted one writer. After 1987, though, reporters increasingly scrutinized him, searching for something sinister—"an inner ruthlessness"—behind his warm, dimpled smile.[20]

For a time, white sportswriters extolled Thomas's life story as a stereotypical tale of despair and triumph: a ghetto boy, the youngest of nine children, raised fatherless by his strong-willed mother on the mean streets of Chicago, enduring unimaginable poverty, redeemed by a sport that extracted Black kids out of the inner city. In this version of events, basketball saved a former "street punk," a welfare kid, from going down the same destructive path as his older brothers, entrapped in a cycle of crime, drug addiction, and imprisonment. Thomas recalled that he found a temporary escape from a desolate world on a West Side basketball court where he could "forget the hunger pangs, the robberies and beatings, and the minute-by-minute threat of violence."[21]

Yet the truth was that not even the blacktop courts could shield him from random gunfire. One time, when he was in middle school, an angry man seeking retribution after a playground fight began spraying bullets. Amid chaos and piercing screams, Thomas sprinted for his life and slid beneath a nearby car, his heart racing with trepidation. Suddenly, a wounded body collapsed right in front of him. Pressing his face against the pavement, young Isiah could see a man gushing blood. Thomas froze, afraid that if he rolled out from under the car and started running he too would get shot. So, he watched the man die. The next day he returned to the court. For a young Black boy who wanted to save his family and lift them out of poverty, playing basketball became a ritual of survival, an obligation, his last hope for "salvation from the ghetto life."[22]

Growing up, Isiah discovered that even the most isolated and invisible Black teens could attract attention from white scouts if they displayed valuable athletic ability. Gene Pingatore, the head basketball coach at St. Joseph's High School in Westchester, a suburb with very few Black faces, offered him a scholarship. Every morning, Thomas made a ninety-minute bus commute—making three transfers along the way—pinning his dreams on a future in professional basketball. At St. Joseph's, Thomas thrived on the court, becoming one of the most coveted college prospects in the country. Indiana University head coach Bob Knight recruited Isiah to Bloomington, where he led the Hoosiers to the NCAA championship in just his second year. Somewhere during his journey between St. Joseph's and Bloomington, he began assimilating into a white world, losing his street accent. He began talking "like a white boy," one of his brothers charged, polishing a sophisticated presentation that would endear him to white fans, writers, and corporate executives. In 1981, after the Pistons drafted him with the second overall pick, he signed a four-year contract that made him a millionaire, fulfilling his destiny as the family's "Chosen One."[23]

By the mid-1980s, Thomas had become a regular NBA All-Star and a local sports hero. Recognizing the power and responsibility that came with being the idol of urban youth, in the summer of 1986, he organized a Detroit campaign calling for a moratorium on crime. Canvassing the city streets, like a politician running for mayor, Thomas visited the most dangerous neighborhoods. He hugged sobbing women who reminded him of his own mother—women who had lost their babies to gun violence. He gave speeches in school auditoriums, urging young people to avoid drugs and gangs. Yet cynics questioned what his "No Crime Day" could really accomplish. Thomas was not naive about the festering underlying conditions that made Detroit a violent city. His campaign focused on recruiting corporate support for creating jobs and raising money to build youth recreation centers. He refused to let Detroit's power brokers ignore the plight of Black people.[24]

On September 27, 1986, Thomas led a "No Crime Day" march through the city with Mayor Coleman Young and one of his best friends—Lakers' star Magic Johnson. Standing before fifteen thousand people, surrounded by children looking up to him, "the smiling basketball star" preached like a minister, talking about hope and courage. He told the crowd that they did not have to live in fear; their voices mattered and so did their lives. It was an important message coming from one of the NBA's emerging stars—a message that Michael Jordan could not have delivered with the same authenticity.[25]

That same determination that fueled his leadership in the community, the aching hunger that made him refuse to surrender to anyone else's idea of limits, drove Thomas on the court. Since childhood, Thomas said, he always had to fight to prove he wasn't weak. Before him, professional-basketball fans had never seen a six-foot-one franchise player who could dominate the game with his dribble, moving players around the court like chess pieces. Yet, more than any other quality, his toughness inspired his teammates. They admired him for his grit and assertiveness. "He was fearless," Bill Laimbeer said.[26]

None of the Pistons would ever forget how Thomas played through a rosary of injuries during Game Six of the 1988 NBA Finals: a throbbing back that required painkillers, a gash on his left cheek, a poked right eye filled with tears, and a dislocated finger on his left hand. Then, in the third quarter, after scoring fourteen consecutive points, he rolled his ankle when he stepped on the foot of Lakers' forward Michael Cooper. Grimacing through excruciating pain, Thomas thought he had snapped his ankle. Somehow, after the team trainer wrapped his swollen ankle, Thomas, barely able to stand, hobbled back onto the floor and scored nine more points, finishing the quarter with an NBA Finals record of twenty-five points. The Pistons lost the game by one point and, ultimately, the series, but his performance sent a clear message: nothing would stop him from competing for a championship.[27]

Two summers later, on June 18, 1990, Thomas basked in the glorious sunshine as the Pistons promenaded along Woodward Avenue on parade floats, past tens of thousands of cheering fans in downtown Detroit. He was a champion, one of the very best players who had ever stepped onto an NBA court. Celebrating the team's second straight title should have been one of the greatest days of his life. But Thomas couldn't completely enjoy the moment because three days earlier, less than twenty-four hours after he had been named MVP of the Finals against the Trail Blazers, a local television station—WJBK Channel 2—dropped a bomb on the city's fans: investigative reporter Vince Wade had linked Isiah to an FBI probe in an illegal multimillion-dollar sports gambling ring. Although the US Attorney's Office clarified that Thomas was not the target of a federal investigation, a collection of personal checks signed by him were subpoenaed by a Detroit grand jury in the context of a case involving his good friend and neighbor Emmet Denha. According to local reporters, Thomas had participated in numerous "high stakes" gambling contests and had cashed hundreds of thousands of dollars' worth of checks through one of Denha's grocery stores—the same supermarket where Denha had laundered millions of dollars for bookmaker Henry Allen Hilf. Federal court records also revealed that Thomas had permitted Hilf and members of the Giacalone crime family to stage casino parties at his redbrick estate in Bloomfield Hills.[28]

Throughout the late 1980s, numerous players on the Pistons socialized with members of the Detroit mob at nightclubs, restaurants, and roaming gambling houses. At a time when there were no legal casinos in Michigan, professional athletes found an outlet for gambling and high-stakes competition at Thomas's home. The players wagered enormous sums of money, and by 1990 Thomas had fallen deeply into debt to Hilf and the Giacalones. The situation became so dire that hours before Game Five of the 1990 Eastern Conference Finals against the Bulls, Mark Aguirre, Thomas's closest friend on the team, someone he had known growing up in Chicago, met with FBI agents at Deli Unique in West Bloomfield. Aguirre told federal agents he was worried that Thomas's liabilities with dangerous mob figures might get his friend hurt. Denha, the godfather of Thomas's son Joshua, also told the FBI he feared for Isiah's safety.[29]

According to Detroit reporter Scott Burnstein, the bureau's informants said that Thomas "had helped the Giacalone crew manipulate point-spreads in Pistons games and washed his gambling money (wins and losses) through Denha's supermarkets." However, the FBI never found enough evidence to support these accusations. Nonetheless, some members of the Pistons suspected that Thomas had shaved points off the spread during two games in December 1989 in order to pay off gambling debts. Years later, a team official acknowledged that the NBA had started a point-shaving investigation into Thomas and his teammate James Edwards before shutting it down the moment the league learned that law enforcement did not plan to charge Thomas.[30]

Initially, Thomas vehemently denied being involved in any illegal gambling operations or point-shaving schemes, but later that summer he testified in front of a grand jury that he staged gambling events at his home and had cashed personal checks at Denha's grocery stores. The wagers, he said, were never "high stakes." He maintained that he gave checks to Denha so that his friend could cash them on his behalf instead of going to the bank, where he was hounded for autographs. Thomas also said that he provided the FBI and the IRS with his accounting records. He insisted that he had done nothing illegal, and he had nothing to hide. But the damage to his reputation was done. "Even though he's cleared," teammate John Salley said, "the man's name is smeared because now people are going to have to wonder."[31]

The gambling story followed Thomas into training camp for the 1990–1991 season. It made him more guarded with reporters, distant and cool. Suddenly writers began describing "the Other Isiah," as if the sweet smile he used to wear was just a mask for a darker and more calculating man than the public knew. The image of the Other Isiah as unpredictable and spiteful, even dangerous, took shape after a confrontation between Thomas and a local sportscaster named Virg Jacques. In early October 1990, after the Pistons finished an informal practice at Oakland University, Thomas began walking toward his car when he spotted the Channel 2 news reporter. According to Jacques, Thomas stared at him and said he wanted to talk. Then Thomas said, "Forget it," and began walking away. Jacques replied, "What's up?" According to Jacques, Thomas suddenly became irate and lunged at him. Thomas pushed him up against a car and grabbed him by the throat, yelling, "Get out of my face! Get the hell out of my way!" After Thomas got into his car, he threatened to run the reporter over.[32]

Thomas denied the accusations, alleging that Jacques had harassed him after practice. "I did not choke him," Thomas said. "I did not strangle him." Pistons spokesman Matt Dobek claimed the reporter blocked Thomas from getting into his car. Jacques countered that Dobek did not witness the incident and that he would take a lie detector test to prove he was telling the truth. From his car, James Edwards saw Thomas pin Jacques against a vehicle but did not see Thomas choke Jacques. Although the sportscaster filed assault and battery charges against Thomas, he ultimately dropped his complaint after the Pistons star apologized to him face-to-face. Regardless of the apology, people began to think that Thomas was spinning out of control, teetering on the brink. And one man in Chicago made it his mission to push him right over the edge.[33]

After losing at the Palace on December 19, Michael Jordan resumed complaining about the talent around him. Even Phil Jackson suggested that management might have to make personnel changes, concerned that his team might not have the fortitude to withstand the physical and mental pressure the Pistons imposed upon them. They needed to get tougher, he thought. Although Jackson liked to tell reporters that he was "trying to instill the peaceful warrior spirit" in the team, urging the players to take a deep breath and walk away from physical altercations with the Pistons, he also believed that the Bulls could only take so many hits until they fought back.[34]

After the Pistons whipped the Bulls, Jackson preached a new message inside the locker room: retaliation. "You've got to hit someone," he told Horace Grant. "When we play Detroit, you've just got to hit guys, anyone. Punch someone. Get thrown out of the game. Just do some damage."[35]

Six days later, on Christmas, the Pistons visited Chicago Stadium for a nationally televised showdown against the Bulls. On a chalkboard inside their locker room, one of the Pistons' coaches had scribbled reminders for how to beat the Bulls. The list included "the Jordan Rules." Everyone on the Pistons knew exactly what these rules meant: Jordan should never be guarded alone or allowed to drive right—his dominant side. And the closer he moved to the basket, the faster he had to be trapped with strategic double-teams.

But the Bulls refused to let the Pistons dictate the rules of engagement. A day after his wife Juanita gave birth to their second son, Jordan collected thirty-seven points in the Bulls' 98–86 victory over the Pistons. Late in the fourth quarter, after catching an elbow in the midsection from Joe Dumars, Horace Grant retaliated, tossing a wild punch, earning an automatic ejection. After the game, Jackson must have grinned inwardly when Grant told reporters, "We can't take crap from anybody."[36]

When it was over, Mark Aguirre, the same player who urged his teammates to return to playing like Bad Boys, complained that the game resembled a no-holds-barred wrestling match. The referees turned a blind eye to Chicago's grappling maneuvers, he complained. It seemed that the tide had turned. The Bulls had found a way to get inside the heads of the Pistons. Not so fast, Jackson warned. "This game was not a measuring stick for us," he said. "We still have to go back to Detroit and win."[37]

No single athlete made more money for Chicago Bulls owner Jerry Reinsdorf than Michael Jordan. According to *Forbes* magazine, between the time Reinsdorf purchased the Bulls in 1985 and when Jordan left the team in 1998, Reinsdorf's investment had grown more than 1,000 percent. Credit: AP Images

Chapter Eight

OTHER PEOPLE'S MONEY

"My father used to tell me that you've got to be in the action. That was one of his favorite expressions. 'Ya gotta be in the action,' he'd say. 'If you're in the action, things'll happen to you.' And I love action. I like to make deals."

—BULLS OWNER JERRY REINSDORF, 1988

efore every game, moments before Michael Jordan laced up a brand-new pair of Nikes, Bulls trainer Chip Schaefer wrapped his ankles with athletic tape. Jordan never broke from his routine, insisting on being the last player Schaefer treated. Typically, he would sit on the training table wearing a T-shirt and his old Carolina blue basketball shorts. This was the time for him to block out the noise and distractions and begin focusing on the game. But on January 16, 1991, inside the Orlando Arena dressing room, breaking news shattered his concentration. President George H. W. Bush had just announced the beginning of Operation Desert Storm, a shock-and-awe bombing campaign of Baghdad and targets across Iraq. Every major television network, including ESPN, aired the president's urgent message from the Oval Office. The sudden news made Jordan's heart sink. He dropped his head and closed his eyes, thinking of his older brother

Ronnie, a sixteen-year Army veteran stationed in Germany, who could be called upon to serve in the Persian Gulf War.[1]

Basketball fans were beginning to file into the arena, but thirty minutes before tip-off everyone on the Bulls was still gathered around a television. They were among the millions of Americans glued to the television, unable to look away from CNN's startling live images of bombs cratering Baghdad's buildings. For the first time in history, satellite technology allowed Americans to watch a war unfold instantaneously.

No one seemed to be thinking about the game against the Orlando Magic. Inside the Bulls' dressing room, Phil Jackson sensed that the team's mood had grown somber. He admitted later that the president's announcement depressed him. But Jordan had no doubt that US military forces would easily expel Iraqi troops out of Kuwait. "We're gonna kick their asses," he said. "We're gonna show them they can't mess with us."[2]

That night the national anthem energized the Orlando Arena, culminating in a crescendo of cheering and applause that seemed a few decibels louder than usual. Whatever inspiration "The Star-Spangled Banner" may have provided the crowd, it didn't help Jordan perform. Although the Bulls beat the Magic by eleven points for the team's seventh straight victory, Jordan missed sixteen of twenty-seven shot attempts. Jackson noticed that Jordan lacked focus, so the coach sat him for the first ten minutes of the second quarter. After the game, Jordan acknowledged that the news of the war weighed on him and made it difficult to concentrate.[3]

It seemed that the entire team was distracted by a rumor that Iraqi dictator Saddam Hussein would send assassins to the United States, seeking retribution for attacks against his soldiers. During a first-quarter break, Craig Hodges turned to Horace Grant and said, "You know, the General [Jordan] is considered a national treasure." If Iraqi sharpshooters were going to target anyone, Hodges said, it would be MJ. Grant gave Hodges a serious look as they backed away from their famous teammate. The very thought of an attack taking place during an NBA game alarmed some players. Over the course of the game, as Jackson shouted instructions during time-outs, some guys avoided Jordan in the huddle.[4]

At halftime, concerned citizens sought updates from Baghdad. In the stadium corridor, a small crowd of fans gathered around a man leaning against a wall, holding a portable TV. People craned their necks trying to catch a glimpse of the small black-and-white screen. By the time the third quarter began, it became increasingly difficult to hear the TV as fans watching the game erupted with shouting. It was a jarring juxtaposition: people cheering grown men playing a game while the news feed reminded basketball fans that US troops were risking their lives so that Americans could enjoy watching that very game in peace. In one moment, the group surrounding the man with the handheld TV could hear a news anchor: "The U.S. Air Force's F-15E Eagle strike fighters have rained destruction on key Iraqi military targets . . . " And in the next instant they could hear the Orlando Magic's public address announcer say, "Michael Jordan, shooting two." At some point the fans returned to their seats. Even during a war, the show had to go on.[5]

The drama put into relief the role thrust upon Michael Jordan at that moment in history. As *Orlando Sentinel* columnist Larry Guest noted, Jordan provided a "momentary escape from the sobering reality half a world away." Sports had always offered spectators a diversion from the routines of daily life, but in the darkness of the Gulf War, Jordan, a nonpareil "cult hero," strengthened his place as an "American institution," a patriotic source for boosting the country's morale. His presence on the court reminded people that the American way of life would endure in a tumultuous time. Expressing gratitude to the troops, he talked about honoring them and praying for their safe return. "We got to do what we got to do," he said. "I hate to see any war. I just hope we can get it over with as quickly as possible and all our people come back safely."[6]

In the coming days and weeks, Americans questioned whether sports should continue as usual. After consulting the White House, NBA commissioner David Stern decided that the NBA would not cancel any games. "It was a tough decision," said deputy commissioner Russ Granik, but guidance from the White House made it easier for the league to play on. President Bush argued that sports offered people an important refuge from the stressful news of combat, just as President Franklin D. Roosevelt did during World War II. If anything, Bush said, continuing America's pastimes, including the upcoming Super Bowl, would send a powerful message around the world that the country would not give Saddam Hussein the power to dictate their lives.[7]

After the game against the Magic, when the Bulls arrived at Orlando International Airport, they learned that the FAA had established heightened security measures out of concern for possible terrorist acts. Under a "Level 4" alert—the highest possible—SWAT teams and bomb squads prepared contingency plans for an attack. Airline passengers were told they could not drop their luggage curbside or have family or friends meet them at the gate. Buses and limos were prohibited from driving on the tarmac. That restriction forced Jordan and his teammates to walk to their chartered jet instead of being bused.[8]

Leading the Pistons by one game in the Central Division, the Bulls landed in Atlanta with a 27–10 record, the team's best start in franchise history. The next day, during the Martin Luther King Jr. holiday, a group of players from the Bulls and Hawks visited the King Center, where they met with the civil rights leader's widow, Coretta Scott King. The NBA and TNT had arranged the event for a halftime segment that would air during the next night's game. The commemoration intended to honor King and connect the achievements of the civil rights movement with the NBA's own history of racial integration—but hours before the ceremony, Jordan called Craig Hodges and asked him to take his place.

The ceremony was intended to feature Jordan and Hawks star forward Dominique Wilkins laying a wreath on MLK's marble grave. Jordan seemed a good fit for the event, considering a year earlier he had said, "[King] will always be one of my heroes. The breakthroughs he made in civil rights, I'm trying to do the same in the business world." But now, presented with the opportunity to pay respects to his hero, Jordan passed the ball. He told Hodges, a player known inside the Bulls' locker room for his community engagement and deep appreciation for Black history, "This is your thing, not mine."[9]

For Jordan, the MLK tribute was just another obligation, one of the countless requests that demanded he perform for the cameras. As a national symbol, the pressures of fame entrapped him in a role he had helped create but couldn't discard. He had grown increasingly tired of being treated like a commodity. Multiple corporations had invested in him; the Bulls, the NBA, Nike, NBC, and the Tribune Company all made money exploiting Jordan's image. "I'm tired of being used by this organization, by the league, by the writers, by everyone," he fumed. Everywhere he went, people expected something from him—an interview, an autograph, a picture. Only his home or a hotel room offered any real escape from crowds or cameras.[10]

On the verge of turning twenty-seven, Jordan was obsessed with winning his first championship, but he also contemplated how his basketball career had completely taken over his life, eroding his love of the game. Jordan started dreaming about the day when he could walk away from the sport and the media machine that consumed him. "Five more years," he told his teammates. "Five more years and I'm out of here. I'm marking these days on a calendar, like I'm in jail."[11]

Michael Jordan was Jerry Reinsdorf's dream come true. When the Chicago real estate developer bought the Bulls with an investment syndicate in 1985 for $16 million, his majority shares—56 percent of the team—cost $9.2 million. He knew at the time that the struggling franchise "came with only one appreciable asset: Michael Jordan." In a sports-crazed town, Reinsdorf thought the Bulls were a "sleeping giant" that Jordan could awaken. He figured the better Jordan played, the more valuable the Bulls would become, which would make him richer and more influential. As Jordan's popularity grew, the demand for tickets at Chicago Stadium skyrocketed, as did the value of the franchise. Before he signed with the Bulls, Chicagoans treated the NBA like a minor league sport. The Ringling brothers' circus had a better chance of selling out Chicago Stadium than the Bulls. "You could shoot a cannon through the place and not hit anybody," recalled one longtime Bulls fan. But since November 20, 1987, every Bulls home game had sold out. On the eve of the 1990–1991 season, more than five thousand fans had joined a waiting list for season tickets, praying for an opening that virtually never happened. Jordan had become so popular that the Bulls sold more team merchandise than the Lakers and Celtics. At that time, the franchise was likely worth about $100 million—a figure that would more than double over the coming decade.[12]

More than anything else, record-breaking television deals drove escalating NBA franchise values. In a new agreement for the

1990–1991 season, NBC and TNT paid the NBA $180 million annually—more than double the combined price of the league's previous arrangement with CBS and TBS. The fees from those TV contracts were evenly distributed among all twenty-seven NBA teams. In exchange for the broadcasting rights, NBC televised twenty-two regular-season games—the Sunday "Game of the Week"—while TNT showed fifty regular-season games—mostly on Tuesday and Friday nights; both networks carried about thirty playoff games. The NBA's television broadcasts attracted major sponsorship agreements with the Miller Brewing Company, McDonald's, Prudential Insurance, Schick Razors, and eight major auto manufacturers. According to David Stern, 80 percent of each club's revenues derived from those national television contracts. They were the very foundation of the league's economic prosperity.[13]

In order to reduce any conflict between the network's games and individual teams, Stern advocated the league impose restrictions on superstation broadcasts. At the time, three superstations—WTBS in Atlanta, WWOR in New York, and WGN in Chicago—televised NBA games locally and nationally. In April 1990, over the objections of Jerry Reinsdorf, the NBA's board of governors voted to limit the number of games each team could broadcast on superstations, effectively cutting the Bulls' appearances on WGN from twenty-five games to twenty. The problem for Stern and most owners was that "the Air Jordan Show on WGN" created direct competition with local telecasts of weaker NBA teams in smaller markets. Stern believed that if fans outside Chicago could see Jordan frequently on WGN, then they would be less likely to tune into Bulls games on NBC and TNT, diminishing the value of those national television deals.[14]

Reinsdorf insisted that Stern was wrong. In fact, he commissioned a survey that showed superstation broadcasts did not harm the NBA's relationship with the networks. Reinsdorf reminded Stern that the NBA's network deals were guaranteed for a minimum of four years and that the league would not receive "one nickel less" from NBC or TNT with the Bulls playing on WGN. Furthermore, he argued WGN broadcasts had no impact on attendance or television ratings for games in other NBA cities. Reinsdorf knew that the Bulls' games on WGN could reach 35 million viewers throughout the country—one-third of all television households. That market share presented him with a rare opportunity: the wide interest in Jordan could grow the team's national audience, making the Bulls "America's Team."[15]

After Stern announced that the NBA planned to eliminate superstation games altogether, Reinsdorf thought he had no choice but to sue the league. Heated debates with Stern had gotten him nowhere. This case was all about money and which NBA owners would profit from the value generated by Michael Jordan. The NBA did not receive a dime of revenue from the Bulls' WGN telecasts; the profits went directly to Reinsdorf and the team's investors. And no one—not Stern or the other NBA owners—was going to prevent Reinsdorf from building his business. "He believed that the Bulls franchise would permanently cripple itself if it did not take advantage of the opportunity, when Michael Jordan was playing, to establish itself on WGN," said NBA general counsel and future NHL commissioner Gary Bettman. "Whether he was right or wrong is not the point. He believed this in his bones."[16]

On October 26, 1990, the Chicago Bulls and WGN filed a suit in federal court against the NBA, alleging that the league's superstation restrictions posed an unreasonable restraint of trade and were a clear violation of the Sherman Antitrust Act. The NBA's attorneys countered that the league's superstation rules were exempt from antitrust lawsuits under the powers of the Sports Broadcasting Act (SBA), which recognized professional sports teams as interdependent partners that could legally contract joint broadcasting agreements. However, the SBA only provided antitrust exemptions for television rights that were transferred or sold *by a league*. In this case, the Bulls owned the rights to any games that the NBA did not sell to NBC or TNT, and, therefore, the SBA did not apply.[17]

On December 18, Jerry Reinsdorf testified before US District Court judge Hubert L. Will, a respected jurist appointed to the Northern District of Illinois by President John F. Kennedy. An energetic and engaging judge who "spoke a mile-a-minute in flat Midwestern tones," Will lived for the conflict of the courtroom, the jousting between attorneys, and what he called "the art of judging." Testifying before him, Reinsdorf, the bespectacled former tax attorney, came across as confident and smart, if uncharismatic. He was a pure businessman, unafraid of playing hardball with Stern. "As an owner," David Halberstam wrote, "he was able to view sports ownership as a very Darwinian business. His view of the process was oddly detached, almost clinical."[18]

Reinsdorf was a shrewd operator, with a reputation for being forceful yet patient enough to wait until he got what he wanted, even if it came at the expense of losing public favor. "Reinsdorf," wrote *Sports Illustrated*'s E. M. Swift, "would rather be respected than loved. It's important to him. Nothing in his manner says, *Hey, I'm one of you*. He does not solicit affection. He solicits something much colder—respect—and it has cost him the common touch."[19]

One of two men who owned two major league sports franchises—Atlanta's Ted Turner owned the Hawks and Braves—Reinsdorf had earned little affection among Chicago sports fans. On the city's South Side, White Sox fans detested him for threatening to move the ball club to St. Petersburg, Florida. That story, played out in the Chicago newspapers, illustrated the politics of professional sports, reflecting the betrayal of trust that many Americans felt when the greedy Lords of the Game manipulated the public for profits. Reinsdorf and his partner, Eddie Einhorn, "the Gepetto and Pinocchio of the affair," were portrayed as "the villains, blackmailers of emotions and unctuous opportunists."[20]

From the moment they took ownership of the White Sox, Reinsdorf and Einhorn complained about the deteriorating condition of Comiskey Park, a poorly aging monument of the dead-ball era. In 1986, they hired an engineering firm, Kennedy and Associates, which released a memo claiming that "Comiskey Park is nearing the end of its useful life." Without any supporting documentation proving that the stadium's structural engineering was beyond repair, Reinsdorf and his old Northwestern Law School friend, Illinois governor James Thompson, set in motion a scheme that delivered a new publicly funded baseball stadium on the city's South Side. Thompson advised Reinsdorf that if he wanted the state legislature to approve a publicly financed ballpark, then he needed to convince everyone that he had a viable stadium project in Florida. "If they [the legislature] don't believe you're going to move, you'll never get a deal," the governor said. "Make them believe it."[21]

Accordingly, in 1988, Reinsdorf and Einhorn flew to Florida, where they began negotiating with the city of St. Petersburg, which had already started building the Suncoast Dome in the hopes of luring a Major League Baseball team. Meanwhile, back in Chicago, Thompson and Illinois House Speaker Michael Madigan began whipping votes on behalf of the Sox owners.

Since the mid-1980s, Reinsdorf had donated thousands of dollars to the election campaigns of both men, one a Republican, the other a Democrat, knowing that each had the power to help him secure public funding for a new stadium. Reinsdorf maintained that he wanted to keep the Sox in Chicago, but if the state legislature did not come through, then he could not afford to keep the club in Comiskey Park. The bitter negotiations over the future of the White Sox cast a pall over him. He received death threats and anti-Semitic hate mail from fanatics who believed that he and Einhorn had held the city hostage.[22]

Ultimately, the Illinois state legislature approved a $150 million stadium subsidy, financed mostly by a tax on hotels. Reinsdorf's sweetheart deal made him "the envy of owners everywhere." He managed to negotiate a twenty-year lease whereby after the first ten years the state would purchase up to three hundred thousand tickets in any year that attendance fell below 1.5 million, a remarkable insurance policy paid for by the public. "Other cities, counties, and states have helped local teams build stadiums," Lester Munson reported in the *National Sports Daily*, "but this is the first time the taxpayers find themselves paying the team's expenses, collecting virtually no rent and subsidizing the team in losing seasons."[23]

It was a classic move by Reinsdorf, who openly boasted that he had made his fortune from "OPM"—"other people's money." In the early 1970s, he constructed tax shelters as cofounder of Balcor, an investment firm that sold real estate partnerships to the general public. In 1982, a year after purchasing the White Sox with a group of fifty investors—again, using OPM—Reinsdorf sold Balcor to Shearson Lehman Brothers, the investment banking and brokerage arm of American Express, for an initial payment of $53 million and further incentives worth another $50 million.

After the sale, Reinsdorf remained chairman of the company. When he left Balcor at the end of 1987, however, the real estate market collapsed and so did Balcor's earnings. Soon, hundreds of thousands of Balcor investors realized that their retirement portfolios were tied to junk mortgages and foreclosures. In Balcor's brochures, Reinsdorf had promised investors a sound future with "well-located and well-managed properties," warning investors that they should act urgently because "the Social Security system appears to be in great jeopardy." Yet instead of enjoying the benefits of a retirement guaranteed by Reinsdorf, investors, crippled by Balcor's mismanagement, filed a multi-billion-dollar class action lawsuit against the company alleging "fraudulently promised and unrealistic returns and understated risks of real estate investment." Reinsdorf, who was not a defendant in the suit, dismissed the charges, eschewing any responsibility for losing other people's money.[24]

Instead, he presented himself as "a respected businessman," which was exactly how the Bulls described him in its game programs and publications. Not as an admired businessman, but as a respected one, though he liked to tell reporters that he was charitable, too. He reminded people that he could have profited more from selling the White Sox broadcasting rights in Florida, an untapped baseball market, but he stayed in Chicago for sentimental reasons, for the fans. "I can only say, having grown up in Brooklyn, and knowing how I suffered when the Dodgers left Brooklyn [for Los Angeles in 1957], and knowing what the loss of the Dodgers meant to Brooklyn, I just didn't want to do it." Years later, though, he admitted that his machination in Florida was all a ruse. "A savvy negotiator creates leverage," he said with a grin. "People had to think we were going to leave Chicago."[25]

Reinsdorf had a habit of complaining that if he did not get the deal he wanted, then he would go broke. It's what he said when he needed a new ballpark and he said it again when the NBA planned to eliminate superstation broadcasts. Testifying before Judge Will, Reinsdorf stated that the NBA's superstation restrictions could cost the Bulls $1 million in advertising revenue for the 1990–1991 season. Although Reinsdorf admitted that he had once voted in favor of constraining the NBA's superstation broadcasts, now, he said, "I would televise as many games on WGN as I could." He explained that he needed to showcase Jordan with impressionable young viewers so that he could grow a loyal fan base that would support the team long after Jordan retired. A convincing witness, Reinsdorf argued that the NBA was depriving Bulls fans of the right to watch their favorite player on TV, as if he had suddenly become the guardian of consumer rights. At one point, Judge Will leaned toward Reinsdorf and asked him if he thought Jordan was the Mikhail Baryshnikov of basketball. "Baryshnikov is the Jordan of ballet," Reinsdorf quipped.[26]

The following day David Stern took the stand. At the time, he was credited as the best commissioner in professional sports and the most important in the history of the NBA. A former Manhattan attorney, Stern prepared for the WGN case around the clock, keeping his legal staff working well into the middle of the night. Losing the case was not an option, he reminded them. "Stern was a maniac about the WGN suit," said an attorney from the league's firm, Proskauer, Rose, Goetz & Mendelsohn. Still, the commissioner claimed he had no personal grudge against Reinsdorf. This was just business and sometimes businessmen had to settle disputes in court.[27]

The NBA owners could not have hired a more effective commissioner. Even Reinsdorf had to admit that Stern had dramatically improved the financial position of a once "dying basketball league" that had now become the fastest-growing professional sports organization in America. In the early 1980s, most NBA teams were losing money. The financial circumstances of the league were so dire that some owners contemplated bankruptcy. But since Stern became commissioner in 1984, the NBA had quadrupled its earnings and broken its attendance record every year. In summer 1989, after NBA owners learned that the NFL had tried to lure Stern away to succeed the football league's Commissioner Paul Tagliabue, Stern received a five-year, $27.5 million contract and a $10 million signing bonus, making him far and away the highest-compensated chief executive officer in professional sports.[28]

Praised as a marketing genius and master salesman, Stern developed a motto for promoting the league: "Sell and sell and sell." Under his direction, the NBA built its business model around the cult of personality, merchandising television stars, celebrities recognized for being entertainers as much as athletes. When NBC bought the rights to broadcast NBA games, what the network really paid for were household names—Michael, Magic, Larry, and Isiah—personalities whose appearances on-screen encouraged audiences to return to the show again and again. Like Hollywood luminaries, basketball stars offered audiences a point of identification. In fact, NBC built the 1990–1991 broadcasting schedule around those four players. The marketing strategy was simple: the more fans saw them play, the more invested they became in their stories.[29]

The NBA's surging popularity—and Jordan's, too—coincided with the emerging revolution in cable television. During the cable boom of the 1980s and 1990s, American viewers enjoyed a whole new variety of sports on multiple channels, including ESPN, and regional sports networks—"mini-ESPNs." These cable outlets, like Chicago's SportsChannel, multiplied the NBA's exposure, which greatly enhanced the league's partnerships with advertisers. Between the 1985–1986 season and the end of the decade, the NBA's cable telecasts increased nearly 40 percent. Professional basketball proved especially appealing on cable TV because most games were played in the evening and during the winter, when television networks provided fewer entertainment alternatives.[30]

The NBA conveyed a telegenic quality that suited American desires for star power and continuous action. In football, a quarterback takes the field only half the time, and in baseball, a slugger comes to bat four or five times each game, but in basketball, stars appear on-screen for almost an entire game. And television cameras provide viewers with an intimacy where the players' faces are not shielded by helmets or hats. Watched on increasingly larger TV sets, the close-ups and slow-motion replays seemed to bring the viewer right onto the court. The NBA delivered suspense and drama, night after night. Looking back on the eighties, Stern said, "We were, without knowing it, entering a new golden era for sports, particularly basketball."[31]

When Stern took the stand before Judge Will, he testified that the NBA's restrictions on superstation broadcasts were necessary in order to sustain the league's revenue-sharing business model. Without shared revenue, he estimated, twenty teams would be swimming in red ink. The NBA's joint-venture agreement was the basis for how the league governed the salary cap, the draft, broadcasting rights, and the distribution of merchandise revenues. The NBA simply could not allow popular teams like the Bulls to encroach on the markets of its partners via superstation broadcasts. Permitting it would make it much more difficult for less popular teams to build their brand, he argued. Stern maintained that the NBA reduced superstation telecasts because the owners wanted to "guarantee the exclusivity and quality of its product in the national market."[32]

Yet his testimony failed to convince Judge Will that the NBA's superstation restrictions did not breach federal antitrust laws. On January 24, 1991, he delivered a seventy-one-page decision in favor of the plaintiffs, ruling that the NBA's policy curbed Reinsdorf's ability to sell the rights of Bulls' games to WGN and that this constituted a "significant restraint of trade." Furthermore, the NBA never provided "evidence that superstations have any significant impact on the league's contracts with NBC or TNT. Both networks signed their present, big-dollar, four-year contracts with the NBA knowing that games would also be carried on superstations and before the vote by the league owners to reduce the number of superstation games from 25 to 20."[33]

Judge Will's ruling delivered a resounding victory for Reinsdorf, but it came at a cost. In the aftermath of the case, the NBA Players Association hired a forensic accountant and former FBI agent named Charles Bennett, who spent five days examining trial records in a Chicago courthouse. Bennett discovered that most owners—including Reinsdorf—had "flagrantly underreported their teams' incomes." That meant the owners had shortchanged the players millions of dollars and that they had artificially reduced the salary cap. The NBA's collective bargaining agreement guaranteed the players 53 percent of the league's gross revenues, but Bennett's findings implied the owners had violated the deal.[34]

In December 1991, the players' union filed a suit with the US District Court in Newark, New Jersey. The complaint charged the owners with fraudulent accounting practices, including a failure to report revenues from luxury skyboxes and foreign broadcast rights. It's unlikely the union would have uncovered the discrepancies without Reinsdorf suing the NBA. As a result of the federal trial, the owners had to disclose financial records in court. "Don't yell at me because I was the vehicle for this being exposed," he said. "If you're doing something wrong you deserve to be caught."[35]

Yet the Bulls owner got caught withholding $3 million in income from local television, advertising, and stadium signs for a single season. Reinsdorf, however, denied any wrongdoing. "It's simply incorrect, at least as it pertains to us," he said. "We have properly accounted for all of our income." The union's executive director Charles Grantham wondered whether the owners conspired to cheat the players out of "tens of millions of dollars over the years." Ultimately, the owners and the union worked out a settlement that paid the players more than $30 million over two seasons, though the owners refused to acknowledge violating the collective bargaining agreement.[36]

Reinsdorf was not the only owner exploiting the system, but his colleagues blamed him for the price they paid. He recalled an owner's meeting where Milwaukee Bucks owner Jim Fitzgerald, a man he once considered a friend, approached his dinner table and asked how anyone could sit with him. "I was a pariah," Reinsdorf lamented. "After that, I stopped going to meetings." Jerry Colangelo, owner of the Phoenix Suns, thought Reinsdorf had no one to blame but himself. "Suing the NBA was no way to deal with his partners," he said. "There's only one way to describe Jerry Reinsdorf's actions—*greed*."[37]

On January 23, 1991, the day before Judge Will delivered his ruling, the Bulls arrived at Byrne Arena in East Rutherford, New Jersey, for a game against the Nets, one of the worst teams in the NBA. Rumors circulated throughout the Bulls dressing room that Jerry Krause was close to making a trade for Denver

Nuggets guard Walter Davis, a thirty-six-year-old veteran averaging eighteen points per game. Davis, an old friend of Jordan's who had played at UNC during the mid-1970s, desperately wanted out of Denver, a franchise that had plummeted to last place in the Western Conference. Convinced that Davis was the player the Bulls needed to back up Scottie Pippen and strengthen the team's bench scoring, Jordan pressed Krause to sign him as a free agent during the off-season, but Davis's wife reportedly did not want to move to Chicago. Now, on the verge of trading for Davis, Krause consulted Phil Jackson and the coaching staff about how one of the Nuggets' leading scorers would fit into the Bulls' rotation. The coaches agreed that Davis posed a defensive liability and that the Pistons would exploit him during the playoffs. Pass on Davis, Jackson advised, and that's exactly what Krause did.[38]

Unaware of the coaches' vote, Jordan was heading to the Nets' court for his pregame practice when he learned that Krause had walked away from the trade. Fuming, Jordan said, "As soon as we get back, I'm calling Reinsdorf. Krause has messed everything up again." Jordan blamed Krause entirely for failing to improve the team, complaining that other team executives did not want to deal with the GM because he couldn't be trusted. "We can't get anything done because of him," he said. "I'm going to tell Reinsdorf when I get back that it's either me or [Krause]. If he wants to keep Krause, fine, I'll tell him to trade me. But this is it. It's got to stop here."

Losing by four points to the lowly Nets, a team with a 13–26 record, reminded Jordan that the Bulls were stuck with Dennis Hopson, a player Krause had acquired in 1990 from New Jersey in exchange for *three* draft picks. Since joining the Bulls, Hopson had struggled in the triangle offense, averaging only four points per game. In Jordan's mind, Hopson was the poster boy for Krause's incompetence. The following morning, when the Bulls returned home to their practice complex in Deerfield, a reporter stopped Jordan in the hallway and asked him about the failed trade. "If I were general manager," he said, "we'd be a better team."

His comments were the strongest public criticism he had ever directed at Krause and fueled rumors about the strife inside the Bulls organization. Jordan had argued that players—labor not management—knew the business of basketball best. *He* was the expert, not Krause. In doing so, Jordan tried to redefine the way the public valued the intellect of players, chipping away at the corporate structure that had allowed an unathletic man like Jerry Krause into professional sports management. Jordan had come to believe that he held the power that mattered most in the organization; yet he was reminded that no matter how much money he made the franchise, Reinsdorf—the owner—called all the shots.

Krause met Reinsdorf with tears in his eyes, devastated that the team's biggest star had ripped him in front of reporters. Reinsdorf had to do something about Jordan, Krause urged. Chastise him in the newspapers. Reinsdorf refused. He would not get into a public feud with Jordan. But he was willing to say that Jordan had crossed a line. Playing the role of peacemaker, Reinsdorf told Chicago reporters how much he admired and respected Jordan. However, the owner noted, "He's still a player. And players, quite frankly, don't know a whole lot about coaching. And they don't know a whole lot about what it takes to make a deal."

When Reinsdorf and Jordan met at the team owner's North Shore home, Jordan complained that Krause's most recent first-round picks—Stacey King, Will Perdue, and B. J. Armstrong—had not improved the Bulls' odds of beating the Pistons. And

Krause's prized draft selections, Pippen and Grant, could not be trusted when it counted most, he said.

Reinsdorf appreciated Jordan's burning desire to win a championship, but he didn't want to argue. He thought that Jordan was being too harsh and was hurting the team's cause when he publicly criticized Krause. The GM had made crucial decisions that helped position the first-place Bulls into contention for a title, and by undermining him, Jordan put him in a weaker negotiating position. Questioning his teammates' abilities was just as damaging. Imagine how your teammates must feel being told that they are not "good enough," Reinsdorf said. How does that inspire them to play better? Jordan sat there for a moment. He didn't know what to say, but he knew Reinsdorf was right.

Still, long after this conversation Jordan found he couldn't extinguish his impatience. Developments in the Eastern Conference convinced him that this season was his best chance to win a championship. By the end of January, the Bulls trailed the Boston Celtics by 2.5 games and the Detroit Pistons by 1.5 games in the conference standings. Yet the Bulls' rivals were facing significant losses due to injuries. Severe back pain forced Larry Bird to wear a cumbersome brace and miss fourteen games. The excruciating spasms and an inflamed nerve root forced him to lie flat on his back for hours. Boston reporters speculated that he would soon have season-ending surgery, eliminating any chance that the Celtics could contend for a championship.

Meanwhile, in late January, the Pistons announced that Isiah Thomas had surgery on his shooting wrist, which would likely cost him at least twelve weeks of the season. He'd been playing all year through the pain, but ligament damage between two middle bones in his right wrist had become unbearable. Without him, the Pistons were no better than an average team. Even if he returned for the playoffs, the Bulls now seemed like a lock for capturing the Central Division and home-court advantage in the Eastern Conference.

That wasn't good enough for Jordan. He'd set his sights on an NBA championship. His dream finally seemed within reach—except he still had to confront a formidable opponent out west, a master of deception as confounding as Houdini himself.

Michael Jordan had long believed that if he was ever going to win an NBA championship and become the true king of the court, he would have to beat Magic Johnson and
the Los Angeles Lakers. Credit: AP Images

Chapter Nine

KING OF THE COURT

"We are in America, where truth does not count. Image does, however. . . . Earvin Johnson, Jr., built himself on images. His task is to be as he appears, now and always. A model, an example, a supermarket of destinies—we are a free country here, choose and enjoy!"

—FRENCH JOURNALIST CLAUDE ASKOLOVITCH, *L'ÉVÉNEMENT DU JEUDI*, JANUARY 9–15, 1992

Jim Murray sized up the competition: "Michael Jordan is a star. Magic Johnson is a team." In early 1990, when HBO television executives floated the idea of a one-on-one, pay-per-view game between the two biggest names in basketball, sportswriters evaluated the matchup like a fight between two heavyweights. Jordan, wrote the legendary *Los Angeles Times* columnist, had it all—everything except a championship ring. "He's rich, famous, good looking. He's the best in the world at what he does. He soars above his sport—literally—the way only a gifted few in history have. His mere image sells shoes, soft drinks, cars and tickets. He's well-liked, well-rounded, and as cheerful as a bluebird." Yet Murray wondered whether Jordan could overcome his reputation as a "trick-shot artist," a one-man scoring machine who often played like he didn't need teammates.[1]

For years, Jordan looked over his shoulder, playing in the shadow of Earvin "Magic" Johnson, an NBA champion celebrated for his charm and selfless leadership. By 1990, Johnson had become *the* standard of success in the NBA, surpassing Larry Bird. Jordan may have been the more successful endorser and richer, but Johnson owned something even more valuable to him than money: championship rings. *Five* of them, to be exact. As much as the press focused on Jordan's rivalry with Isiah Thomas and the Pistons, more than anything, Jordan wanted to prove himself against the player he considered the very best: Magic Johnson. "I used him as a driving force," Jordan admitted.[2]

If a basketball game flowed like a song, Jordan was a virtuoso soloist, while Johnson was a band leader conducting an ensemble, accentuating the talents of the artists around him. Unlike Jordan, Johnson was not particularly quick or explosive, especially as his chronic knee troubles slowed him late in his career. Magic, observed Jack McCallum, moved "with a kind of lumbering grace," but no player could dictate the pace and rhythm of an offense the way he did. Standing six-foot-nine, a giant among point guards, Johnson towered over opponents, pounding the basketball as he orchestrated the convergence between an uncovered teammate and the basket. He directed the Los Angeles Lakers in the half-court, hollering and pointing like a quarterback approaching the line of scrimmage, but when the designed play broke down, he flourished, finding an open man with the flick of a wrist.[3]

In the 1980s, Johnson defined the Showtime Lakers, transforming the team's arena—the "Fabulous" Forum—into a theater of improvisation. His imagination and exuberant personality, his joie de vivre, made the Lakers as brilliant and entertaining as the Harlem Globetrotters' floor routine. Unlike the Globetrotters, however, nothing the Lakers did was choreographed in advance. Johnson thrived most in transition, when the Lakers went on the run. Streaking down the court in the middle of a fast break, his face animated, Johnson compelled the action with his high dribble, drawing two defenders, and then—*in an instant*—zipping a pass to an open teammate under the basket. Running the break, Magic invented entirely new ways to utilize the court's expanse, forcing the opposition to fan widely as he threaded the ball into the passing lanes. He held crowds spellbound, whirling an orange leather basketball like a yo-yo, manipulating the senses through illusion. His unexpected moves—a dribble behind the back or a spin down the lane, his *now you see it, now you don't* sleight-of-hand passes—energized the entire stadium.

The Showtime Lakers were a complete extension of Magic—his mind, his vision, his creativity—and the culture of Los Angeles. He played with ceaseless energy, an unyielding intensity and flair that made the game joyful and intoxicating. During his reign, Showtime became more than a distinct style of play; it was a cultural phenomenon, a brand synonymous with Hollywood glitz and glamour. Like a blockbuster movie, Lakers games had everything audiences wanted: "speed, sweat, and sex appeal." Magic was the reason celebrities bought courtside tickets, turning the Forum into *an event*, a happening, the place to be seen. Playing in La-La Land, surrounded by actors and music stars, Magic produced theater that made Lakers games as entertaining as any Hollywood production.[4]

In an age when sports and entertainment became tightly intertwined, blurring the line between competition and exhibition, show business gimmickry packaged basketball players as products more blatantly than ever before. That's how the idea for the dream matchup between Magic Johnson and Michael Jordan originated in the offices of HBO Sports executives Seth

Abraham and Lou DiBella. Searching for a lucrative sporting event, a pay-per-view as profitable as any prime-time championship boxing bout, Abraham thought in terms of original programming, something sports fans had never seen. The experience of promoting boxing matches inspired him to sell sporting events as stories, compelling dramas where two personalities confronted each other for a crown. Abraham was in the business of making stars out of lesser-known athletes, but staging a contest between Johnson and Jordan required little salesmanship. Who wouldn't pay twenty dollars to watch the two most electrifying basketball players in a shootout?[5]

Abraham pitched Johnson's agent, Lon Rosen. Imagine, he said, a made-for-TV basketball court at Caesars Palace in Las Vegas where Johnson and Jordan would play a half-court game of one-on-one, consisting of fifteen-minute halves in front of thousands of fans. The winner—*the king of the court*—would walk away with a million-dollar purse and lifetime bragging rights.

When reporters first learned about the proposed duel, Johnson took credit for it, confident that he could beat Jordan. "I came up with the idea," he told the *Los Angeles Times*. "We came up with what we wanted to do, and my people contacted Michael's people, and we decided to go ahead with it." Johnson recognized that the times were changing. His rival for the past decade, Larry Bird, was now struggling with various injuries; surgery to remove bone spurs from both heels forced him to miss most of the 1988–1989 season. Everything Bird did—except shooting—hurt; running, jumping, and sliding on defense aggravated the sharp pain he felt in both Achilles tendons. He compared playing basketball to running with "little knives in his shoes." Bird's body betrayed him at the very moment Jordan ascended the East, setting up the possibility for a new rivalry that Johnson undoubtedly hoped would enhance his status as the king of the court.[6]

For Jordan, the challenge of taking Johnson one-on-one, an opportunity to prove who was the best player in the world, appealed to his competitive instincts. He thought playing Johnson would be "fun." Sportswriters and bookies claimed the smart money on him; the Las Vegas Hilton Race and Sports SuperBook listed Jordan as a 2.5-to-1 favorite. Although he gave up three inches in height and about twenty pounds to Johnson, Jordan firmly believed that nobody on the planet could beat him one-on-one. "I'd kill him," Jordan said. "If I'm hitting my jump shot, he wouldn't know what to do. Play me right? Play me left? Lunch."[7]

The more he thought about it, though, the more Jordan wondered if he had more to risk than Johnson. David Falk recalled that Jordan said to him, "If I win, people will say, 'So, what do you expect? That's what Michael is—he's a one-on-player.' And if I lose, then I don't have the rings or the title. So what's the point in doing it?"[8]

Ultimately, the NBA's internal politics prevented Jordan and Johnson from playing at Caesars Palace. Gary Bettman, NBA senior vice president and general counsel, explained that the league explicitly prohibited its players from competing in commercialized games sanctioned by third-party promoters. "We're not interested in seeing our players being promoted like fighters in Las Vegas," he said. Isiah Thomas, head of the Players Association, opposed the king of the court idea, too, citing the collective bargaining agreement's provision that forbade such contests. He also argued that a pay-per-view game between Johnson and Jordan would harm the league's broadcasting contracts. When Jordan learned about Thomas's objections, he told a reporter that the Pistons' star had made it personal against him. "I wonder what Isiah's position would be if he were playing Magic," he said. "But, of course, if he were playing Magic no one would want to see it."[9]

Jordan and Johnson were forced to accept that the king of the court game would not take place. If they ever wanted to answer the question—who's the best player in the game, Michael Jordan or Magic Johnson?—they would have to settle it on an NBA court during the Finals. Only then could Jordan satisfy his greatest ambition and disprove the critics who claimed he would never reach Magic's place in the sport. Otherwise, Jordan said with a smile, they would have to play in somebody's backyard.[10]

Magic Johnson performed as if the world were his stadium. In Los Angeles, his life had become a movie set where he imagined himself the star of his own show, an act that continued when he stepped off the court. During his reign with the Lakers, "Magic" ceased being just a stage name; it became his public persona, a role he produced for the cameras and the crowds that followed him everywhere he went. "I've been an actor," he acknowledged. He talked about Earvin and Magic as if they were two different people leading two different lives. "People may know Magic," he said, "but they don't know Earvin." He understood that everything he did—playing basketball, giving interviews, filming commercials, throwing parties—was for the box office.[11]

His two competing identities—Earvin and Magic—were incompatible. "Where Earvin was eager to be loved," wrote *GQ*'s Charles Pierce, "Magic throve on adulation, which is not the same thing at all." Earvin Johnson Jr., the quiet, contemplative homebody, wanted to settle down and have a family. In 1985, he proposed to his college sweetheart from Michigan State University, Earletha "Cookie" Kelly, but he called off the engagement less than a year later, saying, "I can't get married now. Not while I'm married to basketball." Basketball was not the only reason he did not want to get married. The problem was that too often Earvin succumbed to Magic's temptations. The lure of adoring female fans fulfilled his need for being worshipped and idolized.

When Cookie was not around, he pursued countless women who soothed his aching loneliness. But few of them wanted to know Earvin, he lamented; they simply wanted Magic.[12]

Earvin guarded his privacy, revealing little to the gossip columnists who wanted to know more about him outside his Lakers uniform. Kareem Abdul-Jabbar, his Hall of Fame teammate for much of the eighties, suggested that the man who masqueraded around town as Magic was nothing like Earvin. "It's funny," he said, "Earvin's very shy. To know the real man takes several years." The star that the public knew as Magic had "that smile and easy manner with people, but that's not really him. That's an image he can put out there at will, that kinda gets him by. If you know the real man, he's a very complex person. He's very difficult to know."[13]

Unlike Earvin, Magic was a flamboyant entertainer, a self-indulgent playboy who craved constant affection. He seemed to wear an everlasting smile, as if he was winking at the world, an open invitation to join his rolling party. In the city of stars, Magic became the king of Los Angeles, hitting the clubs and premieres with Eddie and Arsenio. He befriended Michael Jackson, Prince, and Stevie Wonder. He thoroughly enjoyed the perks and privileges that came with fame, wealth, and adulation. Being the star of the Lakers enhanced his sex appeal, making him more desirable than any other athlete in Los Angeles. "During the 1980s," he wrote in his memoir, *My Life*, "the Lakers were seen as the sexiest and most glamorous team of them all. Los Angeles was glamorous. Winning was glamorous. Our fast break was sexy. And being the best team in the league made us seem *very* sexy."[14]

Magic had a strict rule about sex: no fornicating before tip-off. He had to save himself for the game. For Johnson, Roland Lazenby wrote, "sex was the game *after* the game. And the Forum

Club comprised a large part of the playing field." When Lakers owner Jerry Buss bought the team in 1979, he transformed the sports bar inside the Forum into his own personal nightclub, entertaining celebrities, VIPs, and high-profile season-ticket holders. The handsome real estate tycoon with a PhD in physical chemistry had a reputation as the Hugh Hefner of professional basketball, a sugar daddy dating women half his age. A divorced bachelor who once collected stamps as a young boy kept thick photo albums of all the women he had dated; flipping through the album pages, the pictures showed Buss getting older, but the women never did. He was, observed one writer, the archetype of the "Bel-Air millionaire—acquisitive, aggressive, restless, obsessed with good looks and rich in an assortment of playthings, playmates and possessions that ordinary men can only covet." And the Forum Club became his own personal "Fantasy Land," an exclusive pleasure palace where beautiful women came to meet the biggest stars in sports and Hollywood.[15]

For Johnson and his teammates, Showtime continued at the Forum Club. Magic worked the room like he owned it. His favorite dates gained regular access to the club and courtside seats—his own personal cheering section. Wes Matthews, a backup guard who played for the Lakers during the late 1980s, recalled, "Magic had his own section in the back [of the Forum Club] where he had twenty-five to thirty women waiting for him." That was his pickup spot. He was careful not to make any grand overtures. He might sign an autograph on a piece of paper or a napkin and write down his phone number, whispering, "See you in an hour." Sometimes, though, he didn't wait long after a game before getting busy. According to Lakers general manager Jerry West, Magic would retire to the sauna, have sex with a woman, then put on a robe and return to the locker room for his postgame media interviews.[16]

Inside the Lakers organization, he earned a reputation as a libertine, unrestrained by any risks to his reputation or health. In an age of growing fears about AIDS, Magic lived carefree, unconcerned about contracting or spreading the disease from unprotected sexual encounters. Even though more than 150,000 Americans had died of AIDS during his career with the Lakers, he never gave a second thought about how the affliction had devastated the Black community. By 1990, it was the second leading cause of death for Black men and women between the ages of twenty-five and thirty-five. But Johnson didn't worry about it. "AIDS was someone else's disease," he said in 1991. "It was a disease for gays and drug users. Not for someone like me."[17]

At that time, the public knew nothing about Johnson's sexual escapades. From the moment he joined the Lakers in 1979, LA writers polished and protected his carefully manicured image. Unless they compared him to Larry Bird, sportswriters rarely mentioned his race; his Blackness seemed incidental to his success story. One writer called him "the world's first perfect human being." Magic did not smoke, drink, or do drugs. Instead, he got high on fame and the trappings of celebrity. And unlike Kareem Abdul-Jabbar, who was perceived by many white writers as moody and aloof, an outspoken Black critic who refused to appease white America, Johnson enthusiastically flashed his Colgate smile for the cameras, a silent reassurance that he was nothing like his glowering Muslim teammate. Eager to please, Magic was much more accessible and less threatening than Kareem. He never alienated anyone with his political opinions, a conscious choice designed to build an audience. During Johnson's playing career with the Lakers, he virtually never discussed politics or racism. He didn't even vote. Instead, he practiced the politics of comfort, acting as a conciliator who could unify a team, a crowd, and an entire city.[18]

It was easy for him to sell Magic to America. In a country hypnotized by fantasies of wish fulfillment, he embodied an American story of reinvention. Like Walt Disney, he had a unique ability to impose his imagination on the world and make people see him through the lens of animation. As an artist, he sculpted an exaggerated version of himself, a bigger and bolder character who made America love Magic the way he loved being Magic.

In the process of building his heroic image, Johnson romanticized his own life story as the embodiment of the American Dream. The rags-to-riches tale of a poor Black boy, the fourth of seven children, who grew up in a modest two-story yellow frame house in a slumping factory city in the heart of the Rust Belt, followed the archetypal script of a hero born out of an ordinary existence, transformed by extraordinary talent. Sharing his childhood memories, he often talked about how his father, Earvin Sr., grinded on the nightshift assembly line, making Oldsmobile auto bodies in Lansing, Michigan. Then, during the day, he pumped gas at a local Shell station. Later, his father gave up the gas station gig and started a trash-hauling business, but his industriousness barely kept the family afloat. So, his wife, Christine, took a job as a school custodian on top of her household duties raising the children. Despite the family's struggles living in a segregated neighborhood, Johnson remembered that Lansing was "a great place to grow up," a place where "people waved to one another and said hello on the street." He fondly recalled his family eating dinner together every night and how he bonded with his father watching basketball on television. Yet the reality of his parents' hardscrabble existence had a profound impact on his own aspirations. He never forgot the time when he came home from junior high school and saw his mother sitting at the dining-room table, completely drained, her eyes closed, barely able to rest her chin in the palm of her hand. She heard him enter the room and managed a tender smile. "Mother," he asked, "you're really tired, aren't you?" "Yes, Junior, I am," she answered. "Well," Earvin said, "someday I'm going to become somebody and you won't ever have to work again."[19]

His parents' struggles—and their work ethic—inspired dreams and ambitions. Throughout his teenage years, he worked all sorts of jobs: cutting neighborhood lawns, stocking shelves at Quality Dairy, delivering Vernor's ginger-ale, and cleaning office buildings. By the time the Lakers star became a mogul in his own right, "the owner, president, and CEO of Magic, Inc.," he routinely told a story about how two prominent Black entrepreneurs in Lansing—Joel Ferguson and Gregory Eaton—became his role models. Money provided Eaton and Ferguson with the good life, the kind of access and economic mobility that Junior desired. "Everybody admired them," he recalled. "They had nice homes. They drove nice cars. They owned office buildings and had whole staffs of people. They were our heroes." He remembered the weekend evenings when he cleaned their offices, vacuuming carpets, scrubbing floors, and emptying trash bins. When no one was around, he "would sink into their big leather chairs, kick his big feet up on their desks, and imagine a secretary on the other end of the intercom." Then he'd start barking orders and summoning imaginary subordinates. In his daydream, he wielded power and influence, and the whole town looked up to him.[20]

In November 1990, *Sports Illustrated* published a cover story that featured a picture of Magic wearing a black suit and red tie, holding a big cigar, smiling as he leaned back in a leather office chair, the fulfillment of his boyhood dreams. The profile traced his ascendance from player to endorser to dealmaker. Outside his annual NBA salary, he earned millions of dollars from eighteen different sources, a business empire that included endorsements with Converse, Spalding, and Nintendo, a Pepsi-distribution plant he co-owned in Maryland, and his own T-shirt company—Magic Johnson T's, one of the fastest-growing sports apparel companies. During the first five years of his NBA career, he focused mostly on playing, giving little attention to his portfolio outside a few endorsements. Gradually, though, Earvin started thinking about life after basketball and came to realize that branding Magic offered an opportunity to transform iconography into big business.[21]

Part of his motivation for becoming an entrepreneur stemmed from his desire to defy stereotypes about Black athletes as dumb jocks. He didn't want to be seen as another professional athlete who threw away his money. "When kids, especially black youth, look at high-profile people like me and Michael [Jordan], I want them to see us doing more than getting money for wearing somebody's shoes," he said. During his playing career, Johnson conceived of himself as a hero Black kids could emulate. Yet he wielded his cultural influence not by challenging the racial inequalities produced by the American economic system but by working within that system. He adhered to a Black political tradition known as racial uplift, a belief that Black material advancement—particularly, the accumulation of wealth—and the rehabilitation of Black America's image vis-à-vis his place in the NBA would break down racial barriers and open doors, an ideology Michael Jordan shared as well. As the most conspicuous examples of basketball's capitalist fantasies, Johnson and Jordan allowed corporations to "greenwash" them with money, fame, and commercials, Howard Bryant wrote in his book *The Heritage*. Greenwashing meant promoting Black athletes as wealthy and exceptional but "race-neutral," endorsing products rather than political causes.[22]

Although both men built their empires as pitchmen, for years Jordan overshadowed Johnson in endorsements. In fact, Jordan thought that Johnson was jealous over his commercial success. "With Magic I felt a coldness from him, off the court and even when we were playing basketball," Jordan told *Chicago Tribune* columnist Bob Greene. Converse had refused to build a unique Magic Johnson product line comparable to Nike's Air Jordan campaign. Instead, Johnson wore the same Converse shoes as Larry Bird, Isiah Thomas, and other NBA players, though the sneakers came in different colorways. Johnson recalled that in the early years of his career, Converse maintained that "nobody would buy a shoe with a player's name on it"—a dated business theory obliterated by Jordan. In the 1980s, Magic certainly carried as much cultural capital as Jordan. He had an established brand, a memorable nickname, "a thousand-kilowatt smile," a sizable home market, and a handful of championship rings. Yet, instead of developing new products around him, Converse relied on its storied reputation, spending far less on advertising than Nike or Reebok. Lon Rosen, Johnson's agent, complained that Converse kept Magic hidden. Ultimately, Converse failed to capitalize on Johnson's national popularity, costing him and the company an incalculable amount of money. "Way before Michael came into the league," David Falk said, "Magic could've owned the world."[23]

It's important to consider how Johnson helped make it possible for Jordan to succeed in a commercial space long denied to Black athletes. Five years before Jordan joined the Bulls, during the nadir of the NBA's image crisis, when Madison Avenue all but ignored the sport and its Black stars, Johnson arrived in Los Angeles with an infectious joy for the game that captivated America. More than any other player, he helped rehabilitate the image of the NBA—a league still suffering from racialized fears that Black ballplayers could not handle fame, wealth, and the sordid temptations that came with playing in American cities. Johnson's irresistible personality assuaged the anxieties of white fans and corporate America, forging a path for Jordan as the next great Black crossover basketball star.

By 1990, Johnson and Jordan were the most successful Black endorsers in the world of sports. That year, Converse finally released a line of "new treads and threads" with Magic's name on them. The shoe manufacturer produced a provocative commercial centered around "the Magic Johnson lifestyle" that seemed more like an MTV video than a spot for selling sneakers; it completely deviated from past advertisements that emphasized his ingenuous image. The fast-paced short features Johnson "thrillin'" and "chillin'" to a soundtrack of Mantronix's electro-funk "King of the Beats." The story begins with him on a playground court, practicing his moves in his new line of shoes and apparel. The camera cuts to him driving down a palm tree–lined street in a vintage black Cadillac convertible, a summer smile on his face and a bubbly young Black woman cozied beside him. Then the viewer sees a close-up of his sneakers and another shot of him ballin' on the blacktop. Magic peers through the court's chain-link fence and suddenly, out of nowhere, appears a fashionable woman wearing sunglasses and a tight gold dress; she emerges onto the sidewalk toting shopping bags, like a scene out of *Pretty Woman*. A rapid sequence of images flashes on the screen: Magic laughing with one of his white buddies; Magic slappin' skin with one of his Black friends; Magic sitting poolside, enjoying breakfast; a random young Black couple kissing; a close-up of a cover girl wearing sunglasses; back to Magic lounging poolside, where a beautiful Black woman in a bathing suit approaches him—he nods at the camera like he knows what will happen next. The commercial wraps with two images, one with him on the court, the other showing him behind the wheel of the Cadillac. In closing, the sultry voice of a woman intones, "Johnson and Johnson, otherwise known as Magic by Converse."[24]

Promoting Magic as a sex symbol—a swinging single man about town surrounded by women who were nothing more than props for his show—represented a complete break from Converse's long-standing alignment with traditional values. The commercial unfolded the way Johnson lived his life, as though he was "at once both the audience and the actor," blurring the line between the man and the performer. The ad had less to do with basketball than the self-celebration of celebrity and his hedonistic pursuits. It revealed not only his yearning for fame, power, and sex but also his desire to be *seen* enjoying the fruits of his celebrity. It was as if Johnson had peeled back the curtain of his fantasy world, revealing a part of his life that fans did not know about. Soon enough, though, America would learn that staging Magic's reality show came at a devastating cost.[25]

Less than five months before the 1990–1991 season began, most basketball fans concluded that the Showtime era had ended when Lakers head coach Pat Riley announced he was leaving the team. Unquestionably, he was the most successful head coach in the NBA, leading the Lakers to four NBA championships in nine years. The embodiment of cool, tanned and athletic, sporting tailored Armani suits with his hair slicked back, Riley looked like he had come straight out of central casting for Showtime. Beneath his "unwrinkled exterior," observed one *GQ* writer, Riley "was a man possessed," fueled by an incessant drive for perfection. Deep down he always felt he had something to prove—that despite the Lakers' all-star lineup, the team needed him to win. That feeling deepened when Kareem Abdul-Jabbar retired after the 1988–1989 season. Riley—and Johnson—desperately wanted to show the world that the Lakers could win without the Captain. Nicknamed Norman Bates by his players, Riley pushed the team harder than ever before, running excruciating practices that lasted three or four hours.

Gradually, his ego eroded relationships with players who tired of his screaming and berating. Johnson explained that Riley's obsession with winning made him want to "control everything . . . He tried to control the whole arena. He wanted to control the locker room, the band, the Laker Girls. He tried to control everything, and he got away from what he was there to do."[26]

The curtain seemed to close on Showtime after the Phoenix Suns bounced the Lakers from the 1990 Western Conference Semifinals in five games. It did not matter that Riley had won the NBA's Coach of the Year award or that the team had won sixty-three games during the regular season. The players believed that Riley had become a victim of what he called "the disease of me," a self-serving affliction that corrupted the organization from the inside out. Jerry Buss replaced him with Mike Dunleavy, an unaccomplished thirty-six-year-old assistant coach with the Milwaukee Bucks. He may not have been the obvious choice, but GM Jerry West had told Buss that he admired Dunleavy's knowledge of the game and the way he related to players. Dunleavy knew that the Lakers were still a winning franchise, but they had to make changes if they wanted to return to the Finals. He believed that the team could no longer play run-and-shoot basketball like the Showtime Lakers of the eighties. Instead, they would run more selectively, emphasizing a more methodical half-court motion offense.[27]

When the Lakers lost five of their first seven games—the worst start in Magic Johnson's career—spoiled LA fans cried for the return of Riley, but Dunleavy didn't panic. He urged the team to remain patient and made important adjustments, benching longtime starting power forward A. C. Green in favor of Sam Perkins; he also started Serbian sensation Vlade Divac at center and sat Mychal Thompson. Now, he had a starting lineup that included four players who stood about six-foot-nine. The Lakers could easily interchange defensive assignments, employing a size advantage that allowed them to crash the boards and clog passing lanes. Plus, those four players—Johnson, Perkins, Divac, and James Worthy—could pass or score from the post, making it extremely difficult for opposing defenses to double-team any of them. "We have so many weapons now," Johnson said.[28]

By the time the Chicago Bulls arrived at the Forum for their only regular-season visit against the Lakers, Dunleavy's squad carried the second-best record in the NBA, setting up a clash between two of the very best teams in the league. In December, when the Lakers came to Chicago, the Bulls won easily, 114–103. That was the beginning of a crucial stretch when the Bulls won twelve of thirteen games. Now, on February 3, the Lakers were the hottest team in the NBA, riding a fourteen-game winning streak. A *Los Angeles Times* story informed local sports fans that discord inside the Bulls locker room looked nothing like the harmonious unity the Lakers had forged. "After Michael Jordan criticized General Manager Jerry Krause for not landing Walter Davis," Mark Heisler reported, "Horace Grant lashed out at 'selfish' play, Stacey King asked to be traded and Will Perdue said he wasn't happy either." Heisler could have also mentioned Scottie Pippen's ongoing public demand for a contract extension, an unresolved conflict that festered like an open wound. Phil Jackson urged the players to keep private disputes from the press. He reminded them that building trust as a team meant resolving their problems within the group. Allowing reporters—outsiders—into the sacred team circle threatened team unity, he said.[29]

Jackson had grown exasperated with players who were only concerned with themselves. The game against the Lakers illustrated his frustration. In the first half, Scottie Pippen scored eighteen points, making nine of fifteen shots; but in the second half he only took five more shots, blaming his teammates afterward.

"The ball didn't come my way and I wasn't too happy about it," he fumed. "The ball gets in certain people's hands"—*hello, Michael Jordan!*—"and doesn't get moved." Pippen had a point. Jordan had only scored nine points in the first half, and he didn't want to give up the ball after halftime. The Lakers' swarming defense frustrated him; Dunleavy had adopted Chuck Daly's "Jordan Rules," running multiple players into the lane whenever MJ attacked the basket. In the fourth quarter, he scored only four points in the final twelve minutes. After losing to the Lakers, 99–86, he complained about the team's substitutes—six players who scored only four points the entire game. Whenever Jackson replaced him with Craig Hodges or Dennis Hopson, Jordan took it as a personal insult, sitting at the far end of the bench with enough space to drive the team bus between him and his teammates. "Nobody likes to sit next to him and listen to him complain and scream to get back into the game," Bill Cartwright said.[30]

Despite beating the Bulls for their fifteenth consecutive victory, the Lakers' dressing room resembled a funeral parlor. In the closing moments of the third quarter, Magic Johnson backpedaled on defense under the Lakers' basket, bumped into a teammate, fell backward, and smacked his head on the hardwood floor. Sprawled across the court, Johnson lay motionless. Silence washed over the crowd while everyone waited for him to regain consciousness. Every second felt like an hour. "It was a very scary moment," Jordan said. Finally, after about a minute, Johnson opened his eyes. Then he slowly rose to his feet, encouraged by the crowds' cheers. Groggy and confused, he couldn't remember what happened before the fall. A neurologist examined Johnson at a local hospital and diagnosed him with a mild concussion. Fortunately, he only missed a few games.[31]

For all the reported turmoil swirling around the Chicago Bulls, their loss to the Lakers was their only defeat in the entire month of February. The Bulls rattled off ten consecutive wins—including a thrilling two-point victory at the Palace of Auburn Hills. It was the kind of close game that they had always lost at the Palace. In a game where the lead changed twenty-five times, Jordan refused to let anyone else on the court decide the outcome. As he often did in the fourth quarter, he took command and ignored the triangle sets, scoring Chicago's final ten points. When it was over, he walked off the court pumping his fist, a quiet celebration of triumph, confident now that the Bulls could beat Detroit on their home floor.[32]

Chapter Ten

BE LIKE MIKE

"When a person becomes a model for other people's lives, he has moved into the sphere of being mythologized."

—JOSEPH CAMPBELL, *THE POWER OF MYTH*, 1988

"Sometimes I dream
That he is me
You've got to see that's how I dream to be
I dream I move, I dream I groove
Like Mike
If I could be like Mike"

—"BE LIKE MIKE," GATORADE JINGLE, 1991

The heartbreaking letters arrived by the dozens every week, often written in the hurried penmanship of sick children desperate to meet their hero. Scores of dying kids sent their pleas to Michael Jordan, telling him that if they could have one final wish it would be to see him face-to-face. The children often included drawings of themselves with Jordan; others composed poems, rap lyrics, and prayers thanking God for him. Frequently, kids left personal messages on the answering machine at his charitable foundation. Jordan tried to reply to as many requests as he could, but not even Santa Claus could keep up with the volume of incoming mail. If he couldn't meet a child, he sent an autographed basketball or a signed jersey. Sometimes, he mailed a game-worn pair of Air Jordans. One boy, who died from leukemia, was buried wearing the size thirteen sneakers that Jordan had gifted him.[1]

Jordan did not want the suffering of these children reduced to a photo op and resisted publicizing this side of himself. Protecting sick and disadvantaged kids—and his own vulnerability in those meetings—revealed Jordan's discomfort with the way publicists wanted to stage his heroic deeds. Occasionally, though, sportswriters witnessed his kindness and shared those stories with readers. The mythic Jordan made famous by Hollywood and hagiographers—the cartoonish character who possessed the power of a faith healer, a hero whose mere presence could bring people to tears when he entered a room—had much in common with the real Jordan. Although he never cured a sick child by smiling or saying hello, he had a remarkable ability to brighten the lives of countless kids. He knew how to make the most hopeless children feel special by including them in his world, if only briefly. No one in public relations taught him how to connect with kids. The genuine warmth and concern he showed sick and disabled children came from his heart. If someone wanted to see the best of Jordan, all they had to do was watch him interact with kids from the Make-A-Wish Foundation.[2]

On March 10, 1991, before a game against the Atlanta Hawks, a little blonde girl wearing a ruffled dress blushed in his presence. Sam Smith had seen him meet sick children several times before, but this one stood out. The girl started crying when she moved near Jordan, struggling to process a miraculous dream come true. Jordan realized the gravity of the moment and began crying.

Unlike Michael Jordan, Charles Barkley never censored himself. He spoke his mind on and off the court, disregarding the consequences or anyone's notion of how he should behave as a role model. Credit: Steve Lipofsky/Lipofskyphoto.com

Whether they were in a wheelchair or fighting cancer, Jordan had a soft spot for critically ill children. "Relax, take it easy," he said, his voice quivering. She wiped away the tears and found her smile. "Jordan didn't want her to go," Smith wrote. He sat beside her, talking and laughing. The time passed quickly and soon Jordan needed to get his ankles taped for the game. They said goodbye. As the little girl walked away with her family, she looked back over her shoulder, knowing she would probably never see him up close again.[3]

Fighting back more tears, Jordan said aloud, "How do they expect me to play basketball now?"

Carrying the hopes of countless kids and their parents on his shoulders made focusing on his primary job—winning basketball games—a challenge. Jordan needed to concentrate before games and channel his energy toward competing. On March 22, after winning twenty of their previous twenty-one contests, the first-place Bulls arrived in Philadelphia for a contest against the 76ers. By then, Phil Jackson had developed the team into a formidable defensive unit that exerted devastating mid-court pressure, trapping ballhandlers and creating turnovers that led to breakaway dunks. Led by Jordan, Pippen, and Horace Grant, the Bulls' defense forced opponents into approximately seventeen turnovers each game, among the best in the league. As much as the players resisted the triangle offense, they eagerly embraced Jackson's approach to defense. He had long believed that defense—more than offense—shaped the unity of a team because everyone shared the same goal: stopping the enemy.

His coaching philosophy seemed to be working well until the 76ers broke the Bulls' nine-game winning streak, a minor setback that left Chicago holding on to first place in the Eastern Conference over the Boston Celtics by just 1.5 games. That night Jordan and his teammates simply could not stop Charles Barkley, a stout yet explosive forward known for his raw power and surprising speed. "There are two sights in pro basketball better than all others," Mike Lupica once wrote. "One is Michael Jordan on his way to the basket in a flight plan of his own invention. The other is Charles Barkley, not quite six five, 250 pounds, going from one end of the court to the other with the ball." In a blur, Barkley could snatch a defensive rebound, race down court, transfer the ball from one dribbling hand to the other, weave around "defenders like a running-back fooling linebackers," and stuff the ball through the basket. Barging down the lane like a runaway locomotive, Barkley seemed like he might not stop unless he tumbled into the courtside seats.[4]

One of the most tenacious competitors in the NBA, Barkley played with remarkable ferocity. Leveraging his strength and low center of gravity against players four to six inches taller than him, he had a unique ability for gaining position beneath the basket. Bouncing like a pogo stick, he could rise and tap the ball into the basket with his soft, ambidextrous hands. He lived for snatching rebounds. Swinging his elbows like a machete clearing brush, he scratched and clawed for the ball underneath the basket. His back and shoulders were lined with battle scars. "You wouldn't believe how many fingernails there are in the NBA," he said.[5]

Barkley played the way he lived: uninhibited. "He responds to small setbacks—a missed free throw, a sloppy turnover—by clutching his forehead in anguish, or screaming a dozen curses, or kicking a courtside chair, or shaking the press table until a blizzard of notebooks wafts to the floor," Jeff Coplon wrote. Yet he also displayed incredible joy on the court, pumping his fists in the air after a thunderous dunk, high-fiving his teammates during a rally, and waving his arms, imploring the crowd to rise on its feet and pay tribute.[6]

Barkley thought a victory over Jordan and the Bulls might re-focus the middling 76ers, but that idea faded a few nights later in New Jersey, when that same lack of inhibition sparked a national controversy. During the game, a cursing Nets fanatic sitting courtside bombarded Barkley with a barrage of insults. One reporter wrote that the heckler "was calling him nigger this-and-that," and though Barkley tried ignoring him, he eventually couldn't take the abuse anymore. Simmering to a boil, late in the fourth quarter, he erupted and began screaming obscenities at the taunter. "Fuck you!" Barkley shouted. During a break in the action, he approached the heckler near the baseline seats behind the basket and spat toward the court. Barkley said he wasn't aiming at anyone, but it didn't matter. He had inadvertently sprayed an eight-year-old girl.[7]

Immediately, newspaper writers and talk radio hosts vilified him. *Philadelphia Inquirer* columnist Claude Lewis wrote that Barkley's "vile" behavior revealed the utmost "contempt" for the people who paid his salary. It did not help his case that Barkley had once said that "most fans are assholes." Many NBA fans, even in Philadelphia, considered him arrogant and crude, a combative "thug" who had lost all control. After the spitting incident, Lewis suggested Barkley needed psychotherapy. The girl's father, a long-time season-ticket holder named Robert Rose, told reporters that Barkley's behavior was unacceptable and that the NBA should suspend him. Rod Thorn, the league's vice president of operations, fined Barkley $10,000 and made him sit for one game.[8]

Ashamed and embarrassed, Barkley expressed deep regret for spitting on the young girl, though he initially doubted whether he had really sprayed her. The game footage showed him spitting directly downward, not up in the air. He watched the replay repeatedly, but it proved inconclusive. Nonetheless, he met with the Rose family and apologized to the little girl. In the aftermath of the spitting episode, fans booed and cursed him in NBA arenas throughout the league. "I was treated like shit," Barkley complained, "like I'd committed an unpardonable sin."[9]

Reporters wanted to know what the league's greatest spokesman, Michael Jordan, thought about his friend Barkley. In his *Washington Post* column, David Aldridge suggested Barkley should listen to Jordan and learn from him. "Spitting is degrading," Jordan said. Barkley had a lapse in judgment, but Jordan maintained that he deserved forgiveness. In the future, Jordan added, Barkley had to rise above harassment from unruly fans and set a good example because "he, as well as everyone in this business, is a role model."[10]

Yet Barkley thought that parents, not NBA players, should be children's role models. He asked, "Why idolize someone simply because they can run and dunk? Why expect so much of them?" Barkley maintained that athletes should not be put on pedestals, polished and painted like Starting Lineup action figures. He argued that too many adults had become obsessed with the idea that their kids could one day play in the NBA, a long shot by any measure. "What they're really doing is telling kids to look up to someone they can't become," he said, "because not many people can be like we are. Kids can't be like Michael Jordan."[11]

Critics charged that Barkley was simply rationalizing his failure to live up to the responsibilities that came with being a famous athlete. His behavior on and off the court offended NBA officials, fans, and writers. Throughout the season he feuded with his teammates, head coach, and management. Over the past few seasons, the commissioner's office had repeatedly reprimanded him for making lewd gestures toward the crowd. In 1987, while the Celtics thrashed the 76ers, he got into an argument with a woman sitting courtside at the Boston Garden. After the woman admonished him for stomping a folding chair and cursing, Barkley said,

"Shut up, you bitch." Later that season, in Indianapolis, he struck a loudmouth Pacers fan in the face—Barkley called it a slap, an incident settled out of court. Then, in the summer of 1988, a New Jersey state trooper stopped him for speeding through Atlantic City. Searching the car for drugs, the trooper discovered a loaded, unregistered 9-mm pistol behind the passenger seat of his Porsche—though she didn't find any narcotics. (Having witnessed how cocaine destroyed his brother's life, Barkley avoided drugs and told schoolchildren to do the same.) Ultimately, a judge tossed the gun charges against him, ruling that the officer did not have probable cause to search his vehicle. The Philadelphia newspapers had made his arrest a major story but buried the dismissal of all charges, leaving many readers with the impression that Barkley was another dangerous, misbehaving Black man.[12]

Although Barkley was the most famous basketball player in Philadelphia, he knew, too, that there were people in the City of Brotherly Love who despised him. In such a sports-crazed town, Barkley worried about the safety of his wife, Maureen, and their baby girl, Christiana. It was for this reason that he carried a loaded gun: Shortly after the spitting incident, a white man approached Maureen at a local bar, pretending he knew Charles, and asked about their daughter. After Maureen greeted the stranger with a smile, he spat in her face and said, "How do you like that, nigger lover?" It was the kind of vile racism that shattered any notion that America had become a colorblind country, a grim reminder that greenwashing Black athletes didn't insulate them from the worst kinds of bigotry.[13]

Playing in Philadelphia, Barkley had begun to resent the way white writers maligned him, complaining that the local press wanted "Black athletes to be Uncle Toms." He grew increasingly outspoken, calling Philadelphia "one of the most racist cities" in America, lamenting how white people harassed Black folks in "exclusive" (i.e., segregated) neighborhoods. There were white fans in Philadelphia, he charged, who liked him simply because he could dunk a basketball, but many of those same people would lynch him for marrying a white woman. Defiant and unrestrained, he conceived of himself in the image of his hero— Muhammad Ali, a Black rebel who refused to conform to the role of "the All-American boy." Fashioning himself a truth teller, he refused to be silent on any subject, whether he was well-informed or not. He had opinions about everything, discussing race, politics, and the Gulf War (among other subjects) on his local radio show. Unlike Jordan, Barkley insisted on speaking his mind and living by his own code of conduct. After reading a book about Ali, he echoed a line the heavyweight champ uttered in 1964, declaring, "I'm a strong black man—I don't have to be what you want me to be."[14]

The very notion that Barkley—or Jordan, or any Black athlete for that matter—should be a role model, particularly for white kids, was shaped by the nostalgic desires of white adults who wanted Black athletes to follow in the footsteps of the harmless "Good Negro" of yesteryear. As a righteous exemplar, the Good Negro reinforced a belief held by some white people that the only respectable Black folks were those who didn't express anger or confront authority. Over time, the Good Negro athlete of the integration era evolved into "the role model" archetype of the postintegration era. In the context of the NBA, *role models* was a term "often used as a racial code," observed journalist Larry Platt. "It was, after all, a label placed by an overwhelmingly white press on those black athletes who, in Barkley's words, 'played the game.'"[15]

In the narratives produced by the sporting press, Barkley became Jordan's foil; his "bad boy" persona contrasted with Jordan's goodness. For all his wit and charm, Barkley, the most gregarious and accessible player in the NBA, came to be seen as the sports world's antihero or the anti-Jordan, viewed by many Americans as a "scowler, a bully, an angry young man" unbound by propriety or obligatory humility. Yet, in the public imagination, Barkley's iconoclastic personality made him both despised *and* beloved. A certain segment of fans, particularly the younger, urban sect, admired the way Barkley embodied hip-hop culture by "keeping it real" and doing what he wanted. Somehow, he managed to profit from his rebelliousness, selling a subversive, almost radical, message that made him seem more authentic than most pro basketball players. In a famous Nike commercial, Barkley declared, "I am not a role model . . . Just because I can dunk a basketball, doesn't mean I should raise your kids." The commercial, noted a *New York Times* editorial, "shows a sneaker salesman telling us that a sneaker salesman can't save us."[16]

The publicity machine of professional sports—the teams, the networks, the corporate sponsors, and the advertisers—had long sold the public on the idea that professional athletes should provide lessons in morality. There was no greater example of that paradigm than Gatorade's "Be Like Mike" campaign, an advertisement first introduced in 1991 around the joy of being Michael Jordan—and the idea that adults, particularly parents, should see him through the eyes of children. One young fan explained Jordan's ubiquitous appeal. "Everybody wants to be like Michael Jordan," said Cristobal Gutierrez, a sixteen-year-old from Cicero, Illinois. "My white friends, my black friends, my Mexican friends. But you have to pay attention to what people say about him. It's not just being on television that's important. He does charity work. He loves his parents. He always does real good deeds." Celebrated as an example of character and integrity, Jordan became a billboard for traditional American values—self-reliance, hard work, family, faith, and patriotism.[17]

The Be Like Mike commercial positioned basketball as "America's game," a democratic sport played by men and women and boys and girls of all races and ethnicities—a melting pot of young fans brought together on playgrounds by a humble hero who welcomed everyone onto the court. In an age of shifting racial and ethnic demographics, as a surge of immigrants from Asia and Latin America transformed the United States, the children of those immigrants often clumped together in high school cafeterias, sitting among cliques based upon the nationality of their parents or grandparents. Yet those same second- and third-generation children could see themselves in the faces of kids playing with Jordan on the court. Their shared love for basketball—and for Jordan—seemed to dissolve any racial or ethnic differences. At a time when many people wondered whether the United States would "fracture into many separate, disconnected communities with no shared sense of commonality or purpose," Jordan, Gatorade's transcendent role model, represented the ideal champion for a pluralistic society. Thus, the commercial promoted the country's national myth: the idea that people of every racial and ethnic background can be absorbed into "one America"—an America where the great Black basketball hero smudged the color line.[18]

One of the most memorable commercials he ever made, the upbeat, catchy "Be Like Mike" jingle became the soundtrack to the Jordan generation—a chorus of '90s kids singing along and imitating his every move, mostly by purchasing products he endorsed. The commercial shows "Mike"—the friendly, accessible everyman—playing basketball with ordinary men at a local gym, a kind of fantasy camp for his grown-up fans, suggesting he played for the love of the game as much as they did. Integrating highlights of Jordan playing at Chicago Stadium with shots of him drinking Gatorade, the main story—the narrative arc that makes the commercial compelling—is the way Jordan bonds with children over basketball and how the desires of those children make them want to imitate him. Scenes of Jordan playing with kids move the story forward: Mike playfully guarding a small white boy wearing the same Air Jordan uniform as him; Jordan tapping the ball high above the heads of a group of children, teasing them in a game of keep-away; and later, like the Pied Piper, dribbling a basketball across a blacktop court with a crowd of kids dribbling behind him. Then he pulls up for a jumper and all the kids, reverently following behind him, emulate his shot. The commercial makes no claims about the physiological benefits of drinking Gatorade. Kids couldn't have cared less about that anyway. All that mattered was that Michael Jordan drank Gatorade, and if they wanted to be like him, then they should drink it, too.

The Be Like Mike commercial was seen as an advertisement for America's racial advancement. That story, suggested Black cultural critic Stanley Crouch, could be found in the bedrooms of white kids who decorated their walls with posters of Jordan. "In 1960," he said, "if white girls in the suburbs had had posters of a Negro that dark on the wall, there would have been hell to pay. That kind of racist paranoia is not true of the country now. Today, you have white girls who are Michael Jordan fanatics, and their parents don't care."[19]

Perhaps Crouch was right. White parents loved Michael Jordan. And their kids did, too. Undoubtedly, there were white kids who grew up with a more benevolent view of Black people because of Jordan, though it's hard to measure exactly how much he changed racial attitudes. To some degree, embracing him as a role model for white children represented a step away from old prejudices, even if some of those same parents claimed they did not see race. However, the celebration of Jordan also fit into a particular history where the success of prominent Black athletes, like Joe

Louis or Jackie Robinson, became a defense of the country's racial hypocrisies. In their triumphs over racial barriers, Black sports heroes became exemplars of US democracy in ways that white athletes could not.

For Black parents, though, Jordan meant something else entirely: he affirmed the power and beauty of being Black. His example alone was enough to instill racial pride in Black children. In a country that "placed a high value on skin color," noted a writer from the *Chicago Defender*, the city's Black newspaper, many Black children wondered about their own self-worth, but seeing Jordan, "in all his quiet dignity, intelligence, and regal Blackness, they can't help but feel proud themselves."[20]

Jordan knew there were children all around the country who tacked posters of him on their bedroom walls. He also knew that those posters could be ripped down faster than they went up. In the coming years, when critics questioned whether he set a good example, Jordan became defensive and disillusioned with his place on the pedestal. Nearly two decades after Gatorade launched the Be Like Mike ad, Jordan expressed regret that the commercials had turned him into a character he could never sustain. "If I had the chance to do it all over again, I would never want to be considered a role model," he said. "It's like a game that's stacked against me. There's no way I can win."[21]

Yet Jordan had approved the relentless self-promotion campaigns that coalesced consumerism with idolatry. *He* chose to tell the children of the world that they should look up to him as an ideal he could never fulfill—and they did. In the process of producing his pristine image, Jordan may have lost his right to privacy, but he won mightily at the bank. He was the beneficiary of social and economic imperatives that made him famous and wealthy beyond his wildest imagination. That was the point of making all those commercials. That's why he told the youth of

America that they should follow his lead. That was his definition of winning.

Scottie Pippen was never celebrated as a national role model like Michael Jordan. As Pippen complained about his contract throughout the 1990–1991 season, many parents wondered whether he was setting a good example for the kids who looked up to him. During an economic recession, with working parents facing layoffs, Pippen, a professional athlete making more than fourteen times the median household income in Illinois, disappointed some fans when he made it known he felt underpaid. If Jordan had convinced Americans that he played purely for the love of the game, Pippen's ultimatum—"pay me or trade me"—seemed greedy, flying in the face of the concept of team loyalty, an ideal that many fans applied only to professional athletes, not club owners. Those same fans who romanticized the sport ignored the fact that the NBA was a business built on the labor of players who were drafted into an organization that dictated where they could live and practice their craft.[22]

Pippen's critics, including Jerry Krause, complained that he should show more gratitude that the Bulls guaranteed him a salary that the average working stiff would have eagerly accepted without complaint. Krause told Pippen that he "owed everything to him," denying Pippen credit for lifting himself out of poverty, as if no other NBA team recognized his talent on draft day. It was an all-too-common refrain whenever professional athletes, especially Black athletes, exercised their right to negotiate for better compensation. For decades, the game's promoters claimed, "sports have been good to the Negro," a paternalistic cliché that advanced the notion that meritocracy was the central ideology of professional sports. This process of whitewashing the history of sports made it easier for the public to believe that Black athletes had nothing to protest, whether it was economic exploitation or police brutality. It forced Black athletes to confront the idea that they were supposed to "adopt a pose of ceaseless gratitude—appreciation for the waiver that spared them the low status of so many others of their kind," noted historian Jelani Cobb.[23]

Pippen clearly believed he was worth more to the franchise than what his contract paid him. And his mistrust of Krause had only deepened since the beginning of the season. He claimed that Krause had lied to him, breaking a promise to sign him to a better contract before Christmas, though Krause and Jerry Reinsdorf maintained that they had only agreed to start negotiations by that time. In February, Pippen missed a few practices, saying he had an upset stomach. But when he returned to the gym, he seemed to acknowledge to the Chicago writers that he had skipped practice in protest over the team's slow contract negotiations. "I figured we wouldn't be doing much at practice anyway," he said with a mischievous grin. Ever since he reported to training camp after threatening to hold out until the Bulls made him the second-highest-paid player on the team, Pippen regretted showing up. "I felt there'd be a reward down the line," he said in March. "When I think about it now, it's probably the dumbest mistake I made in my life."[24]

One problem for Pippen was that he refused to play to the cameras the way that Jordan did. If Jordan knew how to show the public only what he wanted to reveal, Pippen didn't want to divulge anything at all. He didn't smile for the photographers and video crews that infiltrated the locker room. He shared little of himself with reporters, uninterested in the approval of the game's hero makers. Instead, he "found himself a character in the myth of someone else's making," observed journalist Scott Poulson-Bryant. The only people he really trusted lived in Hamburg. His family and friends back in Arkansas did not want anything from him. Yet the basketball writers needed him to explain himself—not just his play on the court, but his inner thoughts. For Pippen, a quiet and soft-spoken man, answering questions seemed almost painful. Early in his career, "the raw country kid" stuttered through postgame interviews, unable to mask a glaring self-consciousness exposed by the klieg lights shining on his angular face.[25]

In early April, he escalated his demands with team management. If the Bulls did not pay him what he wanted, Pippen reiterated, then he wanted to be traded—at least that's what he said publicly, though he did not really want to leave Chicago. "I've had enough of the Bulls' stall tactics," he fumed. Reinsdorf and Krause "keep saying they're going to give me a new contract, and something else always comes up. I'll finish the season with the Bulls if I stay healthy. But my heart won't be in it. I can't guarantee what kind of effort they'll get out of me because I'm really upset."[26]

Pippen's statement stunned Jerry Reinsdorf when he read it in the newspaper. He could not imagine Pippen loafing on the court. That wouldn't solve anything. Reinsdorf knew that Pippen felt snubbed because he and Krause had been courting Toni Kukoč, the Bulls' second-round draft pick. So, Reinsdorf scheduled a meeting with Pippen and one of his agents in late March, shortly before he and Krause traveled to Yugoslavia to make a final pitch to Kukoč. Reinsdorf tried explaining to Pippen that the team's pursuit of Kukoč would not infringe upon any contract extension with him. But if the Bulls were going to sign Kukoč *this year*, he said, then they needed the remaining $1.8 million of salary cap space. If they failed to sign the Yugoslavian star, then some of that money would go to Pippen. Either way, Reinsdorf guaranteed Pippen a five-year deal of about $18 million. He promised Pippen they would sign the contract after the season. "Even if you get hurt now," Reinsdorf said, "we'll be obligated to pay you. No matter what happens to you, consider that deal done."[27]

"Do you understand, Scottie?" Reinsdorf asked repeatedly. According to Reinsdorf, Pippen agreed—but in the back of Pippen's mind he must have wondered if Reinsdorf's word was worth anything more than counterfeit money.

When Reinsdorf flew to Kukoč's hometown of Split, Croatia, a port city on the Adriatic Sea, he figured that he had resolved the tensions with Pippen. Yet he still worried that Pippen's antagonistic comments about Kukoč might prevent the three-time European Player of the Year from signing with the Bulls. Although Phil Jackson telephoned Kukoč several times, telling him he had the potential to be an NBA star with the Bulls, Pippen and Jordan refused to join the campaign to recruit him. Jordan thought Europeans were too soft to succeed in his NBA—a common criticism leveled against players from the Balkan states, however stereotypical. Foreign players were often diminished in the American mind: the Europeans were considered too fragile—passive and afraid of physical confrontation—to compete with Americans. "Wait until he gets an elbow in the face from Laimbeer," Jordan said. "He won't be going to the basket again." He rolled his eyes when Krause offered Kukoč's highlight reel. And when Krause asked him to call Kukoč, Jordan smirked and famously said, "I don't speak no Yugoslavian."[28]

Nearly five thousand miles away from Chicago, Kukoč could feel the frigid reception from Jordan and Pippen. For years, he had dreamed about playing in the NBA. Like countless young basketball fanatics throughout Yugoslavia, he repeatedly watched Jordan's videocassette *Come Fly with Me*. "Everybody wants to play with Michael Jordan," he said in October 1990. Since then, however, he grew increasingly worried about fitting in with the stars of the Bulls, though Krause maintained that they could all learn to play together. Krause envisioned them thriving in the triangle offense—Jordan, Pippen, and Kukoč were all versatile ball handlers and scorers. With Kukoč and Pippen on the court, he thought, Jordan would never see a double-team.[29]

Standing six-foot-eleven with a slender torso, sloping shoulders, and long skinny arms, Kukoč looked like he had never lifted weights in his life. Gangly yet graceful, an unselfish, clever passer with great shooting range, "White Magic," as he was known across the old continent, had become a European basketball star as a teenager, drawing comparisons to the Los Angeles Lakers' point guard. By the time the Bulls drafted him with the twenty-ninth pick, Kukoč, only twenty-one years old, had already led the Yugoslavian men's national team to the 1990 World Championship and two consecutive European titles. Kukoč, recalled Krause, "was the Jordan of Europe. He was a god. He could not walk down the streets without getting mobbed." If he had heard Krause's comparison, Jordan would have taken it as an insult, another slight from an old basketball scout who didn't know a damn thing. No matter what Krause said, Jordan remained unconvinced that Kukoč could compete with Americans. "Everyone can see for themselves," he said. "No European has ever come here and been a star."[30]

Jordan was right: the NBA had not yet seen a breakout European player, but the basketball world was gradually shrinking. Over the course of the 1990s, NBA teams would draft 130 foreign players, 70 percent of whom came from the six republics of the former Yugoslav federation. Increasingly, during the late 1980s, as NBA franchise expansion created a growing demand for players, league scouts and executives explored Europe for untapped basketball talent. In the past, the cultural exchange around the sport was mostly one directional: American professionals who could not cut it in the NBA found work in Europe, mostly in

Mediterranean countries, playing in the equivalent of the minor leagues. By the late 1980s, as many as one hundred former NBA players were competing on European basketball teams. At the same time, NBA teams began drafting a handful of European prospects. When the 1990–1991 season began, eight European players appeared on NBA rosters, including two of Kukoč's teammates from the unified Yugoslav national squad: Portland Trail Blazers guard Dražen Petrović—soon to be traded to the New Jersey Nets—and Los Angeles Lakers center Vlade Divac.[31]

The dissolution of Yugoslavia's governing political party—the League of Communists—in 1990 portended the eruption of civil war and the breakup of the best national basketball team in the world, intertwining events that shaped the life and career of Toni Kukoč. During the last decade of the Cold War, the Yugoslav national team, an amalgam comprising six major ethnic groups— Serbs, Croats, Slovenes, Bosnian Muslims, Montenegrins, and Macedonians—flourished in international competition under a state-sponsored system. Training under a socialist regime, the players embodied the Pan-Slavic ideology of "brotherhood and unity," but this government-mandated solidarity began to fray under nationalist pressures. In May 1990, Croatia, Kukoč's homeland, formed a multiparty parliament and shortly thereafter established the state's sovereignty. A few months later, at the World Championship in Buenos Aires, as Yugoslavia celebrated its gold medal victory over the Soviets, a fan ran onto the court, waving the Croatian flag. Incensed, Serbian Vlade Divac, "a tousled-haired, soft-eyed giant," snatched the Croatian flag out of the interloper's hands, yelling that a unified Yugoslavia won, not a team of Croats, Serbs, and Bosnians. Red-faced, the Croatian fan shouted that Vlade's Yugoslavian flag was "bullshit." It was the last time the Yugoslav basketball team competed at the World Championship.[32]

In Chicago—dubbed the "Second Croatian Capital" for its large concentration of Croats—few Bulls fans outside those ethnic neighborhoods paid much attention to Kukoč or the Yugoslav national team. But Krause had grown obsessed with his prized draft pick. After drafting Kukoč, Krause visited Yugoslavia on four occasions, including once with Reinsdorf. He had reportedly called Kukoč's home in downtown Split more than one hundred times. Krause gushed talking about how he had "discovered" him. "It was at a playoff game in Detroit in '89 or '90. And Leon Douglas"—a former fringe NBA player—"who had played in Europe came up to me and said, 'Jerry, there's this Yugoslavian point guard you gotta see. He's a 6-foot-ll-inch white guy who plays hungry like a black kid from the ghetto.' That's all I needed to hear."[33]

At a moment when white American players seemed to be disappearing from the NBA, Krause seemed delighted by this Croatian White Hope's ability to dominate Black basketball players. His eyes lit up when he recounted the time Kukoč stunned the American team at the 1990 Goodwill Games in Seattle, blocking a slam attempt by Georgetown star Alonzo Mourning, a muscular player who rarely had his shot rejected. Kukoc *dunked* on Mourning, too, the best shot blocker on the American team, a remarkable play that excited Krause. "Mourning was totally shocked," he recalled. "I don't think a white guy had ever dunked on him."[34]

Phil Jackson viewed Kukoč through an American racial lens, too, suggesting that Kukoč's skills mirrored those of white players born in the United States. He implied that racial characteristics accounted in part for the Croatian's approach to the game. In doing so, he overlooked the fact that the Yugoslav school of basketball valued creativity and improvisation—skills often associated with Black American players—as much as fundamentals and teamwork. Speaking of Kukoč, Jackson explained, "The style of basketball we play and the system we use happens to be conducive to a lot of skills white players have—spot shooting, ball movement, cutting—as opposed to power basketball usually indigenous to the skills black basketball players have—one-on-one moves, quickness, jumping ability."[35] Increasingly, over the course of the 1990s, as NBA scouts, executives, coaches, and reporters evaluated European players, they emphasized how white foreigners, compared to Black American players, had mastered the fundamentals: setting screens, boxing out, moving without the ball, and making the "smart" pass. In short, many NBA observers concluded that European players were more "coachable," efficient, and less individualistic.[36]

Ultimately, Krause's full-court press during the 1990–1991 season failed to deliver Kukoč. Amid an international bidding war for his services and the escalating political turmoil in Yugoslavia, Kukoč chose to sign a six-year contract worth more than $4 million annually with the Benetton Treviso team in the Italian Basketball League. The agreement required Benetton to pay the taxes on Kukoč's salary and allowed him to remain close to his family. Krause could hardly hide his disappointment. But he wasn't giving up on Kukoč yet. He told reporters that Kukoč had an escape clause in his contract with Benetton. And someday, he believed, Kukoč would be *the star* of the Chicago Bulls, finally validating his acumen and judgment and proving he didn't need Michael Jordan.[37]

After Krause and Reinsdorf returned from Croatia, several of Pippen's teammates needled him about management's rumored plans to replace him with Kukoč, feeding his insecurities. It made him think twice about his future with the Bulls. And after reading that Charles Barkley had suffered a knee injury that threatened his season, Pippen called his agent, "nearly hysterical," Sam Smith reported, fearing an injury of his own would shatter whatever assurances Reinsdorf offered. "I want to sign a contract, now," Pippen said. "I've got to sign something now." When his agent called Reinsdorf, the team owner fumed. *Enough*. Reinsdorf had grown exasperated with Pippen, demanding that he tell the press "that there had been a misunderstanding." Pippen backed down. "I was misquoted," he said. "I have always given my best efforts for this team and I always will. I would never do anything to hurt my teammates. And I don't want to be traded."[38]

Even after Pippen backtracked, Krause made sure he had the final word: "You ain't going anywhere, Scottie. We got you and this is where you're staying. No matter what you do and no matter what you say. So get used to it."

Pippen burned over Krause's words. He channeled his frustration into the best year of his career, averaging nearly eighteen points, seven rebounds, and six assists each game. And for all of Michael Jordan's complaints about the triangle offense limiting him, he thrived in the system, again leading the league in scoring with 31.5 points per game. The Bulls completed the regular season with a 61–21 record, eleven games ahead of the Detroit Pistons, the best in the Eastern Conference. When the playoffs began, the Bulls tore through the competition, sweeping the Knicks in the first round, 3–0, and whipping Charles Barkley and the 76ers in four out of five games in the second round, setting up the rematch that everyone in Chicago so desperately desired.

Chapter Eleven

THE GREATEST SHOW ON EARTH

"Magic vs. Michael is the perfect movie script. And that's what this is all about."

—PHOENIX SUNS COACH COTTON FITZSIMMONS
ON THE EVE OF THE 1991 NBA FINALS

Joe Dumars didn't see it coming. About seventy seconds into Game One of the Eastern Conference Finals, while the Bulls set up an inbound play underneath their own basket, Michael Jordan was standing chest-to-chest with Dumars, preparing to set a screen on Bill Laimbeer. In the blink of an eye, Jordan popped Dumars in the chest with his right forearm. Dumars's head whipped back like he'd been stung by a jab from Mike Tyson. Then Jordan hit Laimbeer with a pick that bordered on a shove. Chuck Daly bolted from his seat, shouting above the boisterous Chicago crowd, imploring the referee to call a foul on Jordan. But the game played on.

Seven minutes later, Jordan, setting a moving screen, cracked an elbow into Dennis Rodman's ribs. This time the referee blew the whistle. Then, with about a minute left in the second quarter, Jordan caught a pass on the left wing, blew past Rodman, and scored an easy layup. Returning to defense, Jordan shouted at Rodman, antagonizing him with taunts the whole trip down the court. Jordan needled the NBA's Defensive Player of the Year, telling Rodman that he had no chance guarding him.

Seconds later, after Dumars missed a jumper, Rodman and Jordan turned up court, still jawing at each other, their arms entangled like barbed wire. The referee blew the whistle—this time, calling the foul on Rodman. Jordan charged into Rodman's face, cursing him, nose to nose, until the referee separated them. Jogging toward the Pistons' bench, Rodman's lips curled into a jester's grin as he patted Jordan on the rear. He relished the sparring, the verbal duel, matching wits with the master of the game.[1]

Before tip-off, Jordan had devised a plan to turn the tables on the Pistons: winning, he thought, required attacking them physically and weaponizing wordplay. Verbal battles, or "signifying"— the art of taunting, teasing, and roasting—could give basketball players a psychological edge, affirming an athlete's dominance. Rooted in Black oral tradition, signifying was the competitive equivalent of one-upmanship—elevating oneself while disrespecting or embarrassing an opponent. "Talkin' trash" was the game within the game, a practice Jordan employed to diminish and demoralize opponents. Targeting Rodman, the wiry, tightly coiled forward prone to self-combustion, Jordan delivered a loud message: "I'm comin' after you."[2]

Known for his smothering defense and indifference to scoring, Rodman relentlessly bumped, grabbed, and harassed Jordan. "Every time he'd go past me," Jordan recalled, "boom, knee me in the corner, knee me in the back. He was trying to frustrate me. And I was trying to do exactly what he would do. I'm trying to knock the hell out of Rodman. I'm telling Scottie to bring him off the screen—boom, I knock him. Rodman got pissed off because we were doing the same shit that he would do. I knew I was getting to him."[3]

Still, for much of the game, the Pistons managed to contain Jordan, frequently running double-teams at him. At one point, however, he found himself guarded by John "Spider" Salley, a long-armed six-foot, eleven-inch center. Jordan showed Salley the ball, threatening to drive. Salley challenged him, shouting, "You don't go near the Spider's web!" Jordan didn't hesitate. He drove right at him, reversed direction near the basket, and slammed the ball through the hoop, yelling, "Block that, bitch!" In that moment, Salley knew that whatever power the Pistons once held over Jordan had disappeared.[4]

After they dropped the first two games of the series to the Bulls at Chicago Stadium, it was clear that the Bad Boys had lost their edge. The Pistons looked increasingly like an aging, aching team staggering into the playoffs. Nine of twelve players were thirty years old or older. And several key contributors suffered from nagging injuries. Isiah Thomas hobbled onto the Chicago court with a swollen right ankle, throbbing knees, and a sore shooting wrist that had not fully healed from surgery. When games ended, Joe Dumars, James Edwards, Vinnie Johnson, and Bill Laimbeer all reached for the Excedrin. Younger, quicker, and hungrier, the Bulls were unfazed by the scrums on the court. No matter what, Jordan urged his teammates, *don't back down.*[5]

As the series moved to the Palace, the Bulls stunned the Pistons, sweeping the defending champions and dominating them completely. During the entire series, Detroit led Chicago for just eight minutes and thirty-eight seconds. The Bulls were the best defensive team the Eastern Conference had seen in years, holding their playoff opponents—New York, Philadelphia, and Detroit— to 92.5 points per game, the lowest average in a decade. "They've stolen our playbook," Salley lamented. "Intensity on defense. Corralling the ball. Not letting you get rebounds. Making you beat them with jump shots. Keeping people out of the middle. Talking junk. Talking garbage. Those are all the things we used to do."[6]

The Pistons unraveled in Game Four—a twenty-one-point blowout. The worst moment came midway through the second quarter, when Scottie Pippen drove to the basket and Rodman, completely unprovoked, forcefully shoved him in the back, leveling Pippen into the courtside seats. Pippen had burned Rodman throughout the series, averaging twenty-two points and almost eight rebounds per contest, though he showed little interest in reporters' questions about redeeming himself from "the headache game" a year earlier. As he lay splayed across the hardwood floor with a gash on his chin, Pippen's teammates rushed to his aid. He did not leap to his feet and retaliate. Instead, he sat up, a bit hazy, collected his thoughts, and returned to the court. It was a defining moment for Pippen: his poise and resilience silenced any accusations that he was soft or timid.

In the closing moments of the game, an unforgettable scene unfolded that cemented the Bad Boys' villainous reputation. As the final seven seconds ticked away, after Chuck Daly had pulled the Pistons' starters, several players skipped the postgame handshake and marched right past the Bulls' bench, disappearing into the Palace tunnel. Wearing a sullen expression, Isiah Thomas led the procession with his head down and his shoulders slouched, snubbing Jordan and his teammates in a final act of disrespect. "It made the Pistons look to all the world like losers," wrote *Chicago Tribune* columnist Bob Greene. "It made them seem vanquished and insignificant and yesterday's news. They had been two-time world champions, and in this one moment, on national television, they were throwing away any respect that had accrued to them. Now the Bull's victory was total."[7]

The Pistons were condemned throughout the country in newspaper columns and television commentaries. Critics called them a poor example for America's youth and a disgrace to sportsmanship. The worst vitriol came from Chicago writers, one of whom suggested that Rodman, "the smirking vermin," belonged in prison. One *Sun-Times* writer claimed that the Bulls had saved Detroit from more rioting; had the Pistons won the series, he suggested, Detroit would have witnessed "a repeat of the violence that punctuated last year's championship." In a satirical column for *USA Today*, Mike Lopresti captured the national mood: The Detroit Pistons "were a blight on the land, and all that was standing between us and the further spread of Pistonism was the purity of the Chicago Bulls, who now have preserved the Republic, not to mention the good name of the NBA. Basketball is safe again for women and children. God bless the red and black. Or something like that."[8]

The narratives around the Bulls-Pistons rivalry carried cultural implications, symbolizing the larger moral struggle over the future of the NBA. The ascendance of the Bulls as "America's Team"—and Jordan's rise as a moral force—was tied to trouncing the Detroit Pistons and everything they represented. In the public consciousness, Jordan's crusade restored the mythical—and often undefined—*integrity of the game*, a superior style that embodied the virtues of teamwork, sportsmanship, and humility. The Pistons' style of basketball, Jerry Reinsdorf complained, represented "thuggerism, hoodlumism . . . That's one of the things that made us so popular. We were the white knights; we were the good guys." Jordan echoed Reinsdorf, grumbling that the Pistons didn't play with honor. "You have an obligation to demonstrate good sportsmanship. That's the American way."[9]

Jordan declared the Bulls' victory over the Pistons a triumph of "good overriding evil." From his perspective, the Bulls were the antidote to a team that promoted violence and unruly competition. Beating the Pistons, he thought, transformed the Bulls into a righteous force for uplifting the sport. The public's view of him as a moral figure, therefore, was based on a perception that he safeguarded the NBA from a ruinous team of misfits who disregarded decency and the integrity of the game. During the series, Jordan drew a dividing line between the Good Guys and the Bad Boys: "You have seen two different styles," he said. "Hopefully, the old style"—the Pistons' style—"is going to be eliminated from the game. That's dirty play, flagrant fouls, and what I call unsportsmanlike conduct. We're a clean basketball team. We don't go out and try to hurt people. We don't try to dirty up the game. I don't think people want that kind of basketball."[10]

The Pistons were history, the Bulls the future.

On the Bulls' charter flight home to Chicago, the players celebrated the sweet taste of victory. Jordan smiled widely and imbibed from a bottle of champagne, thinking about the NBA championship ahead. In a matter of days, Magic Johnson and the Los Angeles Lakers would clinch the Western Conference Finals. Jordan would finally get his chance to prove that he was the king of the court.[11]

Dancing in the aisle with a red plastic cup in his hand, Jerry Krause couldn't have been happier. Wearing gray slacks, a white short-sleeve shirt, a loosened tie, and a goofy smile on his face, Krause swung his hips haltingly like he had never danced before in his life. The players busted with laughter, egging him on with chants, "Go Jerry! Go Jerry!" until Scottie Pippen finally said, "Go sit down, Jerry."[12]

After eliminating the Pistons, Jordan owed Krause—and his teammates—an apology. He had underestimated them, complaining repeatedly throughout the season that Krause had failed to build him "a supporting cast" worthy of a championship. When a reporter asked him about his season-long feud with Krause, Jordan said, "I can reconsider my words. I can even eat them."[13]

"Oh yes," Magic Johnson said, a bright smile flickering across his face, "I've dreamed about it."

He could see it all unfolding like an epic movie, a saga starring two of the most recognizable athletes in the world, battling each other, shot for shot, point for point. A championship series featuring Magic Johnson and Michael Jordan blurred the lines between fiction and reality, sports and entertainment.[14]

Magic and Michael. Michael and Magic. The publicity campaign required nothing more than those two names. Stars sold. They were the reason to watch basketball.

Johnson lived for this moment. After the Lakers upset the Portland Trail Blazers, Johnson would appear in his ninth NBA championship series in twelve seasons. He had competed for the title against some of the very best players in the history of the sport—Julius Erving, Larry Bird, and Isiah Thomas—but the prospect of playing against Jordan in his first NBA Finals, *that* was a dream come true. "This is what you live for—to play Michael Jordan in the Finals!"[15]

Jordan had long thought about this moment, too, about what it would take to displace Johnson as the king of the court. After seven seasons of frustration, the twenty-eight-year-old star prepared to step outside of Johnson's shadow and prove his antagonists wrong. For years, he repeatedly heard that he lacked Johnson's leadership. Magic won universal praise for being an unselfish passer who elevated the play of his teammates. He would have never referred to them as "his supporting cast." The endless comparisons irritated Jordan. A year earlier he said, "I could care less about Magic. Personally, I'm trying to be the best basketball player that I can be."[16]

The unprecedented publicity surrounding the 1991 NBA Finals, billed as "the Michael and Magic Show," was largely shaped by its producers: Dick Ebersol and David Stern—business partners who recognized that what attracted viewers to the games were *the stories* about the games, narrative formulas built around characters and conflict. Under the direction of Ebersol, president of NBC Sports, the network promoted storylines that fascinated viewers, emphasizing the morality play of the NBA, its personas and rivalries, heroes and villains. Broadcasting the Finals for the first time, NBC turned a team event into an individual contest, a phantasmal one-on-one match between Johnson and Jordan. For this reason NBC assigned one cameraman to shoot them exclusively throughout the series. Ebersol wanted to capture their every move and emotion, the moments of exhilaration and frustration, the joys and pains of basketball. Those close-up shots of Magic and Michael—every grimace, grin, and glare—created intimacy between the audience and the players and helped build the tension around the subplots of the show. In an entertainment culture that presented sporting events as spectacles, the NBA Finals had become, in the words of *Sports Illustrated* writer Jack McCallum, "the Magic and Michael made-for-TV miniseries."[17]

In that sense each game represented an episode in a serial, a production packaged around the theatrics of its characters. Before Game One, NBC host Bob Costas teased the audience as if he were reading the marquee of a grand movie house: "It's Magic vs. Michael. It's the Bulls vs. the Lakers. It's the NBA Finals. And it's showtime!" The teams were clearly secondary to the stars. It did not matter that Jordan and Johnson were not matched against each other like two centers. Jordan often guarded Johnson, though Johnson rarely covered Jordan. Yet NBC fueled the idea that Johnson and Jordan were competing for something greater than a championship, for some fabled title—the right to claim that they were the very best player in the world. Before Game One, play-by-play announcer Marv Albert declared that the NBA "is the place where fantasy meets reality."[18]

That fantasy world was largely shaped by Stern. Since he became the league's top executive seven years earlier, his mission had been to forge the NBA into a global entertainment conglomerate that could sell its products worldwide. Instead of emulating the marketing strategies of the National Football League or Major League Baseball, he designed the NBA's global brand around the model of the Walt Disney Company. Disney sold family-friendly entertainment throughout the world in its amusement parks, films, and toys. Stern wanted to do the same thing. Under his leadership, the NBA, like Disney, would become a dream factory. "They have theme parks and we have theme parks. Only we call them arenas," he said. "They have characters: Mickey Mouse, Goofy. Our characters are named Magic and Michael. Disney sells apparel; we sell apparel. They make home videos; we make home videos."[19]

Stern recognized that the sport's growing international popularity, coupled with television's enormous power to expose consumers to the NBA overseas, could expand the size of the league's audience. As the United States became saturated with NBA products, Stern, knowing that technology would shape the league's future, strategized that the league would embrace expansion not by planting franchises abroad but by broadcasting the Michael and Magic Show in foreign markets. In the last two decades of the twentieth century, the NBA benefited from two revolutionary technological innovations: fiber-optic cables and direct-broadcast satellite systems, which made possible the transmission of NBA games all over the world. As the Cold War began to wind down, television deregulation opened new European markets, creating virtually unlimited commercial opportunities for the NBA and its advertising partners. By 1991, more than seventy countries broadcast NBA games, and a record number of more than 400 million households worldwide tuned in to watch the Finals.[20]

The Bulls-Lakers series took place in front of a vastly larger television audience than any previous NBA Finals. As a global event, it had become as important as the World Cup and the Olympics, "the Greatest Show on Earth," suggested Lakers' forward Mychal Thompson. Dominating the endorsement market, never had two Black athletes enjoyed such universal popularity. Marketing research showed that Jordan and Johnson were the most "likable" and "familiar" athletes in America, appealing to men and women, young and old, Blacks and whites. During the Finals, sportswriters portrayed Jordan and Johnson as corporate competitors, international spokesmen representing the capitalist rivalries between Nike and Converse, McDonald's and Kentucky Fried Chicken, Coca-Cola and Pepsi. In essence, the NBA Finals had become an extended commercial for advertisers, a vehicle for exporting America's popular culture and its merchandise.[21]

This series had something for everybody. "Everyone's happy," Johnson said. "The fans are happy. The media's happy. The league is happy. Michael's happy and I'm happy." Then he paused, contemplating the monetary value of the Michael and Magic Show. "When it's over," he said with his trademark grin, "we get to renegotiate."[22]

Playing before a frenetic home crowd, Jordan came out firing in Game One. "He seemed intent on showing Magic, and the entire western hemisphere, who was the superior player," recalled Scottie Pippen. Jordan opened the first quarter making seven of ten shots, scoring fifteen points. None of his teammates, however, shot well. After nearly a weeklong pause between beating the Pistons and playing the Lakers—an eternity for a professional basketball player—the Bulls played tight. Some players hardly slept the night before the game. A notorious night owl, Jordan tossed and turned, unable to shut off his mind. By the third quarter, when the Bulls fell behind by seven points, Jordan, nearly drained, asked out of the game, a rarity for him.[23]

In a thrilling game that included twenty-one lead changes and sixteen ties, it all came down to whether Jordan could rescue the Bulls. With twenty-four seconds left, Johnson backed down Jordan with the ball; then he rifled a cross-court pass to Sam Perkins, who drained a wide-open three-point shot, giving Los Angeles a 92–91 lead. The Bulls called time-out with fourteen seconds left on the clock. Everyone in Chicago Stadium knew who would take the last shot. Standing on the sideline, Pippen passed the ball inbounds to Jordan at the top of the key. Guarded by Byron Scott, Jordan dribbled left and drove into a swarm of arms near the basket. Rising above the defenders, he tried to drop off the ball, but it bounced out of bounds off the Lakers. Now, with nine seconds remaining, Jordan crouched in the paint, leaning against his old UNC teammate James Worthy. He darted away from the basket and freed himself from Worthy, catching Pippen's inbounds pass. Perkins picked him up on the switch. Jordan shook loose and launched an eighteen-foot jump shot that rattled around the rim and popped out. The Lakers snatched the rebound and added a free throw to their 93–91 victory. After the game, Jordan said the shot felt good when it left his hand—"All of 'em feel good."[24]

The game—and its stars—had lived up to the hype. Johnson finished with a triple-double: nineteen points, eleven assists, and ten rebounds. Before missing the game-winning shot, Jordan had played brilliantly. The Miller Genuine Draft Player of the Game had thirty-six points, twelve assists, eight rebounds, and three steals. Yet his teammates all but disappeared. In his worst game of the series, Pippen missed twelve of nineteen shots. And the other starters—Horace Grant, John Paxson, and Bill

Cartwright—managed only six points each. "The Bulls," opined Jack McCallum, "looked like the Bulls of old: too much Jordan and too little of everyone else."[25]

One reason Jordan was so exhausted during the first game was because he expended so much energy covering Johnson. Before Game Two, Phil Jackson contemplated assigning Pippen to Johnson, but Jordan resisted the switch. His pride was on the line. He didn't just want to beat the Lakers; he wanted to shut down Magic Johnson. But when Jordan got hit with his second personal foul early in the first quarter of Game Two, Jackson called on Pippen. Taller and longer than Jordan, Pippen put on a tenacious defense that hampered Johnson. Having studied Johnson's passing tendencies, Pippen knew that Johnson did not often pass with his left hand—Magic preferred passing with his right hand off the dribble. So, Pippen, who was quicker than Johnson, picked him up in the backcourt, body to body, moving his feet, giving him little room to breathe. He did not want Johnson running the offense at full speed. Magic was impossible to stop on the break. Instead, Pippen said, he "would come to him" and force Johnson to give up the ball. That strategy worked marvelously as the Lakers struggled helping Magic break the Bulls' press, especially with James Worthy playing on a sore ankle.[26]

In Game Two, the Bulls routed the Lakers, 107–86. Chicago made 61.7 percent of their shot attempts—an NBA Finals record. John Paxson netted all eight of his shots; Horace Grant converted ten of thirteen attempts; and Pippen scored twenty points. But no one played better than Jordan. In the second half, he entered what sports psychologists call "the zone," totally immersed in the moment, playing in the flow of the game at a heightened level of focus, blocking out all the noise and distractions. His shooting felt effortless. At one point he made thirteen consecutive shots. He finished with thirty-three points and thirteen assists.

Of course, what everyone remembers from that game, though, is not Jordan's hot hand, but *the move* that made eighteen thousand Chicagoans rise to their feet in delirium. In the fourth quarter, Jordan caught a pass and drove straight down an open lane toward the basket. As he elevated for a dunk with the ball extended above his head, out of his peripheral vision he recognized "long-armed" Sam Perkins closing in on him—close enough, Jordan thought, that Perkins might block his shot. Suspended in the air, Jordan brought the ball down with his right hand and shifted it to his left, stretching his body across a horizontal plane as he began coming down. In that instant, he flipped the ball off the backboard with just the right amount of spin and into the net. Calling the game for NBC, Marv Albert famously erupted in his baritone voice, "Oh! A spec-TAC-ular move, by Michael Jordan!"[27]

It instantly became Jordan's signature moment, replayed repeatedly on NBC, ESPN, and every local news broadcast in the country. After the play, NBC showed it in slow-motion from five different angles, providing audiences with a complete 360-degree view of a move that became more remarkable with each new frame. That scene became so defining that when Gatorade launched the "Be Like Mike" commercial two months later, it opened with a close-up of the move—the one that Jordan's idolators imitated across playgrounds and gyms everywhere. In a world where SportsCenter could edit an entire game from a feature into a short, highlights virtually deified athletes who could dunk a basketball or hit a game-winning shot. The most popular and influential players were those who provided instant gratification— the athletes who fed the highlight machine. For "the highlight generation"—the people who came of age when everything Jordan did on a basketball court was recorded and replayed—television, noted historian Benjamin Rader, could "transform highlights into an experience bigger and frequently more compelling than the games themselves."[28]

Watching the slow-motion replay of the move was like watching the rise of Superman. It was as if Jordan glided in a slightly different dimension than everyone else on the court. His aerial theatrics—the fluidity, grace, power, and body control—blurred the line between the possible and impossible. But that spontaneous act demonstrated something more impressive than a physical feat. The footage revealed how Jordan's mind worked on the court, the way his vision, training, and creativity allowed him to make a rapid-fire calculation in midair. The move illustrated how he recognized patterns, measuring his position and the position of others in space. That ability to make hot decisions in high-speed, high-pressure situations—assessing risk and reward with the ball in his hand—made it possible for him to play without fear and succeed.

The move exhibited Jordan's improvisational genius and it illustrated the culmination in the making of an icon. The frequent replays of Jordan taking flight against the Lakers compressed his rise as a champion into a single moment of triumph. In the public imagination, that indelible image celebrated and sustained his aura, transforming Jordan into something transcendent: the Jumpman as hero.

The next three games were played in Los Angeles at the Great Western Forum, where the Bulls defied all predictions of withering under the Hollywood spotlight. In Game Three, after trailing the Lakers by thirteen points in the third quarter, the Bulls rallied and tied the game when Jordan dribbled the length of the court, stutter-stepped, and drilled a twelve-foot jumper over Byron Scott with 3.4 seconds on the clock, setting up overtime.

In the next five minutes, the Bulls demoralized the Forum crowd, dominating the Lakers in a 104–96 victory. Jordan, however, had injured his big toe when he landed hard on his right foot making the game-tying jump shot. When he returned to the bench, he thought it might be broken, though it was only sprained. By the next day the toe had grown so swollen that he had the trainer cut a small hole out of the tip of his right sneaker. In Game Four, Jordan played through the pain, scoring thirty-six points and leading the Bulls to victory over the Lakers, 97–82. At one point, he switched shoes because the modified sneaker felt too loose. But he could have played barefoot and it wouldn't have mattered. The Bulls still would have delivered what Magic Johnson called "an old-fashioned ass-kicking."[29]

The Lakers were in trouble and everyone knew it. No team had ever recovered from a 3–1 deficit in a best-of-seven series to win the title. Jordan began imagining what it would feel like to be the champion. After Game Four, on the bus ride back to the hotel, he shouted to Phil Jackson, "Hey, PJ! I ain't goin' to no White House. I didn't vote for that guy. I know you didn't vote for him." Jordan was right. Jackson, a Democrat, definitely had not voted for *that guy*—George H. W. Bush. But the Bulls had not received any White House invitations just yet.[30]

For all his confidence, Jordan could hardly sit still the night before Game Five. He paced his hotel room floor like an expectant father waiting in the maternity ward. Without a basketball in his hand, he didn't know what to do with himself. All he could do was think about the most important game of his career.[31]

Most observers believed the Bulls would roll the Lakers in Game Five, but with about six minutes left, Los Angeles led 91–90. At that point in the fourth quarter, Jordan had taken five of the Bulls' eight shots. Sensing that Jordan was drifting from his teammates, Jackson engaged him in the huddle during a timeout.

All season long, he had urged Jordan to trust his teammates, reminding him that he could not win a championship by himself. And throughout the series, Jackson had pressed him to pass the ball to John Paxson, the team's most accurate long-distance shooter. During the timeout, Jackson pointed out that Magic Johnson was dropping off Paxson so he could double-team Jordan.

Jackson asked, "Michael, who's open?"

Jordan ignored him.

Again, Jackson asked, "Michael, who's open?"

Silence from Jordan.

His voice rising, Jackson asked a third time.

Finally, Jordan answered, "Paxson."

"Then get him the fucking ball," Jackson shouted.[32]

Jordan delivered. In the final minutes, he penetrated the Lakers' defense, finding Paxson wide open for five clean jump shots. Shooting in rhythm with his shoulders squared to the basket, Paxson scored ten of his twenty points in the last four minutes of the game, leading the Bulls down the stretch in a 108–101 victory. Finally, the Bulls were NBA champions, and Jordan would get his ring.

That story has been told and retold by Phil Jackson and the players who witnessed it, forming the myth of the coach as Zen master. It shaped the arc of the Jackson-Jordan legend, intertwining them in a narrative where the coach tamed the Bulls star. Jackson knew that the anecdote made for a great story, so he volunteered it to *Tribune* reporter Sam Smith, who was working on a book about the Bulls' season. After the team returned home from Los Angeles, Jackson recounted the story to Smith and said, "Why don't you save that for your book? Don't put that in the newspaper."[33]

Smith liked the idea. "It was the lesson from when Phil took over—in effect, that you can't win it by yourself. You've got to depend on the group," Sam Smith said. "Now we've come full circle. Michael has bought in, and Phil's theories have been proved: that if you trust the group, you'll have greater success, and you'll be viewed as greater. From that point, Michael was viewed as the greatest player in the league."[34]

Winning the championship—six times with the Bulls during the nineties—and being seen as the guiding light in Jordan's career transformed Jackson into a public pedagogue, an admired moral authority who supposedly brought enlightenment to professional basketball. "His ego," gushed one writer, "rests not in power or control, but in an arching vision, a teacher's sway." Reporters marveled at how he challenged players intellectually and spiritually, assigning books to professional athletes that had nothing to do with sports. Several players on the Bulls said they never read them. Nonetheless, sportswriters described Jackson as part philosopher, part psychologist, a Svengali imparting wisdom upon his team. They recounted stories about how he introduced players to meditation, visualization, and Sun Tzu's *The Art of War*. Yet Jackson was not the gentle, touchy-feely, peace and love archetype the press made him out to be in the early nineties. He was less hippie than Beat poet, observed *Washington Post* writer Michael Leahy. Cool and wry, he could be detached and derisive, rarely offering players praise or gratitude. When players failed to perform, when they stood in the way of winning, he would rip them as harshly as any coach in the league.[35]

His success during the nineties made Jackson into a national icon, who rose "to the status of American Winner," praised as one of the great leaders in the country. Comparing all six of his championship teams with Chicago, the 1991, with their 15–2 playoff record, was the most dominant postseason. In both their playoff losses, the Bulls fell by just two points when an opponent made a game-winning three-point shot in the final twenty seconds.

Furthermore, the Bulls outscored their opponents by an average of 11.7 points per game—second best in playoff history. And the Bulls beat the Lakers with significant contributions from Pippen, Paxson, and Horace Grant. After Game One, Pippen played at an especially high level at both ends of the court, averaging more than 20 points, 9.4 rebounds, and 6.6. assists per game in the series.[36]

Pippen's breakout season earned him the recognition and rewards that came with a contract extension that he so desperately wanted. In order for the Bulls to use the unspent $1.6 million remaining in the team's salary cap budget—money Jerry Krause had reserved for Toni Kukoč—the general manager insisted Pippen sign during the Finals. Because unspent salary cap money did not roll over into the next season, the Bulls had every incentive to spend it now. That way management could front-load the deal, committing most of that remaining $1.6 million to Pippen's salary for the 1990–1991 season. By giving him that money up front, the Bulls could pay him less over the course of Pippen's new five-year, $18 million deal. However, the new agreement did not erase the two remaining seasons Pippen had left on his first contract. That meant that signing the new deal committed him to the Bulls for the next seven years—a period when the salary cap more than doubled and the Bulls paid him substantially below his market value. By the end of his contract, he lived full of regret as the 122nd highest-paid player in the NBA.[37]

In the years to come, as the Bulls built a championship dynasty, Pippen would remain in Jordan's shadow, forever his sidekick. The conversations about him always seemed to revolve around his place in the sport in relationship to Jordan, never the other way around. Of course, Jordan was always the best player on the Bulls, but Pippen became the club's most important *teammate*. He was the one who took the pressure off Jordan, often drawing the most challenging defensive assignments. He was the one who made the triple-post offense work, ensuring that everyone touched the ball. More than any other player on the Bulls, Pippen manifested Phil Jackson's vision of community within the team. If a player missed a few shots, Jordan would stop passing him the ball, but Pippen didn't give up on his teammate; he worked even harder to pass the ball to that player. Jackson believed that sharing came more naturally to Pippen, the youngest of twelve children. He was raised to be selfless and lift up those around him, especially those who struggled. "I was a much better teammate than Michael," he said. "Ask anyone who played with the two of us. I was always there with a pat on the back or an encouraging word, especially after he put someone down for one reason or another."[38]

After beating the Lakers, Pippen celebrated the greatest moment of his career, drenched in champagne. Inside the Bulls' chaotic locker room, a party erupted, packed with people—"a maze of friends and relatives and television cameras." Pippen and his teammates popped corked bottles, shouting and spraying each other. "Emotion and exhilaration washed over the players," Sam Smith wrote. "It was purifying, purging the jealousies, resentments, and feuds of the season. What remained was pure, unrestrained joy."[39]

Amid the chaos, Bob Costas searched the locker room for Jordan, a camera operator following behind him. Frantic, Costas wondered aloud, "Where's Jordan? Where's Jordan?" He found him sitting in front of his cramped cubicle, his body glistening, covered in sweat and alcohol, wearing his red uniform and a white championship hat, hugging the gold championship trophy close to his body like a newborn baby. During the Finals, he had delivered a historic performance, averaging more than 31 points, 11 assists, and 6.6 rebounds per game. Surrounded by a gaggle of photographers and reporters, Jordan sobbed, his eyes turning red, while his father, James, patted him on the back and massaged his neck. He embraced his wife, Juanita, placing his arm around her. Overwhelmed with emotion, Jordan emptied out his feelings in front of the world. Costas asked him what the championship meant to him. Jordan struggled to find the words. Nothing he said revealed how he really felt as much as those tears of joy. He was a champion now and no one could take that away from him.[40]

Across the hallway, in the Lakers' subdued locker room, a somber mood of defeat hung in the air. Reporters asked Magic Johnson about Jordan and if he remembered what it felt like when he won his first championship twelve years earlier. That seemed so long ago. In this moment of disappointment, he was thinking less about the past than the future. Losing in the Finals made him contemplate retirement. Listening to Johnson, reporters predicted that he had played his last game. It seemed that the Showtime era had finally come to an end. But Johnson reassured his fans that he would return. "I'm sure I'll be back," he said.[41]

After talking with reporters, Johnson wandered into the Bulls locker room, searching for Jordan. When he found him, Johnson saw tears in Jordan's eyes. They embraced like brothers, Jordan crying with his head resting on Johnson's shoulder.

"You got one," Johnson said.

"Oh, thank you so much, so very much," Jordan whispered.

"I'm happy for you," Johnson added. It was a bittersweet moment for him, but one that revealed his tremendous respect for Jordan.[42]

In the end, Magic conceded that the show now belonged to Michael.

Chapter Twelve

ALONE AT THE MOUNTAINTOP

"The press can't sully Jordan's image; there's no muck to rake . . . His image is not just an image; it's a reflection of substantial reality."

—George Castle, *SPORT* magazine, January 1991

Jordan snapped. "It's none of your business," he said in a surly tone that few reporters had ever heard him use. During an early October press conference, on the eve of training camp, as the team prepared to defend its championship, a pack of nearly one hundred sportswriters surrounded Jordan at the Deerfield practice gym, pressing him about his absence from the Bulls' ceremony at the White House. It had become a tradition for NBA champions to meet the president. Reporters wanted to know why the team's best player had snubbed President George H. W. Bush. The questions burned him. According to Jordan, the Bulls had scheduled the White House event during his family vacation in Hilton Head, South Carolina. But Jerry Krause told reporters that no one in the organization knew that Jordan wouldn't be traveling with the team. Bombarded with questions, Jordan insisted he didn't owe anyone an explanation, not even the president. "If you want to ask me what I did, I don't have to tell you," he said.[1]

Jordan's frustration with the media began weeks earlier when writers criticized him for considering skipping the 1992 Olympic Games—the first Olympics that included players from the NBA. Jordan figured that since he had already won a gold medal in 1984, there was no reason to compete in Barcelona. After an exhausting nine-month NBA season, he worried that training and playing with Team USA for an additional two months would increase his chances of injury and burnout. He preferred spending the summer resting his body and escaping the spotlight. Despite repeatedly stating that he loved America, the mere suggestion that he would not play in the Olympics made people question his patriotism, as if he were turning his back on the country that made him rich and famous. Critics claimed he had an obligation to represent the United States. He had a patriotic duty to perform when called upon and show gratitude for everything he had—long-standing requirements for successful Black athletes. In short, Michael Jordan, a Black man once hailed as a "true great American hero," had to prove his loyalty to the country by wearing an American uniform.[2]

In late September, a few weeks before the Bulls visited the White House, NBC aired a television special, *The Dream Team: The USA Basketball Selection Show*. Host Bob Costas announced the players' names, one by one, saving Jordan for last. Apparently, Jordan caved after Magic Johnson and Charles Barkley persuaded him to join them in Barcelona. Some reporters suggested that the NBA and his corporate sponsors pressured him too, reminding Jordan how much money was at stake on an international stage. Most important for Jordan, perhaps, was that NBA executive Rod Thorn, the general manager who had drafted him in 1984, reassured him that Isiah Thomas wouldn't be playing on the Dream Team.[3]

For a moment, questions about his patriotism were settled. But when he missed the White House event only a few days after hosting *Saturday Night Live*, commentators excoriated him for disrespecting the president. If Jordan had time to perform a skit, "The First Black Harlem Globetrotter," and introduce the rap group Public Enemy on *SNL*, then he should have made time to meet President Bush, critics charged. "This is about the most disturbing, irresponsible and irrational thing Jordan has ever done in public life," Jay Mariotti wrote in a harsh *Chicago Sun-Times* column. "It makes you wonder if Mike hasn't become too deviant and selfish in his post-title glow." Mariotti maintained that the Bulls should have forced him to appear at the White House or fine him, if necessary, as if Jordan had no say in the matter, no right to exercise his freedom on his own time before training camp began.[4]

Jordan's expected appearance at the White House, though, had nothing to do with his patriotism and everything to do with boosting the image of a president running for reelection despite a poor record on civil rights. During the 1988 presidential race against Michel Dukakis, Bush had endorsed the infamous Willie Horton television ads that showed a mug shot of a violent Black criminal who had raped a white woman after escaping from a weekend prison furlough in Massachusetts. Centering Bush's campaign around white fears of Black men, the television spots implied that Dukakis, the Massachusetts governor, was soft on crime and responsible for the furlough program that set Horton free, even though Dukakis had nothing to do with the case. Defending Jordan, Reverend Jesse Jackson said, "If Michael had gone [to the White House], smiled and posed with a president who used Willie Horton as a scare tactic to get elected, who vetoed the 1990 Civil Rights Act . . . there would have been people who would have been upset with him." Jackson reminded reporters that when Larry Bird missed the Boston Celtics' White House ceremony with Ronald Reagan in 1984, no one complained that Bird insulted the president. The difference between how the public reacted to Bird and Jordan, Jackson suggested, had everything to do with race.[5]

In Chicago, Bulls fans debated whether Jordan should have attended the White House event. Some argued that Bush stood to benefit from a photo op with Jordan, while the Bulls star had nothing to gain from it. A picture of them together on the front page of American newspapers was worth far more to the president than any campaign contribution from Jordan. While some fans thought Jordan was being selfish and had failed to live up to his responsibilities as a role model, others countered that the Bush administration planned to exploit Jordan to court Black voters. "If Bush wants to promote himself so badly and have a buddy-buddy photo with Michael Jordan to send to all the nation's newspapers so he can appeal to African Americans," opined one *Sun-Times* reader, "he should do what Gatorade, Coke, McDonald's and Nike all do: Pay for it."[6]

Although some of Jordan's teammates grumbled under their breath about his absence in Washington, DC, only Horace Grant ripped him publicly. The starting forward complained about the special privileges management afforded the team's star. Jordan didn't appreciate Grant questioning him, especially when reporters could see their tense exchange taking place at the Bulls' practice facility. He suggested the whole story had "been blown out of proportion" by writers trying to "stir things up," though many Chicago scribes defended Jordan's right to skip the photo op with the president.[7]

During his press conference, Jordan shot an icy glare at one writer in particular: Sam Smith. Although several reporters questioned him about his whereabouts during the White House ceremony, Jordan replied that he didn't need Smith telling him what to do with his free time. The *Chicago Tribune* reporter typically got along fine with Jordan. So, he found it odd that the Bulls star repeatedly mentioned his name. He wondered whether Jordan had heard a rumor that his forthcoming book about him was a hit job. Or maybe an editor at *Sports Illustrated* had reviewed an advance copy and shared it with Jordan. Smith didn't know for sure. But, after practice that day, he found himself on Jordan's running list of enemies. Walking out of the gym, Jordan stopped in front of Smith and said, "You're a fucking asshole."[8]

Smith was stunned. Jordan's sneer revealed how much he had hardened over the past year. His success unleashed social forces beyond his control, inviting greater criticism and pressure than ever before. Increasingly, politics and the perils of fame made it impossible for him to live up to the heroic image hyped by television producers and the ad men who made his commercials. Those pressures made him want to hide, but he couldn't evade the cameras that enveloped him every time he appeared in public. Struggling to find some equilibrium between his public and private worlds, he began retreating, searching for a way to close out the intruders. But now that Sam Smith had written a book, *The Jordan Rules*, that exposed his flaws and diminished his mystique, he had more questions to answer. A man who once dreamed about becoming a champion and all the glory that came with it, Michael Jordan learned that basketball could be a cruel business after all.

On November 7, 1991, two weeks before Sam Smith's book hit the shelves, Magic Johnson's agent Lon Rosen called Michael

Jordan and left him an urgent message that he needed to call his client right away. Driving home, Jordan dialed Johnson's number from his car phone. Johnson answered and told him what the rest of the world would learn hours later: he had contracted HIV—the life-threatening virus that causes AIDS. Standing before a packed press room at the Forum, wearing a gray suit, Johnson divulged his personal crisis before the world. He smiled through the pain, as if he was trying to comfort the fans watching him on television. The seven largest Los Angeles television stations plus CNN and ESPN carried the live press conference where he revealed his HIV status and announced his immediate retirement. Later that night, all three TV networks led their evening broadcasts with a story that NBC anchor Tom Brokaw described as "so shocking and so unexpected it is difficult to absorb even as we report it."[9]

Johnson's fans would never forget where they were when they heard the devastating news. Across the globe, the story unleashed an outpouring of sadness, sympathy, and fear. People had so many questions. Why Magic? Why now? He tested positive for HIV just two months after his wedding to Cookie Kelly and only two days after they learned she was carrying their child. Thankfully, neither his wife nor his child was infected with the virus. His press conference, replayed repeatedly across television and radio stations, followed by endless commentary and speculation about his life and eventual death, immediately transformed Magic into a martyr. It did not matter that he did not have AIDS or that he planned on "living for a long time." When he told America that he had HIV, most people heard him announce a death sentence.[10]

During his press conference, Johnson asserted his commitment to being a spokesman for HIV/AIDS awareness. He promised to lead a national discussion about the epidemic, bringing it into the living rooms of Middle America, where it had long been ignored and stigmatized as the "gay plague," a scourge upon gays, prostitutes, and intravenous drug users. Immediately, reporters began digging into his personal life, speculating that he had engaged in sexual encounters with men. Moving to dispel the rumors, he received a frenzied ovation when he declared on the *Arsenio Hall Show*, "I'm far from being a homosexual." Whooping and clapping, the studio crowd expressed its great relief that he wasn't gay, a powerful demonstration of the country's pervasive homophobia. Johnson had reassured his fans that they had not fallen for some sexual deviant. And that meant they didn't have to question their own judgment or their affection for him.[11]

In an interview with *Sports Illustrated*, Johnson admitted that although he did not know exactly who had infected him, he was certain he had contracted HIV from unprotected sex with a woman. "I confess," he told journalist Roy S. Johnson, "that after I arrived in L.A. in 1979, I did my best to accommodate as many women as I could." *Accommodate women? As if he provided some service, letting them sleep with the great Magic Johnson?* His words provoked criticism from feminists who argued that Johnson shifted the blame to women who now wondered whether he had infected them. "Johnson," wrote journalist Sally Jenkins, "has not been a hero to women. He has been a hazard."[12]

Over the next year, Johnson's public battle against HIV became part of the country's daily news, unfolding across television, newspapers, and magazines. His ongoing saga took shape in three phases. First, in the shock stage, the media canonized Johnson for courageously disclosing his sins, hailing him as a role model. Writers, fans, and fellow athletes praised him for saving lives by warning America's youth about the dangers of unprotected sex. But in the second stage, the tabloidization of the news, a backlash against Johnson developed when the press raised invasive questions about his sexual proclivities. Commentators demanded he "tell the whole truth about how he acquired the virus," insinuating that he was hiding something sinister behind his famous smile. The tabloid machine produced stories about his excesses and supposed satyriasis—perpetuating the racist myth about Black male hypersexuality. In the tabloid age, he was the latest example of the truism that while heroes sold newspapers, the downfall of heroes sold even more.[13]

In the third stage, the comeback, Magic tried to regain control of the narrative around his life story, orchestrating a public performance designed to restore his reputation. Almost immediately after going public, he established the Magic Johnson Foundation, a charitable organization devoted to AIDS research and outreach. Embracing his new role as an activist, he accepted President Bush's invitation to serve on the National Commission on AIDS, though a few months later he resigned in protest over the administration's failures to develop any serious prevention policy. He filmed an AIDS awareness video aimed at teenagers and appeared on Nickelodeon's *A Conversation with Magic*, a program that showed Johnson consoling children infected with HIV, a moving scene that garnered him greater empathy.[14]

After Johnson contracted the virus, he began talking more about his faith and how God had directed him to become a messenger in the fight against the disease. He insisted that he was not poisoned by HIV; God chose *him*. It was a master spin move: HIV was not a death sentence but a blessing. At the same time, Cookie became increasingly visible, standing by her husband for photo shoots and television interviews, including a confessional with Oprah Winfrey. Her public devotion to Johnson conveyed a powerful message: he had left his promiscuity in the past. Her presence also helped quiet rumors that he was gay. Cookie insisted that their marriage was strong, and she wasn't afraid to be with him. Pictures of the Johnson family on the covers of *People*, *Ebony*, and *Jet* reminded Americans that he was a good Christian family man. More than any other performance, the demonstration of the health of his wife, child, and marriage helped preserve his image.[15]

In the wake of Johnson's announcement, reporters filed stories about the promiscuous world of the NBA, a fantasy island where the league's stars were hounded by villainous "freaks," "groupies," and "skeezers"—women who were determined to hook up with a baller, whether only for the night or for something more permanent. The players boasted that they could find companionship just about anywhere; NBA arenas, nightclubs, bars, and hotel lobbies were filled with vamps. According to reports, some players shared the same escorts when they traveled on the road, a frightening thought for NBA executives who worried that players would become entrapped, blackmailed, or, worst of all, infected with HIV. According to the *Los Angeles Times*, one woman invited an NBA player to her home on the condition that he provide her with a pair of autographed sneakers. When the player arrived, he found nearly one hundred pairs of signed basketball shoes.[16]

Yet the exaggerated narrative that NBA players were targeted and victimized by shrewd man-eaters diminished the fact that many of these women defied submissive roles and embraced a form of sexual liberation. They rejected the double standard that celebrated men like Magic Johnson for their sexual conquests. Writing for *Esquire*, E. Jean Carroll suggested that the women who pursued professional basketball players were not all gold diggers chasing paternity suits. Rather, they believed "the morals of men and women are the same and refuse to be reduced to the role of sexual objects purely for the pleasure of men. No. These young ladies are the philosophers of the future. They turn *men* into sexual objects. Into beautiful creatures to be won."[17]

Michael Jordan believed that Magic Johnson's travails with HIV set off "an alarm clock" for the entire country. Johnson's HIV scare meant that Jordan could not avoid questions about the NBA's sexual culture or the nation's AIDS crisis. In the age of HIV/AIDS, he said, professional basketball players could no longer ignore the risks of the playboy lifestyle. Johnson inhabited Jordan's worst nightmare, a public scandal that threatened to destroy everything—his reputation, his career, and his family. In the public imagination, though, Jordan, unlike Johnson, was celebrated as a clean-living family man, completely devoted to his wife and children. His fans could hardly imagine him being unfaithful to his wife, Juanita. The beautiful couple, observed a writer from *Ebony*, "have built a solid, loving marriage despite his fame and hectic lifestyle." The image of their harmonious family life was crafted for the public at a time when conservatives lamented the "decline" of the Black family, what Vice President Dan Quayle called "the breakdown of family structure, personal responsibility, and social order." In contrast, the Jordans appeared the ideal family even though they had their first son out of wedlock in 1988, a story Chicago reporters avoided per Michael's request.[18]

The truth was that Jordan had a much bigger secret. Before their September 1989 wedding, he dragged his feet to the altar. He had met Juanita four years earlier, when a mutual friend introduced them at a restaurant after a Bulls home game. At the time, Juanita was an executive secretary for the American Bar Association. Six months later, they began dating "seriously," she said, but after Michael proposed on New Year's Eve in 1987, they agreed to break off the engagement. After about a year, they began making wedding plans again when Juanita discovered she was pregnant. Jordan's parents suggested that she trapped him with the pregnancy, leaving him no choice but to marry her. His unwillingness to commit to Juanita compelled her to hire Chicago attorney Michael Minton. Threatening a paternity suit, Minton employed a private detective named Ernie Rizzo. The notorious gumshoe who worked celebrity cases found Jordan in "compromising situations" with a half dozen women. Within a few months, Jordan admitted paternity and married Juanita at the Little White Chapel in Las Vegas in a 3:30 a.m. ceremony.[19]

Three months after the wedding, however, Jordan began a casual affair, reportedly one of many during his career. In the spring of 1989, after being introduced to her by NBA referee Eddie F. Rush, Jordan began calling Karla Knafel, an aspiring blonde singer from Indianapolis. Over the next two years, they saw each other infrequently in different NBA cities. When Knafel became pregnant in 1991, she thought the baby belonged to Jordan, but after her daughter was born, blood and DNA testing proved he was not the father. Nonetheless, Jordan had agreed to pay her $250,000 to keep the affair quiet. Jordan claimed that he paid her hush money only because she had blackmailed him.[20]

Jordan feared that if anyone knew about the affair, it would destroy his marriage and tarnish his hallowed reputation. But he didn't have to worry about Chicago reporters exposing him. Jordan was untouchable then, insulated by a fawning legion of writers all too eager to ingratiate themselves with him. "We protected him more than I'd like to admit," Sam Smith said. After games, Smith recalled, the local writers would get together in the locker room and try to clean up Jordan's poor grammar or incorrect use of words so that he sounded more polished in the newspapers than he did in person. Jordan benefited from a press that wanted access to him—access that lasted as long as the reporters acted more like publicists than journalists. Generally, Chicago writers portrayed him as a modest gentleman and the quintessential sportsman. They didn't question him about his private life or his politics. Instead, reporters offered him a forum for building a legend—until *The Jordan Rules* hit the shelves.[21]

"Sam Smith wrote a book that was total bullshit." That was Jerry Krause's review, anyway.[22]

In November 1991, about three weeks into the new NBA season, Smith's book, an unfiltered reporter's diary of the Bulls' tumultuous championship season, hit the shelves. The book revealed Jordan's arrogance and his spiteful and sometimes petulant behavior. Smith's reporting surfaced all sorts of gossip about conflicts on the Bulls—the players' jealousies over Jordan's fame; backbiting among teammates over playing time; fights during practice; and the players' open disdain for Jerry Krause. It also raised questions about Smith's sources.

Readers wondered who told the reporter what happened behind closed doors. Jordan's teammates? Phil Jackson? Jerry Reinsdorf? (Answer: all of them.)

The endless speculation preoccupied sportswriters and fans for weeks. It all began when the *Chicago Sun-Times*—Smith's rival paper—tried to beat the *Tribune* in releasing a "sneak peek at the contents." In his November 11 column, *Sun-Times* scribe Jay Mariotti suggested he had read portions of the book. But Smith's publisher had not yet shipped galleys or review copies, though excerpts were given to Simon & Schuster sales reps and editors at the *Tribune* and *Sports Illustrated*. Smith figured that Mariotti likely acquired the excerpts and then predicted that *The Jordan Rules* would "become one of the most damaging books ever written about a sports team."[23]

The hype from Mariotti helped Smith sell a *New York Times* bestseller that nine publishers had rejected. Most New York publishers didn't believe a book about Jordan and the Bulls—a team that had not yet won the championship—would sell outside Chicago. Smith was undeterred, however. He hadn't set out to write an exposé that would shatter Jordan's Madison Avenue image. Rather, his goal was to take readers behind the scenes and on the road with the Bulls. He didn't plan on writing a book focused exclusively on Jordan, either; he wanted it to be about *the team*. In fact, his literary agent came up with the title. Smith patterned his approach after David Halberstam's *The Breaks of the Game*, a chronicle of the Portland Trail Blazers' 1979–1980 season. When Smith started the research process, he told every player on the Bulls, as well as the coaches, that he planned to write a book about the season. He explained that he had no interest in investigating or writing about their private lives. This was a basketball story, Smith insisted.[24]

As a kid growing up in Brooklyn in the late 1950s and early 1960s, he read the New York tabloids voraciously from back to front, always starting with the sports section. Later, Smith devoured the papers on train rides commuting to Pace University, where he majored in accounting and covered sports for the student newspaper. Enchanted by Woodward and Bernstein, he aspired to become an investigative reporter. After covering city hall for the Fort Wayne *News-Sentinel*, a long way from the *Washington Post*, he took a job in DC covering Congress for an upstart news service. Three years later, he took a brief sabbatical from journalism to work as press secretary for Senator Lowell Weicker, a liberal Republican from Connecticut in the mold of Nelson Rockefeller. But he missed the newsroom, and when the *Chicago Tribune* offered him a job on the general assignment desk in 1979, he couldn't resist. Gradually, he began covering sports and gravitated toward the Bulls. As a beat reporter, he became entrenched in the organization. Traveling on the team bus and plane, he often sat near the coaches, earning the trust of Phil Jackson. And because the Bulls still practiced at the Deerfield Complex—a public health club—he became a member so that he could be within earshot of the players lifting weights.[25]

After a few years covering the team, Smith yearned for something more. There wasn't enough room in his eight-hundred-word columns to tell the larger story that he witnessed covering the Bulls. So, after conceiving the book, he found an ideal editor in Jeff Neuman, who five years earlier had published John Feinstein's *A Season on the Brink*, a bestseller about controversial Indiana University basketball coach Bob Knight. Feinstein had spawned a new genre of "insider" sports books built around a single season. After Feinstein sold millions of copies, Neuman was looking for another season on the brink.[26]

The Jordan Rules, reviewers concluded, was the most provocative sports book since Feinstein chronicled Knight and the Hoosiers. When Smith published *The Jordan Rules*, critics wondered why some of the stories from the book did not appear in his regular column. Although the book followed the team almost day by day, much of the material that he collected on background came months after the fact. When he published his column in January, for instance, he was still conducting book research for events that occurred in November. He often met with players and coaches over lunch or dinner, where he learned what happened in the huddle or the locker room. Smith didn't pry into the players' womanizing or Jordan's gambling. Covering salacious stories, he thought, was out of bounds. He cared less about uncovering scandals than reporting what happened within the confines of the team.

For the first time, an NBA reporter portrayed Jordan as a complex human being, not the one-dimensional character who appeared on a cereal box. Smith revealed that Jordan could be moody, self-absorbed, and brutally critical of his colleagues. Jordan regularly cursed and "rarely spoke with his teammates other than to taunt them with his rapier wit," he wrote. Jordan antagonized forward Stacey King for being "fat," lazy, and unable to grab a rebound. He demanded his teammates not pass the ball to Bill Cartwright in the final minutes of games, claiming the long-armed center was too clumsy to handle it. And one time during practice, after Will Perdue set a hard screen on him, Jordan erupted and punched him in the head. These stories must have made Gatorade executives squirm after launching the "Be Like Mike" campaign only a few months earlier.[27]

The tensions and divisions on the Bulls were all too common in the NBA, where the star of a team played by a different set of rules than the rest of the players. Every workplace, noted the *Sun-Times'* Richard Roeper, ranging from the local pizza shop to the largest corporations, treated some employees better than others based on their value to the business. "It's sort of the American way," he wrote. The only difference in this case was that the office drama involved Michael Jordan.[28]

Smith's critics, many of whom never read *The Jordan Rules*, attacked him for trying to tarnish the reputation of Chicago's great hero. Angry fanatics sent hate mail and made threatening phone calls. Some Chicagoans claimed he had betrayed the city and the team, as if Smith was supposed to be a Bulls cheerleader. Jordan suggested that the writer had broken the sacred sports code: what happens in the locker room stays in the locker room. But that rule didn't apply to reporters. They were outsiders. "Sam," Jordan said, "tried to make it seem like he was a friend of the family for eight months." But he was just trying to dig up dirt on him and make money, Jordan claimed. He fumed about writers who had once toasted him as a great role model but now picked him apart like vultures.[29]

Jerry Krause groaned that Smith's book was a work of fiction. He resented being depicted as the frumpy team schlub. "Sam Smith calls me slovenly," he said to one of the assistant coaches. "Have you ever seen me slovenly?" Krause obsessed over the book, underlining passages, mostly unflattering sections about him, that he said were totally false. He told Phil Jackson that he had identified 176 lies in the book. "One hundred and seventy-six lies," Jackson recalled. Krause started going over every single one of them until Jackson interrupted him and said, "Jerry, you have to let go." But he couldn't. Krause wished death upon Sam Smith— and just about every reporter who crossed his path. About a week after the book's release, when the Bulls traveled to Los Angeles for a game with the Clippers, Krause exited the Marina Del Ray Ritz Carlton, crossed the parking lot, and boarded the team bus; there, he noticed an unfamiliar gray-haired man wearing glasses sitting near the front. "Who's that?" Krause asked in an agitated voice. Someone told him it was David Halberstam, a Pulitzer Prize–winning reporter who was working on a profile of Jordan for *Sports Illustrated*. Krause replied loudly enough for everyone to hear, "He's a whore. They're all whores."[30]

If there was one thing Krause and Jordan shared, it was a growing distrust of the press. Up until the past year, the media had mostly helped Jordan sell his greatest product: himself. Or at least the version of himself that he wanted the world to buy. As he became more successful, however, expanding his endorsements and commercials, Jordan became more vulnerable to scrutiny. The press had changed a great deal since he arrived in Chicago in 1984. Back then, most of the media members who covered him regularly were familiar faces he knew well and generally trusted. By the time he won his first title, though, that group of recognizable faces had transformed into a horde of strangers who began chipping away at his protective armor. "The dynamic had changed," Halberstam noted. Jordan wanted to protect his good name but the press, he believed, wanted to besmudge it. "Many a president and movie star had undergone much the same process before him—but his withdrawal, his occasionally hostile tone, and his lack of time for them surprised some of his old friends in the press corps," Halberstam wrote. "He was, they sensed, for all his immense success, beginning to think of himself in some way as a victim of the very system that had helped create him."[31]

Jordan claimed he never read Smith's book. Many who did thought *The Jordan Rules* humanized him and relieved some of the pressure of celebrity. The book, Phil Jackson thought, "had a liberating effect on him. He realized he didn't have to be Mr. Perfect all the time, and that freed him to find out who he really was." But that freedom came at a cost, Jordan said. "People say they wish they were Michael Jordan," he told *Sun-Times* reporter Mark Vancil. "OK, do it for a year. Do it for two years. Do it for five years. When you get past the fun part, then go do the part where you get into cities at three a.m., and you have fifteen people waiting for autographs when you're tired as hell. Your knees are sore, back's sore, your body's sore, and yet you have to sign fifteen autographs at three in the morning."[32]

And what if Jordan didn't stop to sign autographs, like the time the Bulls arrived at their Denver hotel in the middle of the night? Jordan pleaded with a crowd, "I'm sorry, please, I'm tired." Then he walked away. Disappointed, someone muttered, "I guess that's the Jordan rules."[33]

The most famous quote Michael Jordan gave to Sam Smith didn't appear in the pages of *The Jordan Rules*. The story goes something like this: In the fall of 1990, with the midterm elections dominating the news, Smith began talking with Jordan in front of his locker stall before a game about a Senate race that attracted more national attention than any other contest. In Jordan's home state of North Carolina, longtime incumbent Republican Jesse Helms, "the wily parliamentary terrorist who routinely blocks civil rights bills," was defending his seat against Democratic challenger Harvey Gantt, the former mayor of Charlotte aiming to become the state's first Black US senator since Reconstruction. The first Black student enrolled at Clemson University, Gantt, a genial, soft-spoken architect, fully understood his role as a symbol of southern progress fighting what some commentators viewed as the "last apocalyptic battle between Old South and New." As a two-time mayor, he had successfully built an interracial coalition, earning the trust of moderate white voters. During his campaign against Helms, he refused to call the senator a racist and rarely used the terms "Black" or "African American." But when Gantt pulled ahead in the polls, his opponent appealed directly to the racial anxieties of white voters. Eight days before the election, Helms's campaign released the infamous "white hands" television commercial, an overtly racist ad that showed an unemployed white worker crumpling another rejection letter as the narrator intones, "You needed that job. You were the best qualified, but they had to give it to a minority because of a racial quota. Is that really fair? Harvey Gantt says it is." Being an old political reporter, Sam Smith couldn't help but wonder what Jordan thought about the heated election back home. Would he endorse Gantt? Jordan quipped, "Republicans buy shoes, too."[34]

That tagline would come to define Jordan as much as the slogan "Be Like Mike." But Smith didn't divulge the story in 1990. It wasn't until five years later, in his next book, *Second Coming*, that he revealed that the Gantt campaign had approached Jordan for an endorsement. In fact, one of Gantt's most enthusiastic advocates, Deloris Jordan—"Anybody over Jesse Helms"—urged her son to support the Democrat. Still, Gantt's advisers—and Jordan's agent, David Falk—were reluctant to make a formal pitch to him. Falk had long steered Jordan away from engaging in political campaigns. Besides, Falk said, Jordan was naturally apolitical, a misleading characterization belied by the fact that his client made a calculated choice not to engage politicians during his playing career but did endorse candidates after finally retiring from the Bulls in 1998. Nonetheless, Smith's impression of Jordan was that he wasn't interested in politics and didn't know the issues. Jordan scanned newspapers but didn't read books. In *Second Coming*, Smith wrote that Jordan declined Gantt's invitation and "told a friend, 'Republicans buy shoes, too.'" In retelling the story in interviews and other publications, Smith said Jordan delivered the famous line directly to him. However, Smith's initial claim that he learned of the quote secondhand is more in line with Jordan's version of the story. When Jordan finally admitted making the statement in the 2020 ESPN documentary *The Last Dance*, he recalled saying it to teammates on a bus.[35]

Those details aside, the statement contributed to an indelible impression that Jordan was "a soulless capitalist" who cared more about upsetting white people than advocating for the Black community. Perhaps what frustrated Black Americans most was not Jordan's refusal to endorse Gantt but his unwillingness to denounce Helms, a rabid segregationist. His silence has been read as a compromise: if white America was going to accept him, love

him, and idolize him, then he would have to entertain them without offending them. By refusing to endorse Gantt, Jordan made a
business calculation, refusing to risk a single customer.[36]

Many Black Americans have long believed that Black athletes
and entertainers should take a public stand against the forces of
bigotry because of their visibility and influence in America. Jordan's refusal to speak out against racism, therefore, provoked
charges that he had forgotten his roots and responsibilities. After
he won his first championship, prominent Black athletes who
joined the battle for racial equality during the civil rights era—
Arthur Ashe, Jim Brown, and Hank Aaron—scorched him for
his silence against injustice. As the most famous Black man in
America, they said, he had an obligation to use his platform for
a cause larger than himself. But Jordan didn't think it was fair
for people to expect him to jump into politics. His job, he said,
was to entertain basketball fans and relieve some of the pressures
working people experienced in everyday life. In a 1992 interview
with *Playboy*, he complained, "I got criticized for not endorsing
Harvey Gantt, the black guy who was running for the Senate
against Jesse Helms." He knew all about Helms, but Jordan said
he didn't know anything about Gantt. Yet Jordan did know something about him. In 1986, the Charlotte mayor handed Jordan the
key to the city, honoring the former Tar Heel star for inspiring
children. Ultimately, Jordan contributed to Gantt's losing Senate campaign out of consideration for his mother, but like his father, James, he thought politics was a dirty business and preferred
keeping his hands clean.[37]

When reporters asked him why he avoided politics, Jordan
often said his life experience had not equipped him for entering
the partisan arena. Growing up in the rural outskirts of Wilmington made it difficult for him to relate to the struggles plaguing

Black Americans who made up much of the urban underclass. Writing a profile of Jordan in 2020, ESPN writer Wright Thompson suggested, "The conflict between the lessons taught to him in the country and the way the city expected him to act would follow Jordan through his career: his unwillingness to endorse Harvey Gantt; Republicans buying sneakers; the attacks he took for not doing more to help stop the poverty and crime at the Henry Horner Homes, just blocks from the old Chicago Stadium." Nothing in Jordan's country upbringing, Thompson wrote, "prepared him to understand urban decay and poverty. Jordan's experience was rooted in a different kind of decay—the pervasive feeling many country folks, especially black folks, carry in their chests. Only the altar of hard work can offer a way out of this dirt."[38]

Undoubtedly, Jordan internalized a message that countless Black folks heard from their elders: the only way to succeed in America is to work twice as hard as white people. And once Jordan set his sights on an athletic career, he developed tunnel vision, a determination that no one would outwork him or distract him from his goals. His faith in rugged individualism led him to believe that people were largely responsible for their own lives. That view influenced his politics and limited his sense of obligation to help those he thought should help themselves. Charles Barkley recounted the time when he reached into his own pocket to give money to a homeless man, but Jordan swiped at Barkley's hand and said, "If he can say, 'Do you have any spare change?' then he can say, 'Welcome to McDonald's. Can I help you?'"[39]

Jordan's legendary work ethic became central to his identity. Publicists molded his success story into a meritocratic narrative that reminded Black people they could achieve anything they desired in America if they toiled as Jordan did. That fantasy transformed him into an avatar for the country's atomized individualism. In an age of dissolving social solidarity and declining voter turnout, he represented the growing number of Americans who had withdrawn from community affairs and political participation. As the civil rights movement faded into the past, Black professional athletes like Jordan who matured during the seventies and eighties, a time when the Black community lacked a unified social movement, largely avoided activism. In that regard, he wasn't exceptional.[40]

Understanding the gulf between Jordan's experience and the experience of Black professional athletes who came before him— the pioneers who had to endure segregation and fight for their positions in ways he did not—requires situating his life in the context of what Barack Obama called "the Joshua Generation." Born in 1963, the year Martin Luther King Jr. delivered his "I Have a Dream" speech during the March on Washington, Jordan entered the world at the height of the integrationist civil rights movement, though he really came of age after it passed during the late 1970s. King's generation—"the Moses Generation"— marched and fought in pursuit of justice and equality, but many of its members "didn't cross over the river to see the Promised Land." The sacrifices of the Moses Generation made life better for those who followed in their footsteps—the Joshua Generation— even if they didn't fully recognize how they benefited from the struggles of those who came before them. The Joshua Generation defined itself less in terms of protest and more through the pursuit of breakthroughs. That was Jordan. For him, being Black was about aspirations as much as it was about heritage, pursuing the promise of greatness at all costs.[41]

Yet his political insouciance provoked accusations that he did not care about the challenges facing ordinary Black people. Critics suggested his desire for a colorblind society meant he wanted the public to think of him as anything but Black. Those charges stung. "I think that kind of criticism is totally unfair," he said. "I've been trying to have people view me more as a good person than a good black man. I know I'm black. I was born black, and I'll die black." Jordan defended his Blackness by citing his sizable philanthropic contributions to various Black causes and organizations. Although Jordan understood charity, he didn't know how to advocate for social change. As much as he believed "charity starts at home," Jordan maintained he "had an obligation to all people." He had proudly built a fan base that cut across racial lines, a feat he believed reflected the goodness of the country. "All people support me and make me the success I am," he said. "So, regardless of what others say or think, I have a responsibility to help and inspire all kids to fulfill their dreams."[42]

Michael Jordan, the universal hero, belonged to everyone. And that was becoming his biggest problem.

In late December, an early Christmas present arrived in the mailboxes of Jordan's fans, a magazine that quickly became a collector's item. Copies of *Sports Illustrated*'s Sportsman of the Year issue featured a full-color holographic portrait of Jordan wearing his red-and-white team warm-up jacket on the cover. Producing the three-dimensional image required Jordan to sit on a turntable with a special movie camera focused on him. Gradually, at about 1⅓ rpm, holographer Sharon McCormick rotated Jordan 120 degrees as he smiled very slowly without blinking or moving his body. If one holds the magazine about twelve inches away from their face, tilting it left and right, Jordan's face breaks into a radiant smile, as if he is sitting right in front of the beholder. The Jordan hologram was made from a two-hundred-frame strip of film—about ten seconds' worth of action. It was a product of America's ongoing "Graphic Revolution," wherein new technologies replicated and disseminated images of celebrities manufactured by a culture that sold them as "goods and gods." Jordan fully understood that his image—the advertisement, the fabricated spectacle—represented his real power, the power to influence millions of people. It's no coincidence, then, that the most famous athlete in the world was as concerned about optics as the politicians running for office.[43]

If there was a central theme in the three articles *Sports Illustrated* published about the Sportsman of the Year, it was Jordan's unprecedented fame and the exponential expectations that came with it. "At the relatively tender age of 28," Jack McCallum wrote, "he stands alone at the mountaintop, unquestionably the most famous athlete on the planet and one of its most famous citizens of any kind." David Halberstam wrote that it had been more than thirty years since an American experienced anything near the fame Jordan did. Halberstam thought back to 1960, when he covered Elvis Presley's train ride home to Memphis after the King had served in the US Army for two years. Both stars provoked wild crowds wherever they traveled. Being hounded by mobs—swarms of people lunging at him, grabbing his clothes, and shouting in his face—made Jordan feel trapped, like a prisoner of fame, unable to step out into the sunshine. On the road, he rarely ate dinner at restaurants. Teammates and friends had to come to him.[44]

After the Bulls won the championship, his teammates immediately noticed that the spotlight that followed the team flared with an intensity that illuminated everything around them. "This is different," John Paxson observed during the team's 1991–1992 preseason. "I've been playing next to the guy for six years now, but this is a whole different level. The time I really stop and think about what is going on is when he steps to the foul line and all those hundreds of lights start flashing." It was a remarkable phenomenon. Whenever Jordan stepped to the free-throw line, countless camera flashes popped like fireworks. Every fan, Paxson said, wanted to capture the very moment they saw Michael Jordan.[45]

Jordan escaped the cameras on the golf course. Golf provided a refuge from a world that seemed to be closing in on him, a world where privacy no longer existed. During the summers, Jordan could play golf from sunrise to sundown. On the links, nobody could tug on his sleeve. He could have fun and avoid the distractions. He might have bought a fishing boat and drifted away from shore, but witnessing a boyhood friend drown made him afraid of the water. His passion for golf, however, seemed to cure him of all stress. "It's medicine for my mind," he said.[46]

Golf provided more than an escape from the ceaseless demands that came with stardom. The sport fueled his unquenchable thirst for constant action. A notorious gambler, he had an almost compulsive desire to prove a point—that he was the best at whatever game he was playing—with a bet. Whether he was playing a board game or blackjack, he had an incessant need to keep playing until he won. He simply could not walk away a loser.[47]

For a man who didn't get out much, Jordan made life more interesting gambling from his hotel room and the tee box. He could wake up in the predawn hours, play poker with friends, hit the links all day, and spend the evening at a casino table. As he became wealthier, his golf bets grew larger and larger, from $100 a hole to $1,000 a hole. Hubris and his penchant for high-stakes betting made him vulnerable to a hustler like James "Slim" Bouler, a convicted cocaine dealer who owned a pro shop and driving range in Monroe, North Carolina. Bouler first began golfing with Jordan in 1986. Five years later, just a few days before *Sports Illustrated* named Jordan Sportsman of the Year, the *Charlotte Observer* reported that federal officials had seized a $57,000 cashier's check written to Bouler from ProServ—Jordan's management agency. It turned out that while Jordan's teammates were shaking hands with President Bush, his family vacation consisted of golfing and gambling in Hilton Head.[48]

When the news broke, Jordan and Bouler told the same story: the Bulls star had given the old golf pro a loan so that he could build a driving range. But a government wiretap caught Bouler admitting that he was looking to disguise the money Jordan paid him for gambling losses so he could avoid paying taxes. At the time, the US Attorney's Office had opened an investigation into Bouler for drug trafficking and money laundering. In South Carolina, all betting, including wagers on the golf course, was illegal, a misdemeanor punishable by up to six months in prison and a $1,000 fine. Later, during Bouler's drug trial, Jordan would admit from the witness stand that he had lied to the press about loaning Bouler money to protect his image.[49]

In addition to his debts to Bouler, during his gambling spree in Hilton Head, Jordan lost more than $100,000 to Bouler's friend Eddie Dow, a money-washing bail bondsman from Gastonia, North Carolina. In February 1992, intruders broke into Dow's home, busted open his stainless-steel briefcase, and walked away with $20,000 cash after brutally murdering him. The killers left behind three checks from Jordan, totaling $108,000. Although he had nothing to do with Dow's murder and federal authorities made clear he was never an investigation target, being associated with Bouler and Dow stained his reputation and left many people questioning his judgment and character. David Stern announced the league would investigate Jordan's betting, but after warning him about his gambling partners, the commissioner did nothing except release a press statement saying there was no reason for him to punish Jordan.[50]

Jordan insisted he didn't have a gambling problem. He was nothing like Pete Rose, he said, the hypercompetitive Cincinnati Reds player and manager who had bet thousands of dollars on Major League Baseball games. Knowing the accusations Isiah Thomas faced, Jordan told reporters that he never bet on NBA contests, only on himself. He admitted he'd made a mistake socializing with shady characters but maintained his right to make friendly wagers with anyone he wanted. Nothing infuriated him more than when people questioned or criticized his gambling, but in the long run the scandals didn't cost him his fan base. After all, millions of Americans placed wagers on sporting events and saw nothing immoral about it. During the 1990s, when the gaming industry surged, the stigma around gambling became less acute. James Jordan felt the need to defend his son, reminding the press that he was only human. "We are going to have to realize after a while Michael is not God, okay? I feel like Michael should live just like he wants to live."[51]

Jordan's affinity for gambling was rooted in his family's experience in rural North Carolina. Dating back generations, the Jordans worked the cropland in the farm towns near Wilmington. They knew all too well how the elements of chance could shape their lives, how nothing was certain, not even tomorrow. It was a life of unpredictable harvests. Storms and droughts ruined crops. Plows broke down. Farm cattle died. Fieldhands got sick. The list of calamities was endless. Growing up near the country, Jordan never labored on the farm, but he learned that danger often came with life's thrills. One time, when he was riding a horse on his family's land, it bucked him off and his foot got caught in the stirrup. The horse dragged him through a cornfield for about a quarter mile, leaving him bruised and scratched. When he was about six years old, he decided to chop wood with an axe in his backyard. He swung it and nearly sliced off his big toe. Blood spouted everywhere. He screamed as he hopped into the house. A neighbor woman came over to treat him and mistakenly poured kerosene instead of alcohol on his toe. He howled in pain when the doctor stitched it together. Around the same time, he and his brothers thought it would be great fun to slip beneath an electrified hog pen and provoke wild pigs into chasing them. When an aggravated swine attacked Michael, he tried leaping over the fence, but the top wire snagged him and burned his chest. It's no wonder he grew up thinking he would die young.[52]

Those experiences influenced Jordan's outlook on life. He lived moment to moment, seeking the next thrill, the next conquest. That's why he couldn't sit still. That's why he wanted the ball in his hands at the end of the game. Carpe diem. Every wager, whether it was over basketball, cards, or golf, represented something more than his competitiveness. It reflected his desire for independence, the freedom to determine how he would play—to live by his own set of rules.

Yet the confines of fame made it increasingly difficult for him to break free. He grew weary of the countless worshippers who drove by his house. Day and night, fans left flowers, cards, signs, basketballs, and other devotional tokens on his lawn so frequently that his home started to resemble a shrine. There was hardly any buffer between him and the outside world. Increasingly, he felt besieged. He needed space, a sanctuary that could protect him and his family.

In the summer of 1991, a construction crew broke ground on seven acres of forested property in Highland Park, thirty miles north of Chicago. There, Jordan would build a fifty-six-thousand-square-foot palace with an entrance road that seemed as long as Michigan Avenue. If he never wanted to leave home, the villa had everything he needed: nine bedrooms, fifteen bathrooms, and a garage suitable for fourteen cars. It included a home theater, wine cellar, smoking room, casino lounge, full training gym, regulation-sized basketball court, tennis courts, and putting greens. A twelve-foot fence with security cameras surrounded the entire estate. No stranger could knock on his front door. Not even Superman enjoyed a fortress of solitude as impenetrable as the one at 2700 Point Lane.[53]

On November 22, 2016, Michael Jordan received the Presidential Medal of Freedom from President Barack Obama at the White House in Washington, DC. During his tenure as president, Obama gave the Medal of Freedom to three basketball players: Jordan, Kareem Abdul-Jabbar, and Bill Russell. Credit: Pete Souza/Executive Office of the President of the United States

Epilogue

THE LAST DANCE

"Politically speaking, I'm a follower, not a leader. There are things I'd like to change. But there are lots of people who know more and are in a better position to make those changes than I am."

—Michael Jordan, 1992

"I really think that when I'm done [playing basketball] I will take a bigger stand in social and political things. I look at someone like Jackie Robinson, and I see that he became a lot more outspoken after he left the game. Same with Hank Aaron. Because you have more time and energy to devote to causes. I anticipate that happening to me, too . . . I want to do that. But don't criticize me now."

—Michael Jordan, 1998, his last season with the Bulls

This time, Michael Jordan couldn't pass up the White House's invitation. In the East Room, on November 22, 2016, President Barack Obama, a longtime basketball enthusiast, presented an extraordinary collection of artists, actors, athletes, and innovators with the Presidential Medal of Freedom, the highest civilian honor. The medal was a tribute, Obama said, "to the idea that all of us, no matter where we come from, have the opportunity to change this country for the better." The idea that America was a land of possibilities ran throughout his presidency—and Jordan's career. For many Americans, Obama and Jordan were redemptive figures, powerful Black symbols who had helped the country move closer to the nation's democratic promise. Both men had pledged that they would represent everyone, not just Black people, a commitment complicated by the country's racial politics. And both, in their own way, struggled under the weight of public expectations that they should or could rise above racial divisions while critics accused them of being too cautious, muted even, when they were most needed to confront racism and injustice.[1]

If Obama and Jordan could relate to the challenges of representing multiple constituencies, they also found common ground over a love for basketball, a sport that had given them a sense of purpose and community. Like Jordan, when Obama was growing up in the seventies, he thought of the basketball gym as a democratic arena of teamwork and fair play, as a space for building his identity as a young Black man. Playing basketball taught him that "respect came from what you did and not who your daddy was." In his memoir, *Dreams from My Father*, Obama reflected on what the game meant to him as a teenager coming of age in Hawaii: "On the basketball court I could find a community of sorts, with an inner life all its own. It was there that I would make my closest white friends, on turf where blackness couldn't be a disadvantage."[2]

In Obama's America, basketball helped build bridges across the nation's racial divide. The drama of assimilation played out on the court, propelling wider acceptance of Black people in the larger culture. At least, that's what Obama and so many others liked to believe. Maybe there's some truth to it. Maybe white America's acceptance of Jordan helped the country embrace its first Black president. Maybe. But in awarding Jordan the Medal of Freedom, Obama honored a man who vividly defied the limits of Black excellence, a man who illustrated the president's faith and optimism in the vitality of the American Dream.

Living in Chicago during the late 1980s, Obama gained great admiration for Jordan, not just as a basketball player but for how he redefined the way Americans viewed Black athletes. Back then, when Obama was just starting his political career, he could not imagine entering Jordan's ironclad circle of trust. He couldn't even afford tickets to Bulls games. Years later, however, their paths crossed after Obama made a name for himself as an Illinois state senator from Hyde Park. In 2004, Jordan took notice of the Democrats' rising star and donated $10,000 to his US Senate campaign, an endorsement that drew headlines across Illinois. For whatever reason, though, Jordan didn't donate to his 2008 presidential campaign; he did, however, admit to being quite moved when Obama became the first Black president. "I was cryin' like a damn baby," he said. Four years later, during Obama's reelection campaign against Republican Mitt Romney, Jordan joined David Stern as cohost of the incumbent's basketball fundraiser— the Obama Classic, which included a $20,000-a-plate dinner in New York. If Jordan once worried about alienating Republicans, he now recognized that endorsing a candidate from another party posed little risk to him or his bottom line.[3]

During the 2016 White House ceremony, Obama praised Jordan, a six-time NBA champion and the lone Black majority owner of an NBA franchise, for changing American culture and promoting corporate diversity. As the first former NBA player in history to become the primary owner of a team and one of three Black American billionaires, Jordan had amassed unprecedented wealth and power. For all the criticism he faced during his playing career for separating himself from the politics of Black advancement, as the principal owner* of the Charlotte Hornets, he ensured his club hired more people of color in top executive positions than any other organization in North American team sports. And since its inception in 1997, Nike's Jordan Brand has always had a Black American CEO. Unquestionably, "Jordan, Inc." has been far more effective promoting Black empowerment than Michael Jordan the basketball player. But Jordan, Inc., a product of the eighties and nineties, would not exist without the player-turned-pitchman avoiding politics and activism during his career with the Bulls. In the end, cultivating the mystique he created as a player made it possible for the CEO of Jordan, Inc. to build an empire that advocates for social justice today.[4]

After purchasing a majority stake in the NBA's Charlotte franchise from media mogul Robert Johnson—the first Black owner in league history—in 2010, Jordan occupied a rare position in the world of sports, moving beyond labor, beyond performance, and into the ruling class. It was a monumental achievement, the culmination of a career devoted to entrepreneurship and breaking barriers. But it came with a new set of responsibilities. Never was this more evident than in 2014, when Jordan denounced racist comments made by Los Angeles Clippers owner Donald Sterling. A secretly recorded rant during an argument between Sterling and his mistress revealed that the Clippers' owner viewed his franchise as a plantation: he was the boss and the players owed him gratitude for his munificence. Sterling fumed that he did not want Black fans attending Clippers' games and that he didn't want his girlfriend being seen with Magic Johnson. After the story broke, Jordan expressed outrage, calling Sterling's words "sickening" and "offensive."

---

* In June 2023, Michael Jordan agreed to sell his majority stake in the Charlotte Hornets to an investment group led by Gabe Plotkin and Rick Schnall for an approximately $3 billion valuation. The sale ended Jordan's thirteen-year stretch as the team's owner and it meant that the NBA no longer had a Black majority owner.

There was no place in the NBA for Sterling. "In a league where the majority of players are African-American, we cannot and must not tolerate discrimination at any level," Jordan said. Ultimately, NBA commissioner Adam Silver and the league's team owners forced Sterling to sell the franchise and banned him from the sport.[5]

Being the lone Black majority owner and the most famous player in NBA history meant Jordan's words carried enormous weight. He had never publicly expressed such anger against racism. In the past, when he was still a player, he saw little benefit involving himself in political debates or civil rights issues. He didn't see a role for himself joining a movement or an organization where he could not directly influence an outcome. That required ceding too much control to others. But this time it was personal. His statement revealed that he was willing to speak out against racism when it directly affected him. Without saying Jordan's name, Sterling's hate speech was as much an attack on him, his place in the NBA, and everything he had built. There was no way Jordan could continue doing business with a bigot.[6]

A reckoning was coming to the NBA and professional sports. Since the Jordan era began in the 1980s, Black professional athletes had remained conspicuously absent from public protests against racism. That began to change in 2012 when LeBron James, Dwayne Wade, and the other Black players on the Miami Heat posed for a picture bowing their heads and donning hoodies. The gesture honored the life of Trayvon Martin, an unarmed Black teenager who was followed, shot, and killed while wearing a hoodie in Sanford, Florida, by a "neighborhood watchman" named George Zimmerman. Martin's death, the unrest in Ferguson, Missouri, in the aftermath of Michael Brown's killing at the hands of a police officer in 2014, and several other highly visible cases of police brutality and unjust shootings against Black men inspired a new movement: Black Lives Matter.

The Black Lives Matter mobilization of activists drew the attention and involvement of Black athletes across professional and amateur sports in unprecedented numbers, a stark contrast to the Jordan era. Much had changed since the early 1990s, when Jordan refused to say anything publicly about Rodney King being attacked by the LAPD or the uprising that ripped through Los Angeles a year later. In March 1991, King, an unarmed Black motorist, led the police on a high-speed chase that ended when officers stopped him, pulled him out of the car, and beat him with batons for fifteen minutes. When another dozen officers arrived on the scene, none of them intervened on King's behalf. They just watched as four of their colleagues bludgeoned him unconscious—a horrific scene recorded by a local resident. King suffered skull fractures, shattered bones, broken teeth, and permanent brain damage. The raw footage stunned television audiences and sparked outrage across the country. Although the four officers were arrested and charged, a jury acquitted them in April 1992, igniting six days of riots in Los Angeles. Several LA radio stations called the Bulls, urging Jordan to make a public plea for an end to the violence, but he never replied. When pressed on why he had nothing to say about the turbulence in Los Angeles, Jordan replied, "I need to know more about it."[7]

Twenty-five years after the Rodney King beating, Black athletes discovered that linear racial progress was a myth after all. For all the talk about the emergence of a postracial America between the ascendance of Michael Jordan and the election of Barack Obama, suddenly young Black athletes confronted the truth and their own place in the struggle for freedom, power, and equality. Black athletes recognized how their enormous visibility and value to sports and media organizations gave them untapped power—economic power, political power, and cultural power. But that power existed only if they wielded it for change. At the same time, Black Lives Matter created rising expectations for them to join the movement—and lead, in some cases. In an age when most pro athletes engage in social media, there was no escaping the stories and videos about police brutality and claiming ignorance as Jordan once did. "It was one thing to isolate Rodney King, quite another to ignore the list of names and every viral video on Twitter and Facebook of African Americans that grew so fast that people couldn't remember every grisly incident—or the acquittals of the officers who did the killing and walked free," wrote ESPN's Howard Bryant.[8]

On July 13, 2016, standing on a Los Angeles theater stage, NBA stars LeBron James, Dwayne Wade, Chris Paul, and Carmelo Anthony opened the ESPY awards show urging their peers to help them heal a nation fractured by racism, police brutality, and gun violence. The players cited the athlete-activists of the past, including Muhammad Ali, Arthur Ashe, Kareem Abdul-Jabbar, and others, who had redefined the meaning of leadership in sports. Following in their footsteps, James said, meant that professional athletes must renounce violence and help rebuild divided communities. His message occurred against the backdrop of a torrent of confrontations between protestors and police. In the first half of July, the *New York Times* reported, there were at least 112 protests in 88 American cities. Outraged by police violence against Black people, in Dallas and Baton Rouge, unconnected lone gunmen ambushed, shot, and killed officers—eight total in the two cities, raising fears of widespread Black retaliation against police, a fear that never materialized. The violence in America had become so pervasive that Michael Jordan finally declared, "I can no longer stay silent."[9]

In a cautious open letter shared with ESPN's Undefeated website, Jordan persisted in the same guise of universal hero as he always had, trying not to offend the pro-police crowd in Middle America by supporting the Black community exclusively. As a proud American and a Black man, he expressed sadness for "the deaths of African-Americans at the hands of law enforcement" and anger over "the cowardly and hateful targeting and killing of police officers." Calling for peace and unity, he wrote, "I have decided to speak out in the hope that we can come together as Americans." Citing the dedication of law enforcement officers who had protected him and his family for years, not to mention the investigators who worked to solve his father's murder in 1993, Jordan conveyed his admiration for cops who worked jobs that were often dangerous. He also recognized that there were Black folks who had very different experiences with police than he did. Imploring his fellow Americans to embrace colorblindness as his parents had taught him, Jordan stated that Black people deserved better treatment from police and that officers deserved respect and support from the public they served. Hoping to build a bridge between the Black community and law enforcement, he announced $1 million donations to two organizations: the NAACP Legal Defense Fund and the Institute for Community-Police Relations.[10]

Increasingly, in the age of Black Lives Matter, Jordan couldn't ignore the bloodshed on America's streets. In the summer of 2020, millions of Americans participated in nationwide demonstrations against racism and police violence, the largest wave of protests in the country's history. In late May, shortly after a Minneapolis police officer suffocated to death a forty-six-year-old Black man named George Floyd, an unprecedented number of protests took place across the country in large cities and small towns. According to the *New York Times*, by early July, the United States had witnessed more than 4,700 demonstrations, or an average of 140 per day. In response to Floyd's murder and the largest social movement of Jordan's lifetime, the owner of the Charlotte Hornets issued a statement of support for peaceful protests against police brutality: "I am deeply saddened, truly pained and plain angry. I see and feel everyone's pain, outrage and frustration. I stand with those who are calling out the ingrained racism and violence toward people of color in our country. We have had enough."[11]

In partnership with Nike's Jordan Brand, he announced a Black Community Commitment, pledging $100 million over ten years to organizations dedicated to promoting social justice, economic opportunity, and access to education, a substantial contribution that could not be dismissed by cynical pundits. One of Jordan's longtime critics, African American columnist William Rhoden, praised him for "joining the war against racism." Fifteen years earlier, in his provocative book, *$40 Million Slaves: The Rise, Fall, and Redemption of the Black Athlete*, Rhoden skewered Jordan for abdicating any responsibility to the Black community "with an apathy that borders on treason." During his playing career, Rhoden wrote, Jordan's competitiveness fueled his "willingness to criticize publicly and abrasively anyone he deemed counter to his cause." Winning was all that mattered. "No one was spared: coaches, teammates, front-office staff. He reveled in confrontation. Except when it came to confronting racism."[12]

Nothing more vividly illustrated Rhoden's argument than ESPN's ten-part docuseries *The Last Dance*, a film centered around Jordan's desire for greatness at any cost. In April and May 2020, during a pandemic that deprived sports fans of any live content, ESPN Films filled the void, delivering two episodes per night for five consecutive Sundays. *The Last Dance* became a must-see national television event that evoked nostalgia for a time when Jordan reigned the sports world. Viewers were promised exclusive never-before-seen footage documenting the Chicago Bulls' final championship run during the 1997–1998 season. Yet the film is less about the Bulls' journey as a team than it is about Jordan's entire career in Chicago.

Director Jason Hehir frames the rise of Jordan around his brilliance and his ruthlessness, how he had to overcome his own internal struggles with perfectionism and the perceived weaknesses of those around him. Repeatedly, viewers witness Jordan's competitiveness in the extreme: during practices and road trips, he pounds his teammates into submission, forcing them to capitulate to his will. The glorification of him bullying teammates—and Jerry Krause—on-screen goes largely unchallenged and becomes central to his success story, validated by Jordan's six championship rings. "Winning has a price," he says. "And leadership has a price. So, I pulled people along when they didn't want to be pulled."[13]

The portrait of Michael Jordan in *The Last Dance* is not entirely flattering, but it reflects his vision of himself as the greatest basketball player who ever lived. When Mandalay Sports Media producer Michael Tollin pitched the project to Jordan on June 23, 2016, the same day LeBron James and the Cavaliers held their championship victory parade in Cleveland, he convinced Jordan that *now* was the time to make the film. After leading the Cavs to the NBA championship in a historic comeback from a 3–1 series deficit to the Golden State Warriors, a team that had won a record seventy-three regular season games, James came to believe that *he* was the greatest basketball player who ever lived—a view shared by countless basketball fans. The question—James or Jordan?—fueled debates on sports talk shows and social media. Tollin stressed how *The Last Dance* could remind people—and educate a new generation of fans who wore Jordan's shoes but had not seen him compete in his prime—that the greatest player in history wore a Chicago Bulls jersey. Jordan liked that idea and said, "I'm in."[14]

Tollin admitted that *The Last Dance*—coproduced with the NBA, ESPN, Netflix, and Jordan's production company, Jump 23—is not an example of investigative journalism. Nor is it an objective documentary intended to uncover the truth. Rather, it's another product endorsed by Jordan, an uncontested exercise in mythmaking designed to polish his brand. Although he is not the most reliable narrator for explaining what his life has meant to others, Jordan has long understood the power of television and how the medium can enhance his image. Back in 1997, when NBA Entertainment president Adam Silver—today, the league commissioner—persuaded the Bulls to let a film crew follow the team for an entire season, Jordan agreed on one condition: the tapes could not be released without his approval. So, for nearly twenty years, the archival footage from the Bulls' last championship season, more than five hundred hours of film, sat unexamined in the NBA Entertainment archives in New Jersey until Jordan agreed to participate in the production of *The Last Dance*.[15]

From the moment NBA Entertainment began filming his last season with the Bulls until ESPN released *The Last Dance*, Jordan made sure that he remained in total control over his story, revealing very little about his private life or his family. He retained final approval over the involvement of anyone interviewed for the film and reviewed the rough cut, offering notes to the director before its release. The result, noted sportswriter Will Leitch, is that virtually every talking head, a group that includes countless NBA legends, teammates and rivals, appears on-screen only to bolster the Jordan legend. His contemporaries can only recount his greatness and ferocity on the court but have little to say about him as a person without a basketball in his hand. Jordan remains closed off, distant from teammates who once shared the joy of a championship locker room. Now that joy is long gone. After the series aired, several of his former teammates, including Scottie Pippen, complained that the film diminished them just as Jordan did during their playing days when he referred to them as his "supporting cast."[16]

In *The Last Dance*, Michael Jordan always gets the last word. Throughout the series, whenever someone says something questionable or potentially controversial about him, Hehir hands Jordan an iPad so he can react in real time. Sitting comfortably in a stranger's living room with a whiskey glass and a cigar resting on a table at his side, Jordan, who did not want cameras in his own home, offers candid and often entertaining replies to the other interviews. Quick with a wisecrack, he spares no one who dares to challenge him or his legend. As the camera captures his reaction, Jordan becomes, in the words of critic Wesley Morris, "an incredulous Zeus in these moments, lightning bolts falling from his toga as he laughs, zapping lesser gods."[17]

The Last Dance, Morris correctly observes, does not offer any larger ideas about Jordan's place in history or American culture. It does not ask questions about race or politics in the way that Ezra Edelman did in his Academy Award–winning documentary, *OJ: Made in America* (2016), a compelling feature that explores the life and times of O. J. Simpson. Instead, Hehir's film, like its protagonist, looks inward, away from the broader world. It spends about as much time showing Jerry Seinfeld wandering through the Bulls' locker room as it does on Jordan's refusal to campaign for Harvey Gantt. "The doc's myopia is Jordan's myopia," noted *Mother Jones* editor Jacob Rosenberg. "Its obliviousness is his obliviousness. It can't see beyond the basketball to realize that it is telling a deeply political story in spite of itself."[18]

Ultimately, though, for Jordan's fans, his politics and pronouncements matter far less than the way his performance on the basketball court made them feel. *The Last Dance* reminds us that making Michael Jordan into an American hero has always been about the production and repetition of manicured images and sound bites, transforming his life story into a series of highlights and clips that we have seen repeatedly but can't quite get enough of. Yet Jordan himself remains elusive and untouchable, a man living with no regrets or any acknowledgment of weakness. In the end, the mystique endures in the public mind precisely as Jordan imagines himself: invincible and triumphant.

ACKNOWLEDGMENTS

Jumpman is built on a vast literature about Michael Jordan and the history of the NBA. I have consulted countless books, articles, and critical essays about him. I am indebted to several outstanding writers who covered Jordan during his career. I relied especially on the work of Sam Smith, his columns in the *Chicago Tribune* and his thought-provoking book *The Jordan Rules*. I also drew extensively from David Halberstam's impressive biography, *Playing for Keeps*. Roland Lazenby's biographies of Michael Jordan and Phil Jackson proved indispensable. Anyone interested in the history of the NBA during the Jordan era should read Jack McCallum's writing at *Sports Illustrated* and his book *The Dream Team*. I also benefited from the insights of several writers who have situated Jordan in a larger context, including Wright Thompson, Howard Bryant, and William Rhoden. Their ideas influenced my interpretation of Jordan.

This book would not have been possible without the incredible support of my publisher at Basic Books, Lara Heimert. Lara has long been a champion of my writing and it is a privilege to work with a publisher who has shown such great confidence in me. Although much has been written about Michael Jordan, Lara didn't hesitate when I approached her with the idea for this book. Her encouragement helped me think more critically about how I could frame Jordan's story from a historical perspective.

Basic Books has been a great publishing home. Executive Editor Brandon Proia gave the manuscript a close reading and helped me refine my arguments. He pushed me in the right direction and found a way to make every page better. I am grateful, too, to Melissa Veronesi and Irina du Quenoy for helping me get the manuscript across the finish line.

I am especially thankful for the wisdom and enthusiasm of my literary agent at United Talent Agency, Melissa Chinchillo. Melissa is a tireless advocate for her authors, and she has made so much possible in my writing career. Thank you, Melissa.

When I decided I wanted to be an author, I knew I wanted to write books like Randy Roberts. Randy taught me just about everything I know about writing history. I am fortunate to have written three books with him. More than anyone else, he helped me find my writer's voice.

Randy and several colleagues read a draft of the manuscript and offered constructive feedback that helped me tremendously. Aram Goudsouzian is my go-to reader, and he always helps me figure out what I am trying to say and how to make it better. Ryan Swanson provided great critiques and asked thoughtful questions. Eric Hall's enthusiasm for the project made me believe that I should undertake this project and that it would succeed.

At Georgia Tech, my academic home, I benefited from the support of several people while writing this book. Writing a book during the pandemic proved challenging and stressful at times, but having caring colleagues like Dan Amsterdam, Doug Flamming, and Mary McDonald helped me find peace of mind. Hanchao Lu, chair of the School of History and Sociology, and Kaye Husbands Fealing, dean of the Ivan Allen College of Liberal Arts, made sure I had every opportunity to complete my manuscript and deliver it on time. I am especially grateful to the family of Bud Shaw, a generous supporter of Georgia Tech. The resources that come with the Shaw Professorship make it possible for me to conduct research and write. The professorship also allows me to hire outstanding graduate research assistants like Declan Abernethy and Eric Stegall. And I would be lost without the support of Administrative Manager Robert Hampson, who makes everything I do at Georgia Tech easier and more efficient.

I am most thankful of all to my family, starting with my parents, Jay and Kim. My mom taught me how to read and how to believe in myself. She nurtured my love for reading at an early age, encouraging me to check out as many books as I wanted from the local Bookmobile. My dad's subscriptions to *Sports Illustrated* and the *Sporting News* began my lifelong interest in great sports stories. I'll never forget when my dad bought me my first pair of Air Jordans at Nike Town in Chicago when I was fourteen years old. They were expensive for any working father, but he knew what they meant to me. Wearing a white pair of Air Jordans with red and black trim, a limited-release sneaker, made me feel special, like so many other kids who wore the Jumpman on their feet. Watching six NBA Finals with my brother, Paul, and sharing in the joy of those Bulls' championships remains among my greatest childhood memories. And although my sister McKenna was too young to care about Michael Jordan and the Bulls dynasty, she has always been my great fan, cheering me on.

Finally, and most importantly, I want to thank my wife, Rebecca, and my daughter, Madison. They are my inspiration and my purpose. I love you both more than words can say.

NOTES

PREFACE: THE MYSTIQUE

1. Jack McCallum, "Alone on the Mountaintop," *Sports Illustrated*, December 23, 1991, 69.

2. Bob Greene, *Hang Time: Days and Dreams with Michael Jordan* (New York: Doubleday, 1992), 24, 65–66.

3. Wright Thompson, "Michael Jordan: A History of Flight," ESPN.com, May 19, 2020.

4. David Breskin, "Michael Jordan, in His Own Orbit," *GQ*, March 1989, 397.

5. Breskin, "Michael Jordan, in His Own Orbit," 396.

6. Black scholar W. E. B. DuBois originally used the term "double consciousness" in his essay "The Strivings of the Negro People," *Atlantic*, August 1897, 194–195.

7. David Halberstam, *Playing for Keeps: Michael Jordan and the World He Made* (New York: Random House, 1999), 416–417. In 1991, *Washington Post* columnist Michael Wilbon noted that there were only four Black sports columnists nationwide and one Black sports editor at major metro newspapers. See Wilbon, "Progress Easy to Measure," *Washington Post*, August 10, 1991.

8. Gay Talese, "Silent Season of a Hero," *Esquire*, July 1966.

9. Michael Wilbon, "Needing to Play the Game Just Like Mike," *Washington Post*, January 14, 1998.

ONE: THE HERO BUSINESS

1. Bob Sakamoto, "Jordan Takes Time Out for '60 Minutes,'" *Chicago Tribune*, January 19, 1987.

2. Michael Jordan, interview by Diane Sawyer, *60 Minutes*, CBS, February 15, 1987.

3. Michael Jordan, *For the Love of the Game: My Story*, ed. Mark Vancil (New York: Crown Publishers, 1998), 5.

4. Curry Kirkpatrick, "In an Orbit All His Own," *Sports Illustrated*, November 9, 1987, 93–94.

5. Jordan gave a similar answer in other interviews. See Phil Patton, "The Selling of Michael Jordan," *New York Times Magazine*, November 9, 1986; Sally B. Donnelly,

"Great Leapin' Lizards," *Time*, January 9, 1989, 52; David Breskin, "Michael Jordan, in His Own Orbit," *GQ*, March 1989, 396; Mark Vancil, "Playboy Interview: Michael Jordan," *Playboy*, May 1992.

6. William Rhoden, *$40 Million Slaves: The Rise, Fall, and Redemption of the Black Athlete* (New York: Crown Publishers, 1996), 205.

7. Kirkpatrick, "In an Orbit All His Own," 93; Jim Naughton, "The Slam-Dunk Joy of Michael Jordan," *Washington Post*, April 14, 1990.

8. David Falk, *The Bald Truth: Secrets of Success from the Locker Room to the Boardroom* (New York: Gallery Books, 2009), 40–41; Henry Louis Gates Jr., "Net Worth," *New Yorker*, June 1, 1998, 52.

9. Lynn Norment, "Black Agents," *Ebony*, August 1992, 121; Terry Lefton, "Donald Dell: Ace Agent," *Sports Business Journal*, March 4, 2013; Eric Allen Hall, *Arthur Ashe: Tennis and Justice in the Civil Rights Era* (Baltimore: Johns Hopkins University Press, 2014), 116–117; Raymond Arsenault, *Arthur Ashe: A Life* (New York: Simon & Schuster, 2018), 261–262.

10. David Halberstam, *Playing for Keeps: Michael Jordan and the World He Made* (New York: Random House, 1999), 134–135; Jim Naughton, *Taking to the Air: The Rise of Michael Jordan* (New York: Warner Books, 1992), 69–70.

11. Bernie Lincicome, "Apologetic Bulls 'Stuck' with Jordan," *Chicago Tribune*, June 20, 1984; Maria E. Recio, "Michael Jordan Scores Big—On and Off the Court," *Business Week*, December 3, 1984, 78, 82; Francis Clines, "Reagan Delivers a Pep Talk," *New York Times*, July 29, 1984; Scott Ostler, "Newest Living Legend Really Looks the Part," *Los Angeles Times*, December 3, 1984; Michael Weinreb, *Bigger Than the Game: Bo, Boz, the Punky QB, and the Making of the Modern Athlete in the Eighties* (New York: Gotham Books, 2010), 8.

12. Breskin, "Michael Jordan, in His Own Orbit," 322.

13. Falk, *Bald Truth*, 52; Bryan Burwell, "Super Deals for Superstars," *Black Enterprise*, July 1984, 42; Jim Naughton, "Bull Market," *Washington Post Magazine*, February 9, 1992.

14. Chris Cobbs, "NBA and Cocaine: Nothing to Snort At," *Los Angeles Times*, August 19, 1980.

15. Jordan, *For the Love of the Game*, 15; Larry Platt, "The Graying of Dr. J," *Philadelphia*, May 1993, 78.

16. Curry Kirkpatrick, "The Master of Midair," *Sports Illustrated*, May 4, 1987, 80; Burwell, "Super Deals for Superstars," 37–39; Platt, "Graying of Dr. J," 77–78, 121–122; Julius Erving, interview by author, September 9, 2022.

17. Nicholas Smith, *Kicks: The Great American Story of Sneakers* (New York: Crown Publishing, 2018), 169–170.

18. J. B. Strasser and Laurie Beckland, *Swoosh: The Unauthorized Story of Nike and the Men Who Played There* (New York: HarperCollins, 1993), 424, 431–432; Falk, *Bald Truth*, 39.

19. Smith, *Kicks*, 161; Donald Katz, *Just Do It: The Nike Spirit in the Corporate World* (New York: Random House, 1994), 6, 101.

20. Strasser and Beckland, *Swoosh*, 425–429.

21. Falk, *Bald Truth*, 52.

22. George Castle, "Air to the Throne," *Sport*, January 1991, 34; Falk, *Bald Truth*, 58; Patton, "Selling of Michael Jordan."

23. Falk, *Bald Truth*, 58; Leon E. Wynter, *American Skin: Pop Culture, Big Business, and the End of White America* (New York: Crown Publishers, 2002), 93–98, 110–111; Richard Grenier, "Eddie Murphy's Comic Touch," *New York Times*, March 10, 1985; David Sirota, *Back to Our Future: How the 1980s Explain the World We Live in Now—Our Culture, Our Politics, Our Everything* (New York: Ballantine Books, 2011), 178.

24. Bob Sakamoto, "Jordan's Glamour Fills League Arenas," *Chicago Tribune*, December 16, 1986; Patton, "Selling of Michael Jordan"; Naughton, *Taking to the Air*, 137.

25. Dan Baum, *Smoke and Mirrors: The War on Drugs and the Politics of Failure* (Boston: Little, Brown, 1997), 221–226.

26. Theresa Runstedtler, "Racial Bias: The Black Athlete, Reagan's War on Drugs, and Big-Time Sports Reform," *American Studies* 55, no. 3 (2016): 85–87, 90–94; "A Killer Stalks the Locker Room," *U.S. News & World Report*, July 14, 1986, 6; "Jordan Backs Drug Tests 'For Sake of Kids,'" *Chicago Sun-Times*, September 8, 1988; Jeff Davis, "Jordan Takes Over Where Dr. J Left Off," *Fresno Bee*, June 27, 1987.

27. Breskin, "Michael Jordan, in His Own Orbit," 319–320; Bob Sakamoto, "Drug Trap No Worry to Jordan," *Chicago Tribune*, April 5, 1987; "Message from Michael," *Chicago Sun-Times*, May 8, 1987; Pete Axthelm, "Michael Jordan's Life at the Top," *Newsweek*, January 5, 1987, 47; "An All-American Drug," *Los Angeles Times*, September 21, 1986.

28. Kirkpatrick, "In an Orbit All His Own," 93.

29. Leola Johnson and David Roediger, "'Hertz, Don't It?' Becoming Colorless and Staying Black in the Crossover of O. J. Simpson," in *Birth of a Nation'hood: Gaze, Script, and Spectacle in the O. J. Simpson Case*, ed. Toni Morrison and Claudia Brodsky (New York: Random House, 1997), 203–209.

30. Kara Swisher, "O. J. and Hertz: The Rise and Fall of a Rent-A-Star," *Washington Post*, July 10, 1994; Robert Lipsyte, "O. J. Didn't Play," *New York Times*, August 2, 1969.

31. Breskin, "Michael Jordan, in His Own Orbit," 396.

32. Michelle Alexander, *The New Jim Crow: Mass Incarceration in the Age of Colorblindness* (New York: New Press, 2012), 100; Leonard Steinhorn and Barbara Diggs-Brown, *By the Color of Our Skin: The Illusion of Racial Integration and the Reality of Race* (New York: Dutton, 1999), 173; "Whites Less Biased Survey Finds; Stereotypes About Blacks, Hispanics Persist, Center Says," *Chicago Tribune*, January 9, 1991.

33. Alexander, *New Jim Crow*, 243; "Reagan Quotes King Speech in Opposing Minority Quotas," *New York Times*, January 19, 1986; Doug Rossinow, *The Reagan Era: A History of the 1980s* (New York: Columbia University Press, 2015), 149.

34. Bob Sakamoto, "The Forces Behind Jordan," *Chicago Tribune*, April 15, 1990; Donnelly, "Great Leapin' Lizards," 52; Jeff Weinstock, "In Pursuit of Michael Jordan," *Sport*, December 1991, 66; Tim Layden, "Inside Interview: David Stern," *Inside Sports*, May 1990, 23.

35. E. M. Swift, "Reach Out and Touch Someone," *Sports Illustrated*, August 5, 1991, 54.

36. Sakamoto, "Forces Behind Jordan"; Howard Bryant, *The Heritage: Black Athletes, a Divided America, and the Politics of Patriotism* (Boston: Beacon Press, 2018), 74.

37. Ron Rosenbaum, "The Revolt of the Basketball Liberals," *Esquire*, June 1995, 104; John Hoberman, *Darwin's Athletes: How Sport Has Damaged Black America and Preserved the Myth of Race* (New York: Houghton Mifflin, 1997), 34; Steinhorn and Diggs-Brown, *By the Color of Our Skin*, 144–146; Henry Louis Gates Jr., "TV's Black World Turns—But Stays Unreal," *New York Times*, November 12, 1989.

38. Breskin, "Michael Jordan, in His Own Orbit," 320.

39. Kirkpatrick, "In an Orbit All His Own," 88; Skip Bayless, "That Nasty Side to Jordan Helped Make Him Great," *Chicago Tribune*, January 17, 1999; Breskin, "Michael Jordan, in His Own Orbit," 322.

40. John Edgar Wideman, "Michael Jordan Leaps the Great Divide," *Esquire*, November 1990, 141, 210.

TWO: THE SPIKE AND MIKE SHOW

1. "It's Gotta Be the Shoes," Nike commercial, aired in 1990.

2. Donald Katz, "Triumph of the Swoosh," *Sports Illustrated*, August 15, 1993, 67.

3. David Halberstam, *Playing for Keeps: Michael Jordan and the World He Made* (New York: Random House, 1999), 183–184.

4. Katz, "Triumph of the Swoosh," 60.

5. Ann Cooper, "He Just Did It," *Advertising Age*, January 1, 1990, 13; William Schmidt, "A Growing Urban Fear: Thieves Who Kill for 'Cool' Clothing," *New York Times*, February 6, 1990.

6. Stephen W. Colford, "Athlete Endorsers Fouled by Slayings," *Advertising Age*, March 19, 1990, 64; Nick Paumgarten, "Phil Mushnick's Dangerous Game: Work for Murdoch, Blast TV Schlock," *New York Observer*, March 16, 1998; Phil Mushnick, "Sports World's Silence Deadly," *New York Post*, March 12, 1990.

7. Harold Evans, "A Typology of the Lurid," *Harper's*, September 1984, 56–59; Edwin Diamond, "The Tabloid Sports Wars," *New York*, October 21, 1985, 19–20.

8. Mushnick, "Sports World's Silence Deadly"; Phil Mushnick, "Shaddup, I'm Sellin' Out . . . Shaddup," *New York Post*, April 6, 1990.

9. Donald Katz, *Just Do It: The Nike Spirit in the Corporate World* (New York: Random House, 1994), 7; Jim Naughton, *Taking to the Air: The Rise of Michael Jordan* (New York: Warner Books, 1992), 89–90; Craig Neff, "Leaping Lizards, It's Almost Iguana," *Sports Illustrated*, November 17, 1986, 21. Sources offer conflicting figures about the total sales for the Air Jordan I, but they typically fall within the $110 million to $130 million range.

10. Nicholas Smith, *Kicks: The Great American Story of Sneakers* (New York: Crown Publishers, 2018), 176; J. B. Strasser and Laurie Beckland, *Swoosh: The Unauthorized Story of Nike and the Men Who Played There* (New York: HarperCollins, 1993), 508–509, 525–526.

11. Strasser and Beckland, *Swoosh*, 533–534; E. M. Swift, "Reach Out and Touch Someone," *Sports Illustrated*, August 5, 1991, 57; Frank Deford, "Running Man," *Vanity Fair*, August 1993, 62, 66.

12. Curry Kirkpatrick, "In an Orbit All His Own," *Sports Illustrated*, November 9, 1987, 94.

13. James Cox, "Air Jordan Ads Discover Mars," *USA Today*, February 10, 1988; Cooper, "He Just Did It," 20; Spike Lee with Ralph Wiley, *Best Seat in the House: A Basketball Memoir* (New York: Crown Publishers, 1997), 134–135; Halberstam, *Playing for Keeps*, 180–181.

14. Halberstam, *Playing for Keeps*, 182.

15. Katz, *Just Do It*, 148; Rick Reilly, "He's Gotta Pitch It," *Sports Illustrated*, May 27, 1991, 76; Stuart Mieher, "Spike Lee's Gotta Have It," *New York Times Magazine*, August 9, 1987, 26.

16. Reilly, "He's Gotta Pitch It," 82; Marcus Mabry and Rhonda Adams, "A Long Way from 'Aunt Jemima,'" *Newsweek*, August 14, 1989, 34; Halberstam, *Playing for Keeps*, 181–182.

17. Mark Whicker, "Michael Just Doesn't Have Magic Touch," *Orange County Register*, June 2, 1991.

18. Mieher, "Spike Lee's Gotta Have It," 26; Elvis Mitchell, "Playboy Interview: Spike Lee," *Playboy*, July 1991, 62.

19. Ray Fisman, "Cos and Effect," *Slate*, January 11, 2008.

20. Smith, *Kicks*, 157.

21. Bill Brubaker, "Athletic Shoes: Beyond Big Business," *Washington Post*, March 10, 1991; Katz, "Triumph of the Swoosh," 56–57.

22. Robert M. Collins, *Transforming America: Politics and Culture During the Reagan Years* (New York: Columbia University Press, 1997), 158–163; Tom Wolfe, "The Years of Living Prosperously," *U.S. News & World Report*, December 25, 1989/January 1, 1990, 117.

23. Randy Harvey, "Taking to Air," *Los Angeles Times*, April 26, 1985.

24. Rick Telander, "Senseless," *Sports Illustrated*, May 14, 1990, 37–38; Ed Bruske, "Police Theorize Arundel Youth Was Killed for His Air Jordans," *Washington Post*, May 6, 1989.

25. Telander, "Senseless," 38.

26. Chicago murder statistics compiled from the Chicago Police Department annual reports for 1989 and 1990; Carolyn Rebecca Block, "The Killing That Can Be Prevented," *Chicago Tribune*, January 22, 1991; Eric Harrison, "'Murder Epidemic' Alarms Chicago," *Los Angeles Times*, June 23, 1990; David Wilson, *Inventing Black-on-Black Violence: Discourse, Space, and Representation* (Syracuse: Syracuse University Press, 2005), 18; "The War at Home: How to Battle Crime," *Newsweek*, March 25, 1991, 35.

27. Wilson, *Inventing Black-on-Black Violence*, 48.

28. Wilson, *Inventing Black-on-Black Violence*, 134; Michael James, "Athletic Shoe Makers Accused of Catering to Violence," *USA Today*, May 7, 1990; Tony Kornheiser, "The Insidious Sneaker," *Washington Post*, March 28, 1990; John Leo, "The

Well-Heeled Drug Runner," *U.S. News & World Report*, April 30, 1990, 20; Warren Berger, "They Know Bo," *New York Times Magazine*, November 11, 1990, 48.

29. James, "Athletic Shoe Makers Accused"; Telander, "Senseless," 44.

30. Spike Lee, "Don't Blame Shoes for Society's Problems," *National Sports Daily*, April 19, 1990.

31. Lacy Banks, "NBA Report," *Chicago Sun-Times*, April 22, 1990.

32. Telander, "Senseless," 38; Fred Bayles, "The Sneaker Business Grows Up," *Los Angeles Daily News*, June 24, 1990.

33. Telander, "Senseless," 44.

34. Telander, "Senseless," 43; Phil Mushnick, "The Write Thing Ain't Right," *New York Post*, April 27, 1990; Lee, "Don't Blame Shoes."

35. Raymond Coffey, "Senseless Story Blames the Wrong People," *Chicago Sun-Times*, May 17, 1990; Joseph H. Brown, "Letter to the Editor," *Sports Illustrated*, July 2, 1990, 4.

36. C. L. Cole, "Nike's America/America's Michael Jordan," in *Michael Jordan, Inc.: Corporate Sport, Media Culture, and Late Modern America*, ed. David Andrews (Albany: State University Press of New York, 2001), 77; Telander, "Senseless," 38.

37. Bob Greene, *Hang Time: Days and Dreams with Michael Jordan* (New York: Doubleday, 1992), 207–209.

38. Marcia Froelke Cobun and Steve Rhodes, "The Sad Saga of Bob Greene," *Chicago Magazine*, March 3, 2003.

39. Bob Greene, "In Jordan's Wake, a Trail of Magic," *Chicago Tribune*, November 21, 1990; Greene, *Hang Time*, 5–12; Froelke Cobun and Rhodes, "Sad Saga of Bob Greene"; John Schulian, "Michael Jordan: Color Him Greene," *Los Angeles Times*, November 22, 1992.

40. Bob Greene, "Savor the Era of Michael Jordan," *Chicago Tribune*, June 10, 1990.

THREE: SWEET HOME, CHICAGO

1. Rick Telander, "'Da Stadium,'" *Sports Illustrated*, June 1, 1992, 67.

2. Telander, "'Da Stadium,'" 62.

3. Eric Zorn, "Glitz Meets Grit Outside the Stadium," *Chicago Tribune*, May 17, 1992; John Edgar Wideman, "Michael Jordan Leaps the Great Divide," *Esquire*, November 1990, 141–142.

4. Achy Obejas, "Waiting for the Stadium: A Walk on the West Side," *Chicago Reader*, August 27, 1987; Telander, "'Da Stadium,'" 66.

5. Alex Kotlowitz, *There Are No Children Here: The Story of Two Boys Growing Up in the Other America* (New York: Anchor Books, 1992), 156, 160.

6. Kotlowitz, *There Are No Children Here*, 8, 12–13, 159; Adam Walinsky, "What It's Like to Be in Hell," *New York Times*, December 4, 1987.

7. Kotlowitz, *There Are No Children Here*, 157.

8. Jim Naughton, *Taking to the Air: The Rise of Michael Jordan* (New York: Warner Books, 1992), 1–2.

9. David Maraniss, *Barack Obama: The Story* (New York: Simon & Schuster, 2012), 513–514.

10. Barack Obama, *Dreams from My Father: A Story of Race and Inheritance* (New York: Three Rivers Press), 141–142; David Remnick, *The Bridge: The Life and Rise of Barack Obama* (New York: Vintage Books, 2011), 142, 158–160; Andrew J. Diamond, *Chicago on the Make: Power and Inequality in a Modern City* (Oakland: University of California Press, 2017), 241–242.

11. Remnick, *Bridge*, 158–159.

12. Remnick, *Bridge*, 158–159.

13. Thomas Byrne Edsall, "Black vs. White in Chicago," *New York Review of Books*, April 13, 1989, 21–22; Dirk Johnson, "Chicago's Raw Nerve," *New York Times Magazine*, February 19, 1989, SM34.

14. Leonard Steinhorn and Barbara Diggs-Brown, *By the Color of Our Skin: The Illusion of Racial Integration and the Reality of Race* (New York: Dutton, 1999), 154; David Protess, "The News in Black and White," *Chicago Magazine*, March 1990, 15–16.

15. Naughton, *Taking to the Air*, 206.

16. Diamond, *Chicago on the Make*, 247.

17. Sam Smith, *There Is No Next: NBA Legends on the Legacy of Michael Jordan* (New York: Diversion, 2014), 18.

18. Michael Kiefer, "Chicago," *Sport*, March 1989, 66; Telander, "'Da Stadium,'" 71; Douglas Bukowski, "When the Game Mattered More Than the Skybox," *Chicago Tribune*, June 13, 1989; Ron Rosenbaum, "The Revolt of the Basketball Liberals," *Esquire*, June 1995, 104.

19. Orlando Patterson, *Rituals of Blood: Consequences of Slavery in Two American Centuries* (New York: Basic Civitas, 1998), 236; Michael Eric Dyson, "Be Like Mike? Michael Jordan and the Pedagogy of Desire," *Cultural Studies* 7, no. 1 (January 1993): 64; Jim Naughton, "The Slam-Jam Joy of Michael Jordan," *Washington Post*, April 14, 1990; Neal Gabler, *Life: The Movie* (New York: Alfred A. Knopf, 1998), 174; Dan Carson, "Reggie Miller Says Michael Jordan Once Referred to Himself as 'Black Jesus,'" *Bleacher Report*, March 6, 2015.

20. Jim O'Donnell, *Daily Herald* (Arlington Heights, IL), October 27, 1984.

21. Ralph Wiley, *What Black People Should Do Now: Dispatches from Near the Vanguard* (New York: Ballantine Books, 1993), 251.

22. Wideman, "Michael Jordan Leaps the Great Divide," 141.

23. For Bird quote see Rick Telander, "Ready . . . Set . . . Levitate!," *Sports Illustrated*, November 17, 1986, 20; Wiley, *What Black People Should Do Now*, 249; Jonathan Cohen, "Alan Parsons, Writer of Chicago Bulls' Theme Song and Former Beatles Engineer, Talks 'Sirius' and 'Let It Be,'" *Variety*, August 24, 2020.

24. Unless otherwise cited, the section on Ray Clay and the Bulls' introduction at Chicago Stadium comes from Jake Malooley, "Aaaand Now . . . An Oral History of the Greatest Starting Lineup Introduction in Sports History," *Ringer*, November 13, 2018.

25. Telander, "'Da Stadium,'" 66.

26. Bob Greene, "'And Now, the Starting Lineup . . .,'" *Chicago Tribune*, June 5, 1991.

FOUR: RAGING BULL

1. Wright Thompson, "Michael Jordan Has Not Left the Building," *ESPN The Magazine*, February 22, 2013; Filip Bondy, *Tip-Off: How the 1984 NBA Draft Changed Basketball Forever* (New York: Da Capo Press, 2007); *ESPN SportsCentury*, "Michael Jordan," aired December 26, 1999, on ESPN.

2. David Halberstam, *Playing for Keeps: Michael Jordan and the World He Made* (New York: Random House, 1999), 230.

3. Bill Simmons, "Gambling and the Alpha Dog," *ESPN The Magazine*, June 19, 2006.

4. David Halberstam, "Jordan's Moment," *New Yorker*, December 21, 1998, 48–49.

5. Michael Leahy, *When Nothing Else Matters: Michael Jordan's Last Comeback* (New York: Simon & Schuster, 2004), 386.

6. John Jackson, "Vintage Michael Shoots, Scores—Emotional Jordan Thanks Those Who Lit His Competitive Fire but Saves Best Shot for Krause," *Chicago Sun-Times*, September 12, 2009; Tom Sorenson, "The Passion: Jordan Wants to—Must—Win," *Charlotte Observer*, March 8, 1984; Halberstam, *Playing for Keeps*, 19–20; *The Last Dance*, directed by Jason Hehir, aired from April 19, 2020, to May 17, 2020, on ESPN.

7. *Last Dance*; Mark Vancil, "Playboy Interview: Michael Jordan," *Playboy*, May 1992; Roland Lazenby, *Michael Jordan: The Life* (New York: Little, Brown, 2014), 47–49.

8. Vancil, "Playboy Interview: Michael Jordan"; Michael Jordan, interview by Tim Russert, *Meet the Press*, aired on NBC, April 23, 2000.

9. Jack McCallum, "Mission Impossible," *Sports Illustrated*, November 6, 1989, 46.

10. Halberstam, *Playing for Keeps*, 241.

11. Johnette Howard, "Breakthrough," *Sport*, February 1992, 68; Lazenby, *Michael Jordan*, 402.

12. Leigh Montville, "Out of the Shadow," *Sports Illustrated*, February 24, 1992, 78–79; Sam Smith, "Pippen as Far from a Quitter as He Is from a Role Model," *Chicago Tribune*, May 17, 1994.

13. Howard, "Breakthrough," 68; Phil Jackson and Hugh Delehanty, *Sacred Hoops: Spiritual Lessons of a Hardwood Warrior* (New York: Hyperion, 1995), 53–54.

14. Jackson, *Sacred Hoops*, 54; Ben Joravsky, "Nobody Cheers for Jerry Krause," *Chicago Reader*, April 26, 1990; Mark Vancil, "Inside Interview: Phil Jackson," *Inside Sports*, October 1991, 23.

15. Jackson, *Sacred Hoops*, 127; Bryan Smith, "Inside the Start of the Chicago Bulls' Championship Run," *Chicago Magazine*, April 11, 2011.

16. Joravsky, "Nobody Cheers for Jerry Krause."

17. Smith, "Inside the Start."

18. Halberstam, *Playing for Keeps*, 262.

19. Smith, "Inside the Start"; Sam Smith, *There Is No Next: NBA Legends on the Legacy of Michael Jordan* (New York: Diversion, 2014), 136–137.

20. Unless cited otherwise, this section on Jordan and Grover draws from Halberstam, *Playing for Keeps*, 267–271.

21. Tim Grover with Shari Lesser Wenk, *Relentless: From Good to Great to Unstoppable* (New York: Scribner, 2013), 10–12.

22. Grover, *Relentless*, 12.

23. The editors of *GQ*, "Michael Jordan's Trainer, Tim Grover, on Counting MJ's Steps and Carrying His Clubs," *GQ*, April 17, 2020.

24. Lazenby, *Michael Jordan*, 405–406, 411.

25. Lazenby, *Michael Jordan*, 407; Michael Wilbon, "How to Push When the Shoe's on the Other Foot," *Washington Post*, August 17, 1990; Eric Harrison and Bruce Horovitz, "Nike Feels Heat, Sets Minority Goals," *Los Angeles Times*, August 18, 1990; Lillian Williams, "Nike Exploits Blacks, Jackson Says," *Chicago Sun-Times*, July 26, 1990; Jim Naughton, *Taking to the Air: The Rise of Michael Jordan* (New York: Warner Books, 1992), 213.

26. "When Shove Came to PUSH," *Economist*, September 22, 1990, 28; William Braden, "Nike Favored over PUSH in Chicago Poll," *Chicago Sun-Times*, September 14, 1990; Isabel Wilkerson, "Challenging Nike, Rights Group Takes a Risky Stand," *New York Times*, August 25, 1990.

27. Phil Jackson, "Where the Zen Master Finds Inner Peace," *Wall Street Journal*, September 19, 2013.

28. Jackson, *Sacred Hoops*, 131; Sam Smith, "Jackson Teaches Bulls to Win," *Chicago Tribune*, June 2, 1991; Phil Jackson and Hugh Delehanty, *Eleven Rings: The Soul of Success* (New York: Penguin Books, 2014), 80.

29. Jackson, *Eleven Rings*, 96–97; Roland Lazenby, *Mindgames: Phil Jackson's Long Strange Journey* (Chicago: Contemporary Books, 2001), 158–159.

30. Jackson, *Sacred Hoops*, 100–101; Sam Smith, "Less from Jordan, More for Bulls?," *Chicago Tribune*, October 5, 1990; Harley Tinkham, "Bulls Have a Play for When It's Beyond 'Hail Mary' Time," *Los Angeles Times*, May 28, 1990.

31. Naughton, *Taking to the Air*, 30–31.

32. Dave Hoekstra, "The Offense Even Bulls Don't Understand," *Chicago Sun-Times*, December 23, 1990.

33. Dan Devine, "How the Point-MJ Experiment Foreshadowed the Modern NBA," *Ringer*, March 11, 2020.

34. Jackson, *Sacred Hoops*, 85–86; Jackson, *Eleven Rings*, 5.

35. Phil Jackson with Charles Rosen, *Maverick: More Than a Game* (Chicago: Playboy, 1975), 134–136.

36. Jackson, *Maverick*, 138.

37. Lawrence Shainberg, "In a Game of Individuals, They Are a Community: The Amazing Knicks," *New York Times*, January 25, 1970. For an insightful discussion about the myths around "the Old Knicks" of the 1970s as a team that symbolized "the promise of liberalism," see Yago Colas's *Ball Don't Lie: Myth, Genealogy, and Invention in the Cultures of Basketball* (Philadelphia: Temple University Press, 2016), 71–81.

38. Dave Hoekstra, "Phil Jackson: Bulls' Man of Many Face(t)s," *Chicago Sun-Times*, July 16, 1989; Lazenby, *Mindgames*, 2; Tom Callahan, "The New Age

of Coaching," *U.S. News & World Report*, May 11, 1992, 61; Dirk Johnson, "Once Free-Spirited Jackson Leads Calmly," *New York Times*, January 21, 1990; Halberstam, *Playing for Keeps*, 190–191.

39. Jackson, *Sacred Hoops*, 87.

40. Jack McCallum, "Helping Hands," *Sports Illustrated*, December 17, 1990, 42.

41. Jackson, *Sacred Hoops*, 105. In his book *The Meaning of Sports*, Michael Mandelbaum argues that basketball represents the "post-industrial game." See Mandelbaum, *The Meaning of Sports: Why Americans Watch Baseball, Football, and Basketball and What They See When They Do* (New York: Public Affairs, 2004), 199–207.

42. Naughton, *Taking to the Air*, 225–226.

43. Jeff Coplon, "The Age of Jackson," *New York Times Magazine*, May 17, 1992; Sam Smith, *The Jordan Rules* (New York: Simon & Schuster, 1992), 62.

44. McCallum, "Helping Hands," 40; Melissa Isaacson, *Transition Game: An Inside Look at Life with the Chicago Bulls* (Champaign, IL: Sagamore, 1994), 13.

45. Smith, "Less from Jordan, More for Bulls?"

FIVE: BOBOS AND WARRIORS

1. Phil Jackson with Charles Rosen, *Maverick: More Than a Game* (Chicago: Playboy, 1975), 5.

2. Jackson, *Maverick*, 85, 126; "Phil Jackson's Courtly Attitude," *GQ*, February 1992, 43.

3. Don Pierson, "The Bulls Aren't Easy to Coach, but Phil Jackson Gets His Point Across," *Chicago Tribune Magazine*, April 19, 1992, 16–17; Dave Hoekstra, "Phil Jackson: Bulls' Man of Many Face(t)s," *Chicago Sun-Times*, July 16, 1989.

4. Peter Richmond, "Phil Jackson: Then and Now," *National Sports Daily*, April 29, 1990.

5. Dirk Johnson, "Once Free-Spirited, Jackson Leads Calmly," *New York Times*, January 21, 1990.

6. Phil Jackson and Hugh Delehanty, *Sacred Hoops: Spiritual Lessons of a Hardwood Warrior* (New York: Hyperion, 1995), 75–76, 93; Mark Vancil, "Inside Interview with Phil Jackson," *Inside Sports*, October 1991, 22.

7. Vancil, "Inside Interview with Phil Jackson," 19; David Halberstam, *Playing for Keeps: Michael Jordan and the World He Made* (New York: Random House, 1999), 200; Jeff Coplon, "The Age of Jackson," *New York Times Magazine*, May 17, 1992.

8. Elizabeth Kaye, "Servant of the Cause," *Los Angeles Magazine*, June 2002.

9. Sam Smith, "Reinsdorf Saw Imminent Disaster," *Chicago Tribune*, July 9, 1989.

10. Sam Smith, "Reinsdorf Saw Imminent Disaster."

11. Sam Smith, *There Is No Next: NBA Legends on the Legacy of Michael Jordan* (New York: Diversion, 2014), 113.

12. Coplon, "Age of Jackson."

13. Jim Naughton, *Taking to the Air: The Rise of Michael Jordan* (New York: Warner Books, 1992), 201.

14. Greg Donaldson, "Flying with the Bulls," *Sport*, February 1990, 26; Johnson, "Once Free-Spirited, Jackson Leads Calmly."

15. Sam Smith, *The Jordan Rules* (New York: Simon & Schuster, 1992), 60; Halberstam, *Playing for Keeps*, 250.

16. Johnson, "Once Free-Spirited, Jackson Leads Calmly"; Sam Goldaper, "A Flower Child Turns on the Bulls," *New York Times*, June 12, 1991.

17. Jackson, *Maverick*, 17; Jackson, *Sacred Hoops*, 27–28; Phil Jackson and Hugh Delehanty, *Eleven Rings: The Soul of Success* (New York: Penguin Books, 2014), 45–46; Roland Lazenby, *Mindgames: Phil Jackson's Long Strange Journey* (Chicago: Contemporary Books, 2001), 62.

18. Jackson, *Maverick*, 19; Jackson, *Sacred Hoops*, 26–28.

19. "A Timeout to Talk About Words," *Chicago Tribune*, November 29, 1992; Kaye, "Servant of the Cause."

20. Jackson, *Sacred Hoops*, 29–30.

21. Halberstam, *Playing for Keeps*, 254.

22. Jackson, *Eleven Rings*, 47; Jackson, *Sacred Hoops*, 31.

23. Jackson, *Maverick*, 49–50; Peter Richmond, *Phil Jackson: Lord of the Rings* (New York: Penguin, 2013), 24; Jack McCallum, "For Whom the Bulls Toil," *Sports Illustrated*, November 11, 1991, 114.

24. Jackson, *Maverick*, 51; Jackson, *Sacred Hoops*, 32.

25. Thomas Rogers, "Injured Jackson Has a Healthy Outlook," *New York Times*, April 6, 1969; Jackson, *Maverick*, 49, 194.

26. Jackson, *Maverick*, 8; Lazenby, *Mindgames*, 74, 101; Coplon, "Age of Jackson"; Johnson, "Once Free-Spirited, Jackson Leads Calmly."

27. Jackson, *Maverick*, 69–70; Pat Joseph, "Jack Scott and the Jock Liberation Army," *California Magazine*, Spring 2020; Jack Scott, *The Athletic Revolution* (New York: Free Press, 1971).

28. Richard Hoffer, "Sitting Bull," *Sports Illustrated*, May 27, 1996, 84; Sam Smith, "Phil Jackson: An Unlikely Coach," *Chicago Tribune*, April 29, 1990; Jackson, *Sacred Hoops*, 32–33.

29. Skip Myslenski, "Phil-abbergasting," *Chicago Tribune*, June 24, 1993.

30. Bill Bradley, *Life on the Run* (1976; New York: Vintage Books, 1995), 178; Lazenby, *Mindgames*, 41–43, 48; Pierson, "Bulls Aren't Easy to Coach."

31. Jackson, *Sacred Hoops*, 108–109.

32. Jackson, *Sacred Hoops*, 109–110.

33. Jackson, *Eleven Rings*, 3.

34. Melissa Isaacson, "Bulls Pushed into Title Condition," *Chicago Tribune*, October 15, 1992.

35. Jackson, *Sacred Hoops*, 11–12.

36. Gerald Vizenor, "A Pale Look at Tribal Life," *Los Angeles Times*, May 20, 1984; Stephen Farber, "5-Hour TV Saga of the Sioux," *New York Times*, May 17, 1984.

37. Jackson, *Sacred Hoops*, 111. This section on Jackson's cultural appropriation of Native American life draws from John Bloom and Randy Hanson's insightful article, "Warriors and Thieves: Appropriations of the Warrior Motif in Representations of Native American Athletes," in *Sports Matters: Race, Recreation, and Culture*, ed. John Bloom and Michael Willard (New York: NYU Press, 2002), 246–263.

38. The picture of Jackson wearing the Native American headdress can be found on ESPN's Outside the Lines webpage, "The Native American Sports Experience," November 10, 1999, www.espn.com/espninc/pressreleases/991110otlnative americans.html.

39. Philip J. Deloria, *Playing Indian* (New Haven, CT: Yale University Press, 1998), 170–175; Hugh Delehanty, "Buddha and the Bulls: An Interview with Phil Jackson," *Tricycle: The Buddhist Review*, Summer 1994.

40. Shunryu Suzuki and Trudy Dixon, *Zen Mind, Beginner's Mind* (New York: Walker/Weatherhill, 1970), 22.

41. Bloom and Hanson, "Warriors and Thieves," 255–256; David Brooks, *Bobos in Paradise: The New Upper Class and How They Got There* (2000; New York: Simon & Schuster, 2004), 10–11, 41–42.

42. Brooks, *Bobos in Paradise*, 224–226, 241–242; Phil Jackson, "Where the Zen Master Finds Inner Peace," *Wall Street Journal*, September 19, 2013.

43. Jackson, *Sacred Hoops*, 5; Hoffer, "Sitting Bull," 84.

44. Jackson, *Sacred Hoops*, 47–50, 116–117; Jackson, *Eleven Rings*, 50–54.

45. Jackson, *Sacred Hoops*, 173–174; Michael Jordan, *For the Love of the Game: My Story*, ed. Mark Vancil (New York: Crown Publishers, 1998), 77; Michael Jordan as told to Rick Telander, "Flinch First? Not Me," *ESPN The Magazine*, April 6, 1998.

46. Jordan, *For the Love of the Game*, 73.

47. McCallum, "For Whom the Bulls Toil," 118.

48. Lazenby, *Mindgames*, 147; Jackson, *Sacred Hoops*, 122.

SIX: CRUMBS

1. Melissa Isaacson, "Jerry Krause Is the Man Primarily Responsible for Putting Together the Bulls' Three World Championship Teams. So . . . Why Do People Hate This Guy?," *Chicago Tribune*, February 5, 1995.

2. Rick Telander, "The Sleuth," *Sports Illustrated*, March 15, 1993, 63.

3. David Halberstam, *Playing for Keeps: Michael Jordan and the World He Made* (New York: Random House, 1999), 167–168; Rick Telander, "Ready . . . Set . . . Levitate!," *Sports Illustrated*, November 17, 1986, 20.

4. Bob Sakamoto, "Reinsdorf Weakens in Jordan Tug of War," *Chicago Tribune*, March 22, 1986; Bob Sakamoto, "Jordan Rails at Reinsdorf, Krause," *Chicago Tribune*, April 3, 1986.

5. *The Last Dance*, directed by Jason Hehir, aired from April 19, 2020, to May 17, 2020, on ESPN.

6. Sakamoto, "Jordan Rails at Reinsdorf, Krause."

7. Telander, "Sleuth," 71; Bob Sakamoto, "Jordan, Reinsdorf Decide to Bury the Hatchet—For Now," *Chicago Tribune*, April 6, 1986.

8. For an incisive history of the NBA's labor battles and racial confrontations during the 1970s, see Theresa Runstedtler, *Black Ball: Kareem Abdul-Jabbar, Spencer Haywood, and the Generation That Saved the Soul of the NBA* (New York: Bold Type Books, 2023).

9. Henry Louis Gates Jr., "Net Worth," *New Yorker*, June 1, 1998, 50.

10. Jack McCallum, *Dream Team: How Michael, Magic, Larry, Charles, and the Greatest of All Time Conquered the World and Changed Basketball Forever* (New York: Ballantine Books, 2013), 57–58; Johnette Howard, "Breakthrough," *Sport*, February 1992, 68–69; Scottie Pippen with Michael Arkush, *Unguarded* (New York: Atria, 2021), 2–6.

11. Pippen, *Unguarded*, 1; McCallum, *Dream Team*, 58.

12. Unless otherwise cited, this section on Pippen draws from Sam Smith, *The Jordan Rules* (New York: Simon & Schuster, 1992), 67–75.

13. Lacy Banks, "Pippen 'Beefs Up' for Big Year," *Chicago Sun-Times*, October 10, 1990; Sam Smith, "Surgery on Pippen Will Hurt the Bulls," *Chicago Tribune*, July 26, 1988; Pippen, *Unguarded*, 56.

14. "N.B.A. Salary Cap Rises," *New York Times*, August 2, 1990.

15. Lacy Banks, "Scottie Pippen," *Chicago Sun-Times*, May 29, 1989; Roland Lazenby, *Michael Jordan: The Life* (New York: Little, Brown, 2014), 326; Shane Tritsch, "Foul Trouble," *Chicago Magazine*, December 1, 2005.

16. Data for 1990–1991 NBA player salaries found at *USA Today Sports*, Hoops Hype website, accessed April 4, 2023, https://hoopshype.com/salaries/players/1990-1991.

17. Ben Joravsky, "Nobody Cheers for Jerry Krause," *Chicago Reader*, April 27, 1990; Telander, "Sleuth," 63.

18. Jerry Krause, *To Set the Record Straight* (unpublished memoir); Bruce Newman, "Now You See Him," *Sports Illustrated*, November 30, 1987, 67, 68; Joravsky, "Nobody Cheers for Jerry Krause."

19. Telander, "Sleuth," 62.

20. Mark Vancil, "Enraging Bull," *Chicago Magazine*, April 1992, 114–115.

21. Ira Berkow, "Not Fitting the Profile," *New York Times*, May 11, 1992; Joravsky, "Nobody Cheers for Jerry Krause."

22. Halberstam, *Playing for Keeps*, 197; Telander, "Sleuth," 69.

23. Joravsky, "Nobody Cheers for Jerry Krause."

24. "Letters: Jerry Krause (Cont.)," *Sports Illustrated*, May 10, 1993, 4.

25. Robert Markus, "After a Long Chase, Krause Finds Dream in His Backyard," *Chicago Tribune*, June 3, 1976; Robert Talley, "Can Gym Rat Jerry Krause Lead Bulls to Promised Land?," *Chicago Tribune*, June 6, 1976.

26. David Condon, "Krause Should Get Blame," *Chicago Tribune*, June 10, 1976; Joravsky, "Nobody Cheers for Jerry Krause."

27. Joravsky, "Nobody Cheers for Jerry Krause."

28. McCallum, *Dream Team*, 59; Smith, *Jordan Rules*, 70.

29. Newman, "Now You See Him," 71; Halberstam, *Playing for Keeps*, 222.

30. Harvey Araton, "Pippen's Stunning Leap into Jordan's League," *New York Times*, October 27, 1991.

31. Gene Wojciechowski, "His Turn," *ESPN The Magazine*, February 22, 1999.

32. Howard, "Breakthrough," 70.

33. Halberstam, *Playing for Keeps*, 206.

SEVEN: BAD BOYS

1. Jim Naughton, *Taking to the Air: The Rise of Michael Jordan* (New York: Warner Books, 1992), 221; David Halberstam, *Playing for Keeps: Michael Jordan and the World He Made* (New York: Random House, 1999), 235.

2. Sam Smith, "Bulls Can't Help Looking Ahead to Pistons," *Chicago Tribune*, December 18, 1990.

3. Lacy Banks, "Bulls' Goal: Measure Up to Pistons," *Chicago Sun-Times*, December 19, 1990.

4. "Jordan Fights Pistons with Points; Bulls Win," *Los Angeles Times*, January 17, 1988; Bob Sakamoto, "Bulls KO Pistons in Slugfest," *Chicago Tribune*, January 17, 1988; Jeff Coplon, "Motor City Madmen," *Rolling Stone*, May 4, 1989, 96.

5. Mitch Albom, "Pistons? Bad Guys? It's Only Because They're Good," *Detroit Free Press*, January 20, 1988; Corky Meinecke, "Are the Bad Boys Really Bad?," *Detroit Free Press*, April 11, 1989; Cameron Stauth, *The Franchise: Building a Winner with the World Champion Detroit Pistons, Basketball's Bad Boys* (New York: William Morrow, 1990), 100; Coplon, "Motor City Madmen," 70.

6. Kevin Boyle, "The Ruins of Detroit: Exploring the Urban Crisis in the Motor City," *Michigan Historical Review* 27, no. 1 (Spring 2001): 122; Isabel Wilkerson, "After Four Terms, Us versus Them Still Plays in Detroit," *New York Times*, September 17, 1989; Jack McCallum, "Palace Coup," *Sports Illustrated*, November 5, 1990, 88, 95; Armen Keteyian, Harvey Araton, and Martin Dardis, *Money Players: Inside the New NBA* (New York: Simon & Schuster, 1997), 138; Terry Foster, "It's Plain as Black and White: Pistons' Move Was Based on Green," *Detroit News*, March 19, 1989.

7. Jim Cavan, "Motor City's Yearning," *SB Nation*, October 30, 2013; Stauth, *Franchise*, 71.

8. McCallum, "Palace Coup," 94; Keteyian, Araton, and Dardis, *Money Players*, 246.

9. Charlie Vincent, "Jordan Sees That Pistons Haven't Lost Their Drive," *Detroit Free Press*, December 20, 1990.

10. Bill McGraw, "8 Die as Detroit Revels in NBA Victory," *Washington Post*, June 16, 1990; Doron Levin, "Detroit Basketball Celebration Turns Violent," *New York Times*, June 16, 1990; Scott Martelle, "Violence after Pistons' Victory Blamed on Tension and Poverty," *Detroit News*, June 17, 1990; William Oscar Johnson, "Nothing to Celebrate," *Sports Illustrated*, June 25, 1990, 35.

11. "Poverty Caused Friday Morning Violence, Some Say," *Detroit News*, June 17, 1990.

12. Alan Greenberg, "A Championship Can't Hide Tragedy of a City in Trouble," *Hartford Courant*, June 20, 1990; Brenda Ingersoll, "Detroit Loses No Matter Who Wins," *Detroit News*, June 13, 1989; Coplon, "Motor City Madmen," 72; Todd Boyd, *Young, Black, Rich, and Famous: The Rise of the NBA, the Hip Hop Invasion, and the Transformation of American Culture* (New York: Doubleday, 2003), 108.

13. Jack McCallum, "The Mystique Goes On," *Sports Illustrated*, June 8, 1987, 31; Clifton Brown, "Isiah Clears Air About Remarks," *Detroit Free Press*, June 4, 1987.

14. Shelby Strother, "I'm Sorry, Isiah Tells Larry Bird," *Detroit News*, June 4, 1987; Mitch Albom, "We All Need the Chance to Explain," *Detroit Free Press*, June 4, 1987; "Who's Right? Who's Wrong? Opinions Vary," *Detroit Free Press*, June 7, 1987; Melvin Durslag, "Al Campanis Case in Reverse for NBA," *Los Angeles Herald-Examiner*, June 3, 1987.

15. Ira Berkow, "The Coloring of Bird," *New York Times*, June 2, 1987.

16. Berkow, "The Coloring of Bird"; David Halberstam, "The Stuff Dreams Are Made Of," *Sports Illustrated*, June 29, 1987, 39; Gary A. Sailes, "The Myth of Black Sports Supremacy," *Journal of Black Studies* 21, no. 4 (June 1991): 481.

17. Martin Kane, "An Assessment of Black Best," *Sports Illustrated*, January 18, 1971, 72–83; "Black Dominance," *Time*, May 9, 1977, 57–60; "The Black Athlete: Fact or Fiction," television special, aired on NBC, 1989; David K. Wiggins, "'Great Speed but Little Stamina:' The Historical Debate over Black Athletic Superiority," *Journal of Sport History* 16, no. 2 (Summer 1989): 158–185.

18. William Rhoden, "Searching to Bridge Racial Divide in Athletics," *New York Times*, January 5, 1998; Douglas S. Looney, "Two for the Show," *Sports Illustrated*, October 15, 1979, 40; Frank T. Bannister, "Search for 'White Hopes' Threatens Black Athletes," *Ebony*, February 1980, 130, 132; John Papanek, "Gifts That God Didn't Give," *Sports Illustrated*, November 9, 1981, 82–96; Jim Murray, "Here's a Rube Who's Master of City Game," *Los Angeles Times*, February 15, 1981; Bob Schron, "Bird's Eye View: How the Best Rates the Rest," *Sport*, May 1986, 46; Jeff Lenihan, "Larry Bird Shows That the Best Can Get Better," *Basketball Digest*, April 1987, 26, 30.

19. William Sampson, "Thomas Told Truth About Larry Bird," *Chicago Sun-Times*, June 6, 1987; David Bradley, "The Importance of Being Isiah," *Sport*, May 1988, 27.

20. Stephen Metcalf, "The Devil Wears Nikes: Liking Isiah Thomas Against My Better Judgment," *Slate*, June 29, 2006; Isiah Thomas, *The Fundamentals: 8 Plays for Winning the Games of Business and Life* (New York: HarperBusiness, 2001), 84.

21. Johnette Howard, "Fame and Fear," *Detroit Free Press*, October 22, 1985; Charlie Vincent, "Crime or No Crime, Isiah Knows Whereof He Speaks," *Detroit Free Press*, September 27, 1986; William Nack, "'I Have Got to Do Right,'" *Sports Illustrated*, January 19, 1987, 60, 64, 66–68, 70; Bradley, "Importance of Being Isiah," 27; Thomas, *Fundamentals*, 9.

22. Johnette Howard, "One Man's Dream Day," *Detroit Free Press*, September 25, 1986; Loren Feldman, "Isiah's Prophecy," *GQ*, February 1988, 240; Liz Robbins, "The Lessons of Chicago's West Side," *New York Times*, January 27, 2004; Thomas, *Fundamentals*, 9.

23. Nack, "'I Have Got to Do Right,'" 70.

24. Howard, "One Man's Dream Day."

25. "Thousands of Detroiters Show They've Had Enough," *Detroit Free Press*, September 28, 1986.

26. Thomas, *Fundamentals*, 31; Keteyian, Araton, and Dardis, *Money Players*, 141.

27. Isiah Thomas with Matt Dobek, *Bad Boys! An Inside Look at the Detroit Pistons' 1988–1989 Championship Season* (Grand Rapids, MI: Masters Press, 1989), 50–51;

Stauth, *Franchise*, 13–14; Charlie Vincent, "For All Thomas Did, Pistons Couldn't Win," *Detroit Free Press*, June 20, 1988.

28. Jocelyn Zablit and Jack Kresnak, "A Day of Glory, Grief and Anguish," *Detroit News and Free Press*, June 16, 1990; Allan Lengel, "Feds: Isiah Not Target of Inquiry," *Detroit News*, June 19, 1990; Keteyian, Araton, and Dardis, *Money Players*, 256–257; Scott Burnstein, "News of Isiah Thomas' Affairs with the Mob Came to Light as Pistons Repeated in 1990," *Gangster Report*, July 14, 2021.

29. "'I Don't Deserve This,'" *Detroit News and Free Press*, June 17, 1990; Keteyian, Araton, and Dardis, *Money Players*, 256, 267–271; Scott Burnstein, interview by author, July 14, 2021.

30. Burnstein, "News of Isiah Thomas' Affairs."

31. "Thomas Says Ex-Neighbor Did Him a Favor," *Detroit Free Press*, June 18, 1990.

32. Keteyian, Araton, and Dardis, *Money Players*, 143; Tim Kiske, "Isiah, TV-2's Jacques Scuffle; Was It Assault?," *Detroit News*, October 3, 1990; "Isiah Thomas Hit with Assault, Battery Charge," *Jet*, October 22, 1990, 48.

33. Kiske, "Isiah, TV-2's Jacques Scuffle"; Drew Sharp, "TV Reporter Says Isiah Choked Him," *Detroit Free Press*, October 3, 1990.

34. Sam Smith, "Pistons Shake Up Bulls Again," *Chicago Tribune*, December 20, 1990; Greg Donaldson, "Flying with the Bulls," *Sport*, February 1990, 26; Phil Jackson and Hugh Delehanty, *Sacred Hoops: Spiritual Lessons of a Hardwood Warrior* (New York: Hyperion, 1995), 136.

35. Sam Smith, *The Jordan Rules* (New York: Simon & Schuster, 1992), 132.

36. Paul Sullivan, "Bulls Deliver Sweet Holiday Punch," *Chicago Tribune*, December 26, 1990.

37. Dave Hoekstra, "Bulls Enjoy the Present," *Chicago Sun-Times*, December 26, 1990.

EIGHT: OTHER PEOPLE'S MONEY

1. Larry Guest, "News Stuns Jordan, but Game Goes On," *Orlando Sentinel*, January 17, 1991.

2. Barry Cooper, "Basic Bulls Ground Magic," *Orlando Sentinel*, January 17, 1991; Sam Smith, *The Jordan Rules* (New York: Simon & Schuster, 1992), 154.

3. Sam Smith, "Bulls Find Magic Touch," *Chicago Tribune*, January 17, 1991; Lacy Banks, "Bulls, Jordan Top Stubborn Magic," *Chicago Sun-Times*, January 17, 1991.

4. Smith, *Jordan Rules*, 155–156.

5. Brian Schultz, "It's All Right to Enjoy Diversions of Sports,"*Orlando Sentinel*, January 18, 1991.

6. Guest, "News Stuns Jordan"; "Sports World Reacts," *Chicago Sun-Times*, January 18, 1991.

7. Ailene Voisin, "NBA Plays with Eye on Gulf," *Atlanta Journal-Constitution*, January 18, 1991.

8. Jim Leusner, "Orlando Airport on Highest Alert in Its History," *Orlando Sentinel*, January 18, 1991.

9. Lacy Banks, "Bulls Bits," *Chicago Sun-Times*, January 16, 1990; Sam Smith, "Bulls, Hawks Players Join King Day Tribute," *Chicago Tribune*, January 18, 1991; Craig Hodges, *Long Shot: The Triumphs and Struggles of an NBA Freedom Fighter* (Chicago: Haymarket Books, 2017), 138.

10. Smith, *Jordan Rules*, 147.

11. Smith, *Jordan Rules*, 146–147.

12. Bob Sakamoto, "Reinsdorf Buys Bulls," *Chicago Tribune*, February 9, 1985; David Greising, "The Toughest #&?!%* in Sports," *Business Week*, June 15, 1992, 101; Sam Smith, *Second Coming: The Strange Odyssey of Michael Jordan* (New York: HarperCollins, 1995), 17; E. M. Swift, "Misunderstood?," *Sports Illustrated*, June 30, 1997, 85; David Halberstam, *Playing for Keeps: Michael Jordan and the World He Made* (New York: Random House, 1999), 25; Henry Louis Gates Jr., "Net Worth," *New Yorker*, June 1, 1998, 51; Jeff Rude, "Bulls 25: Ultimate Saga of Success," *Chicago Sun-Times*, November 4, 1990; "Jordan, Inc.," *Sports Illustrated*, April 23, 1990, 24; Roy S. Johnson, "The Jordan Effect," *Fortune*, June 22, 1998.

13. Chicago Professional Sports Ltd. Partnership v. NBA, 754 F. Supp. 1336 (N.D. Ill. 1991), hereafter, *Chicago Professional Sports*; "NBC and TNT Bring the Game Home," *Hoop*, December 1990, 74; John McManus, "NBC Scoring Big with NBA Gamble," *Advertising Age*, November 5, 1990, 24.

14. *Chicago Professional Sports*, 1345; Greising, "Toughest #&?!%* in Sports," 104.

15. Steve Nidetz and John Gorman, "Bulls, WGN Sue NBA for Telecast Cut," *Chicago Tribune*, October 27, 1990; Sam Smith, "Reinsdorf Turns Bulls' Answer Man," *Chicago Tribune*, November 1, 1990; Jerry Reinsdorf witness testimony, Transcript of Proceedings, *Chicago Professional Sports*.

16. *Chicago Professional Sports*; Bill King, "Bulls' Boss Finds Different Need, Role in NBA," *Sports Business Journal*, May 20, 2013; Swift, "Misunderstood?," 80.

17. Nidetz and Gorman, "Bulls, WGN Sue NBA"; *Chicago Professional Sports*, 1350–1351.

18. Richard Mertens, "A Federal Judge Who Did It His Way," *University of Chicago Magazine*, July/August 2009; Edward Kiersh, "Playing Hardball," *Cigar Aficionado*, Summer 1995; Halberstam, *Playing for Keeps*, 26.

19. Swift, "Misunderstood?," 78, 84.

20. Bill Granger, "Celebrating Disgrace: Leave It to the White Sox to Air Their Dirty Hosiery," *Chicago Tribune*, May 8, 1988; Linnet Myers, "Neighbors Love Sox, Not Owners," *Chicago Tribune*, May 12, 1988; Bernie Lincicome, "Will Sox Become Worth Keeping?," *Chicago Tribune*, July 3, 1988.

21. E. M. Swift, "The Sunshine Sox?," *Sports Illustrated*, May 30, 1988, 40–44; David Peterson, "Reinsdorf's Secret," *Chicago Reader*, September 26, 1996; Sam Smith, "It's a Bittersweet Repeat for Reinsdorf," *Chicago Tribune*, June 19, 1992.

22. John Kass, "Sox May Pick Up Some Heavy Hitters," *Chicago Tribune*, June 10, 1988; Linda Kay, "At Long Last, Jerry Reinsdorf's Side of the Story," *Chicago Tribune*, November 6, 1988; Sean Dinces, *Bulls Markets: Chicago's Basketball Business and the New Inequality* (Chicago: University of Chicago Press, 2018), 202.

23. Lester Munson, "'Ways of Doing Things,'" *National Sports Daily*, December 4, 1990.

24. John Heylar, *Lords of the Realm: The Real History of Baseball* (New York: Villard, 1994), 243; "Jerry Reinsdorf Pulls a Double Play in Chicago," *Business Week*, October 10, 1983, 53; Munson, "'Ways of Doing Things'"; Greising, "Toughest #&?!%* in Sports," 101.

25. Heylar, *Lords of the Realm*, 243; Kay, "At Long Last, Jerry Reinsdorf's Side of the Story"; Kiersh, "Playing Hardball."

26. Tom Seibel, "Reinsdorf Says Superstation Cap May Cost Bulls $1 million," *Chicago Sun-Times*, December 19, 1990; Jerry Reinsdorf witness testimony, Transcript of Proceedings, *Chicago Professional Sports*.

27. E. M. Swift, "From Corned Beef to Caviar," *Sports Illustrated*, June 3, 1991, 78; Armen Keteyian, Harvey Araton, and Martin Dardis, *Money Players: Inside the New NBA* (New York: Simon & Schuster, 1997), 28.

28. Matthew Grimm, "The Big Rebound at the NBA," *Adweek's Marketing Week*, February 19, 1990, 19; Swift, "From Corned Beef to Caviar," 84; "NBA Chief Gets $27.5-Million, 5-Year Contract," *Los Angeles Times*, February 15, 1990.

29. N. R. Kleinfield, "How One Man Rescued Basketball, and Its Bottom Line," *New York Times*, March 4, 1990.

30. Chuck Stogel, "Era of Explosion Continues for TV Sports," *Sporting News*, April 23, 1990, 48; Pete Croatto, *From Hang Time to Prime Time: Business, Entertainment, and the Birth of the Modern-Day NBA* (New York: Atria Books, 2020), 78; Mark C. Wyche et al., *Sports on Television: A New Ball Game for Broadcasters* (Washington, DC: National Association of Broadcasters, 1990), 6.

31. Halberstam, *Playing for Keeps*, 125, 131–132.

32. "Stern Defends NBA's TV Restriction Policy," *Tampa Tribune*, December 21, 1990; David Stern witness testimony, Transcript of Proceedings, *Chicago Professional Sports*; Richard Sandomir, "Bulls, Superstations and Power Moves," *New York Times*, April 16, 1991.

33. James Warren, "WGN-TV, Bulls Take Early Lead in Court Over NBA," *Chicago Tribune*, January 25, 1991; *Chicago Professional Sports*, 1357, 1360. In April 1992, the US Court of Appeals for the Seventh Circuit voted 3–0, affirming the Federal District Court's ruling in favor of the Bulls and WGN.

34. Lester Munson, "The Athletes' New Best Friend," *Sports Illustrated*, April 25, 1993, 10.

35. Greising, "Toughest #&?!%* in Sports," 104.

36. "BA Players 'Short-Changed,' Suit Says," *Chicago Sun-Times*, December 13, 1991; David Aldridge, "NBA, Players Association Settle Revenue Dispute," *Washington Post*, February 10, 1992.

37. King, "Bulls' Boss Finds Different Need"; Charley Rosen, *The Chosen Game: A Jewish Basketball History* (Lincoln: University of Nebraska Press, 2017).

38. This section on the Jordan-Krause rift and Jordan's meeting with Reinsdorf comes from Smith, *Jordan Rules*, 168–170, 173–177.

NINE: KING OF THE COURT

1. Jim Murray, "King of the Air Is Missing Crown," *Los Angeles Times*, February 11, 1990.

2. Sam Smith, *The Jordan Rules* (New York: Simon & Schuster, 1992), 322; "One on One with Ahmad Rashad: Michael Jordan," NBATV, 2013, YouTube video, www.youtube.com/watch?v=GDbOs5LMATM&t=517s; Armen Keteyian, Harvey Araton, and Martin Dardis, *Money Players: Inside the New NBA* (New York: Simon & Schuster, 1997), 212.

3. Jack McCallum, "Unforgettable," *Sports Illustrated*, November 18, 1991, 35.

4. Jack McCallum, *Unfinished Business: On and Off the Court with the 1990–1991 Boston Celtics* (New York: Summit Books, 1992), 22.

5. Jonathan Abrams, "The Greatest Game Never Played," *Bleacher Report Magazine*, February 14, 2017.

6. Garr Kluender, "Magic-Jordan Matchup Looks Like a Hard Sell," *Los Angeles Times*, January 15, 1990; Jack McCallum, "The Bird Is Grounded," *Sports Illustrated*, November 28, 1988, 52–54, 59.

7. "Up-Close with Roy Firestone," interview with Michael Jordan, February 2, 1990, YouTube video, www.youtube.com/watch?v=mzCHxFE3aRQ; Ira Berkow, "One on One with Magic and Michael," *New York Times*, February 3, 1990; Rudy Martzke, "Striking Match: Magic, Jordan Go One-On-One," *USA Today*, January 9, 1990; David Aldridge, "With New Director, 'Showtime Closes,'" *Washington Post*, December 26, 1990.

8. Abrams, "Greatest Game Never Played."

9. "NBA Holds Key to Match-Up of Magic, Michael," *Los Angeles Times*, January 11, 1990; Lacy Banks, "Magic, Jordan One-on-One Is Under Attack," *Chicago Sun-Times*, January 10, 1990; Lacy Banks, "Jordan, Magic Duel? No Chance," *Chicago Sun-Times*, January 14, 1990; Jack Craig, "ProServ, NBA to Go 1-on-1?," *Boston Globe*, January 21, 1990; Abrams, "Greatest Game Never Played."

10. Jan Hubbard, "Magic Imagined How He Won the Duel," *Sporting News*, February 26, 1990, 16.

11. Mike Lupica, "Do You Believe in Magic?," *Esquire*, April 1990; Richard Hoffer, "Magic's Kingdom," *Sports Illustrated*, December 3, 1990, 109.

12. Charles P. Pierce, "The Magic Act," *GQ*, February 1993, 124, 126; Diane K. Shah, "Magic's Kingdom," *GQ*, March 1987, 294; Bruce Newman, "The Business of Being Magic Johnson," *Los Angeles Times Magazine*, September 10, 1995.

13. Bruce Newman, "Magic Faces the Music," *Sports Illustrated*, May 13, 1985, 94; Mark Heisler, "He's Still Taking Care of Business," *Los Angeles Times*, November 2, 1990.

14. Earvin "Magic" Johnson with William Novak, *My Life* (New York: Fawcett Crest, 1992), 249–251; Jesse Katz, "Master of Illusion," *Los Angeles Magazine*, October 2003.

15. Roland Lanzenby, *The Show: The Inside Story of the Spectacular Los Angeles Lakers in the Words of Those Who Lived It* (New York: McGraw-Hill, 2006), 278; William

Oscar Johnson, "Jerry Is Never Behind the Eight Ball," *Sports Illustrated*, June 18, 1979, 22, 29; Johnson, *My Life*, 261, 275.

16. Jeff Pearlman, *Showtime: Magic, Kareem, Riley, and the Los Angeles Lakers Dynasty of the 1980s* (New York: Gotham Books, 2014), 202–203; Johnson, *My Life*, 251–252; Roland Lazenby, *Jerry West: The Life and Legend of a Basketball Icon* (New York: Ballantine Books, 2009), 376.

17. Dawn K. Smith, "HIV Disease as a Cause of Death for African Americans in 1987 and 1990," *Journal of the National Medical Association* 84, no. 6 (1992): 481–487; Magic Johnson with Roy S. Johnson, "I'll Deal with It," *Sports Illustrated*, November 18, 1991, 19.

18. Barry Farrell, "It's the Magic Show," *Sport*, February 1980, 23; David Halberstam, *The Breaks of the Game* (1981; New York: Hachette Books, 2009), 195; William Knoedelseder Jr., "Magic Johnson Casts No Shadow," *Los Angeles Times*, October 25, 1980; Cheryl L. Cole and Harry Denny III, "Visualizing Deviance in Post-Reagan America: Magic Johnson, AIDS, and the Promiscuous World of Professional Sport," *Critical Sociology* 20, no. 3 (1994): 129. According to reporter Jesse Katz, Johnson did not register to vote in California until 1992. See Katz, "Master of Illusion."

19. Johnson, *My Life*, 3; Earvin "Magic" Johnson and Richard Levin, *Magic* (New York: Viking Press, 1983), 31–33.

20. Heisler, "He's Still Taking Care of Business"; Johnson, *My Life*, 5–6; Richard Hoffer, "Magic's Kingdom," *Sports Illustrated*, December 3, 1990, 109–110; Katz, "Master of Illusion."

21. Hoffer, "Magic's Kingdom," 108–109; Newman, "Business of Being Magic Johnson"; Michael Wilbon, "Off the Court, Magic Minds His Business," *Washington Post*, August 6, 1990.

22. Harvey Araton and Filip Bondy, *The Selling of the Green: The Financial Rise and Moral Decline of the Boston Celtics* (New York: HarperCollins, 1992), 220; Lacy Banks, "'Magic' a Winner On, Off Court," *Chicago Sun-Times*, December 21, 1990; Howard Bryant, *The Heritage: Black Athletes, a Divided America, and the Politics of Patriotism* (Boston: Beacon Press, 2018), 82–87, 96, 131–132.

23. Bob Greene, *Hang Time: Days and Dreams with Michael Jordan* (New York: Doubleday, 1992), 200; Johnson, *My Life*, 243; Jack McCallum, *Dream Team: How Michael, Magic, Larry, Charles, and the Greatest of All Time Conquered the World and Changed Basketball Forever* (New York: Ballantine Books, 2013), 13.

24. Converse print ad, "Magic by Converse," 1990; Thomas Vannah, "Converse Is in the Game," *Boston Globe*, September 16, 1990; "Converse—Magic Johnson Thrillin' and Chillin' Commercial," 1990, YouTube video, www.youtube.com/watch?v=CUQ5fPwDMXY.

25. Pierce, "Magic Act," 124.

26. Diane K. Shah, "The Transformation of Pat Riley," *GQ*, January 1989, 138; Michael Stone, "A Whole New Ball Game," *New York*, November 25, 1991, 47; Ken Auletta, "The Life of Riley," *Vanity Fair*, April 1992, 128; Mark Heisler, *The Lives of Riley* (New York: Macmillan, 1994), 127–129, 136–137, 146; Pearlman, *Showtime*, 385.

27. Pat Riley, *The Winner Within: A Life Plan for Team Players* (New York: Berkeley Books, 1994), 39–54; Hank Hersch, "A Change in the Water," *Sports Illustrated*, February 25, 1991, 15–17.

28. Hersch, "Change in the Water," 17.

29. Mark Heisler, "All's Not Well in Chicago with These Bulls," *Los Angeles Times*, February 3, 1991.

30. Mike Davis, "Turns Out the Los Angeles Lakers Have Their Own Set of Jordan Rules," *USA Today*, February 3, 1991; Smith, *Jordan Rules*, 181–183.

31. Sam Smith, "Magic's Sub Floors Bulls," *Chicago Tribune*, February 4, 1991; Mark Heisler, "Magic's Fall Gives Lakers Biggest Scare," *Los Angeles Times*, February 4, 1991.

32. Ted Cox, "The Sports Section," *Chicago Reader*, February 14, 1991; Dave Hoekstra, "Bulls' Palace Coup," *Chicago Sun-Times*, February 8, 1991; Smith, *Jordan Rules*, 188.

TEN: BE LIKE MIKE

1. David Remnick, "Back in Play," *New Yorker*, May 8, 1995, 41; Jim Naughton, *Taking to the Air: The Rise of Michael Jordan* (New York: Warner Books, 1992), 3.

2. Bob Greene, "In Jordan's Wake, a Trail of Magic," *Chicago Tribune*, November 21, 1990.

3. Sam Smith, *The Jordan Rules* (New York: Simon & Schuster, 1992), 217–218.

4. Mike Lupica, "Has Mouth, Will Shoot," *Esquire*, March 1992, 73; Nelson George, *Elevating the Game: Black Men and Basketball* (Lincoln, NE: Bison Books, 1999), 228.

5. Jeff Coplon, "Headstrong," *New York Times Magazine*, March 17, 1991; Jack McCallum, "On a Mission," *Sports Illustrated*, December 12, 1988; Charles Barkley and Roy S. Johnson, *Outrageous! The Fine Life and Flagrant Good Times of Basketball's Irresistible Force* (New York: Simon & Schuster, 1992), 55.

6. Thomas Boswell, "Playboy Interview: Charles Barkley," *Playboy*, May 1993, 61.

7. Barkley, *Outrageous!*, 18, 22; Skip Myslenski, "With 76ers' Barkley the Spirit Always Is Willing," *Chicago Tribune*, April 28, 1991; Phil Jasner, "Now, Little Leaves Barkley's Mouth," *Philadelphia Daily News*, March 29, 1991.

8. Claude Lewis, "Barkley Went Too Far This Time," *Philadelphia Inquirer*, April 1, 1991; Barnett Wright, "Has Barkley Mellowed? No, but He's Matured," *Philadelphia Tribune*, May 9, 1989; Barnett Wright, "Barkley Won't Tone Down Image," *Philadelphia Tribune*, June 1, 1990; Phil Jasner, "Barkley: 'Stupid Mistake,'" *Philadelphia Daily News*, March 28, 1991; David Aldridge, "Of So Many Images, Barkley's Talent Clear: Forward Heads 76ers' Charge," *Washington Post*, May 1, 1990; Barkley, *Outrageous!*, 37, 47.

9. Bob Ford, "Barkley Regrets Spitting Incident, But . . .," *Philadelphia Inquirer*, March 31, 1991; Barkley, *Outrageous!*, 21.

10. David Aldridge, "When Barkley Spits, Jordan Gets Upset," *Washington Post*, April 10, 1991.

11. Timothy Dwyer, "The Life of Barkley: Struggling for Peace off the Court," *Philadelphia Inquirer*, January 21, 1990; Stan Hochman, "Emotional Rescue," *Philadelphia Daily News*, February 9, 1990; Larry Platt, "The Round Mound Bids Farewell," in *New Jack Jocks: Rebels, Race, and the American Athlete* (Philadelphia: Temple University Press, 2002), 128.

12. Barkley, *Outrageous!*, 46–47; Gloria Campisi and Phil Jasner, "Sixers' Barkley Faces Gun Charge," *Philadelphia Daily News*, August 18, 1988; Gloria Campisi and Phil Jasner, "Barkley Case a Puzzle," *Philadelphia Daily News*, August 19, 1988; Phil Jasner, "Barkley Car Search Illegal, Judge Rules," *Philadelphia Daily News*, September 17, 1988; Rick Reilly, "Interview: Charles Barkley," *Sports Illustrated*, March 9, 1992, 187.

13. Barkley, *Outrageous!*, 157, 243, 253, 308.

14. Chris Wilder, "Nineties Niggers," *Source*, December 1992, 42; Barkley, *Outrageous!*, 243, 246; Ray Didinger, "Barkley Looking at the Bright Side," *Philadelphia Daily News*, June 30, 1989; Platt, "Round Mound Bids Farewell," 128–129.

15. Platt, "Round Mound Bids Farewell," 128.

16. Platt, "Round Mound Bids Farewell," 126, 129; Nelson George, *Hip Hop America* (New York: Penguin, 1998), 148–149; Didinger, "Barkley Looking at the Bright Side"; Donald Katz, *Just Do It: The Nike Spirit in the Corporate World* (New York: Random House, 1994), 249.

17. Naughton, *Taking to the Air*, 188.

18. William Booth, "One Nation, Indivisible: Is It History?," *Washington Post*, February 22, 1998.

19. S. L. Price, "Whatever Happened to the White Athlete?," *Sports Illustrated*, December 8, 1997, 33.

20. Chester Blair, "The Regal Blackness of Michael Jordan," *Chicago Defender*, June 24, 1991.

21. *The Last Dance*, directed by Jason Hehir, aired from April 19, 2020, to May 17, 2020, on ESPN.

22. Sam Smith, "Pippen to Bulls: Pay Me or Trade Me," *Chicago Tribune*, February 21, 1991.

23. Smith, *Jordan Rules*, 247; William Oscar Johnson, "How Far Have We Come?," *Sports Illustrated*, August 5, 1991; Jelani Cobb, "From Louis Armstrong to the N.F.L.: Ungrateful as the New Uppity," *New Yorker*, September 24, 2017.

24. David Moore, "Overshadowed No More," *Sporting News*, March 4, 1991; Alan Boomer, "The Sports Section," *Chicago Reader*, March 14, 1991; Lacy Banks, "No Deal: Pippen to Get $— Bulls Aims to Satisfy Player's Ultimatum," *Chicago Sun-Times*, February 22, 1991; Lacy Banks, "Pippen Is Set to Play," *Chicago Sun-Times*, March 1, 1991.

25. Scott Poulson-Bryant, "The Shadow Knows," *Vibe*, March 1995, 60; Boomer, "The Sports Section"; Jeff Coplon, "Legends. Champions?," *New York Times Magazine*, April 21, 1996; Bob Greene, *Hang Time: Days and Dreams with Michael Jordan* (New York: Doubleday, 1992), 137.

26. Scottie Pippen with Michael Arkush, *Unguarded* (New York: Atria, 2021), 103; Lacy Banks, "Pursuit of Kukoc Irks Pippen," *Chicago Sun-Times*, April 2, 1991.

27. Banks, "Pursuit of Kukoc Irks Pippen"; Smith, *Jordan Rules*, 246.

28. Dave Hoekstra, "Kukoc to Get Taste of Chicago—Bulls Planning Yugoslavian's Visit," *Chicago Sun-Times*, October 30, 1990; Smith, *Jordan Rules*, 32–33.

29. David Dupree, "The Name Is Toni Kukoc, Pronounced Coo-Cotch," *USA Today*, October 11, 1990.

30. Bryan Smith, "Inside the Start of the Chicago Bulls' Championship Run," *Chicago Magazine*, April 11, 2011; Peter Vecsey, "Yugoslavia's Fabled Toni Kukoc Has Committed to Treviso's Benetton Team," *USA Today*, February 28, 1991.

31. Vjekoslav Perica, "United They Stood, Divided They Fell: Nationalism and the Yugoslav School of Basketball, 1968–2000," *Nationalities Papers* 29, no. 2 (2001): 286n1; "Basketball Talent: Imports Are Up," *New York Times*, August 20, 1989; Greg Boeck, "NBA Dabbles in International Trade," *USA Today*, November 2, 1990. Between 1988 and 1989, the NBA added four new teams: the Charlotte Hornets, Miami Heat, Minnesota Timberwolves, and Orlando Magic.

32. Perica, "United They Stood," 267; Alexander Wolff, "Prisoners of War," *Sports Illustrated*, June 3, 1996, 80; Bob Baker, "A Sensation in Serbo-Croatian," *Los Angeles Times Magazine*, October 14, 1990, 25.

33. Peter Richmond, "The Toni Kukoc Wars," *GQ*, January 1993, 92, 94; Ben Joravsky, "The X Factor," *Chicago Reader*, April 28, 1994.

34. Richmond, "Toni Kukoc Wars," 94. In the 1990s, reporters increasingly wrote about the declining numbers of white American professional basketball players. See, for example, Bruce Schoenfeld, "The Loneliness of Being White," *New York Times Magazine*, May 14, 1995.

35. Melissa Isaacson, *Transition Game: An Inside Look at Life with the Chicago Bulls* (Champaign, IL: Sagamore, 1994), 34.

36. Leigh Montville, "The Yugos Are Coming," *Sports Illustrated*, March 12, 1990, 45–46; Alexander Wolff, "The Toni Awards," *Sports Illustrated*, June 22, 1992, 63; Jeffrey Lane, *Under the Boards: The Cultural Revolution in Basketball* (Lincoln: University of Nebraska Press, 2007), 200.

37. Sam Smith, "Kukoc Snubs Bulls to Join Italian Team," *Chicago Tribune*, May 11, 1991; Richmond, "Toni Kukoc Wars," 96.

38. Smith, *Jordan Rules*, 247–248; Sam Smith, "Jackson, King Talk; Pippen, Too," *Chicago Tribune*, April 3, 1991.

ELEVEN: THE GREATEST SHOW ON EARTH

1. Skip Myslenski, "Pistons Lose a Game, Not Their Trademark Defiance," *Chicago Tribune*, May 20, 1991; Game One footage of the 1991 Eastern Conference Finals, "Bulls x Pistons 1991 ECF Game 1," YouTube video, www.youtube.com/watch?v=RXIW8QNIbww.

2. Gena Dagel Caponi, ed., *Signifyin(g), Sanctifyin' and Slam Dunking: A Reader in African American Expressive Culture* (Amherst: University of Massachusetts Press, 1999), 2–7, 22; Nelson George, *Elevating the Game: Black Men and Basketball* (Lincoln, NE: Bison Books, 1999), xiv; Peter De Jonge, "Talking Trash: The Art of Conversation

in the N.B.A.," *New York Times Magazine*, June 6, 1993; Sam Smith, *The Jordan Rules* (New York: Simon & Schuster, 1992), 305.

3. Mark Vancil, "Playboy Interview: Michael Jordan," *Playboy*, May 1992.

4. David Halberstam, *Playing for Keeps: Michael Jordan and the World He Made* (New York: Random House, 1999), 273.

5. Skip Myslenski, "Pistons Warn Time for Talking Done," *Chicago Tribune*, May 19, 1991.

6. Skip Myslenski, "End of Era Passing with Nary a Whimper," *Chicago Tribune*, May 26, 1991.

7. Bob Greene, *Hang Time: Days and Dreams with Michael Jordan* (New York: Doubleday, 1992), 237.

8. Ira Berkow, "The Pistons Were a Disgrace," *New York Times*, May 29, 1991; Bernie Lincicome, "NBA's Garbage Swept Out Door," *Chicago Tribune*, May 28, 1991; Dave Hoekstra, "Let's Get Physical? Bulls Just Say No," *Chicago Sun-Times*, May 27, 1991; Richard Roeper, "Bulls' Victory Saves Detroit from Itself," *Chicago Sun-Times*, May 29, 1991; Mike Lopresti, "The Detroit Pistons Are Gone. Good," *USA Today*, May 28, 1991.

9. Michael Jordan, *For the Love of the Game: My Story*, ed. Mark Vancil (New York: Crown Publishers, 1998), 52; Roland Lazenby, *Mindgames: Phil Jackson's Long Strange Journey* (Chicago: Contemporary Books, 2001), 162; Johnette Howard, "The Trials of Isiah," *Sport*, June 1992, 69.

10. Vancil, "Playboy Interview: Michael Jordan"; the last Jordan quote is a composite from two Chicago newspapers that offer slightly different versions of his comments. See Hoekstra, "Let's Get Physical?"; Sam Smith, "Bulls Make NBA Safe for 'Solid' Basketball," *Chicago Tribune*, May 28, 1991.

11. Smith, *Jordan Rules*, 320.

12. *The Last Dance*, episode 4, directed by Jason Hehir, aired April 26, 2020, on ESPN.

13. Jack McCallum, "Watch Out, World," *Sports Illustrated*, June 3, 1991, 29.

14. Lacy J. Banks, "Underdog Role OK to Lakers," *Chicago Sun-Times*, June 1, 1991.

15. Johannes Tesselaar, "Magic in the Air," *Los Angeles Daily News*, June 2, 1991.

16. Terry Boers, "Getting Better All the Time," *Inside Sports*, May 1990, 33.

17. Stuart Silverstein, "Courting Consumers," *Los Angeles Times*, June 1, 1991; Sam Smith, "Manifest Destiny: Michael vs Magic," *Chicago Tribune*, June 2, 1991; Frank Deford, "Rings Master," *Newsweek*, July 22, 1996, 53; Brian Hewitt, "NBC Gets Lost, Finds a Story," *Chicago Sun-Times*, June 10, 1991; Jack McCallum, "Show of Shows," *Sports Illustrated*, June 10, 1991, 20.

18. Game One footage of the 1991 NBA Finals on NBC, "Bulls x Lakers 1991 Finals Game 1," YouTube video, www.youtube.com/watch?v=1gPRkSAT8ew.

19. E. M. Swift, "From Corned Beef to Caviar," *Sports Illustrated*, June 3, 1991, 84.

20. Bill Gloede and C. L. Smith Munoz, "NBA Goes Global," *Sports Inc.*, November 16, 1987, 29–30; Jack McCallum, "Tomorrow the World," *Sports Illustrated*, November 7, 1988, 60–63; Greg Boeck, "NBA Players Find Fortune in Europe," *USA Today*, October 10, 1990; Walter LaFeber, *Michael Jordan and the New Global*

Capitalism (New York: W. W. Norton, 2002), 69–71; Dave Hoekstra, "70 Countries Will Get Look at NBA Finals," *Chicago Sun-Times*, May 31, 1991.

21. Michael Wilbon, "Michael vs Magic: The Clash of Titans," *Washington Post*, June 2, 1991; Silverstein, "Courting Consumers"; "The Stuff of Dreams," *Advertising Age*, June 3, 1991; McCallum, "Show of Shows," 21.

22. Harvey Araton, "No Kisses, Just Great Players in Final," *New York Times*, June 2, 1991.

23. Scottie Pippen with Michael Arkush, *Unguarded* (New York: Atria, 2021), 112; Alan Boomer, "The Sports Section," *Chicago Reporter*, June 6, 1991; Ira Berkow, "For Michael and Magic, It Was All a Dream," *New York Times*, June 3, 1991.

24. Game One footage of the 1991 NBA Finals on NBC; David Aldridge, "Bulls Just Miss as Lakers Take Game 1, 93–91," *Washington Post*, June 3, 1991.

25. McCallum, "Show of Shows," 23.

26. Pippen, *Unguarded*, 112–114.

27. "Michael Jordan—Famous Switch Hands Layup in 1991 Finals! (All Angles)," YouTube video, www.youtube.com/watch?v=IiSdb16N_Dg.

28. Jack Silverstein, "The 1991 NBA Finals Were David Stern's Godsend," A Shot on Ehlo (Substack website), June 11, 2021, https://readjack.substack.com/p/the-1991 -nba-finals-were-david-sterns?s=r; Mike Lupica, "Amazing Grace," *Esquire*, February 1995, 61; Benjamin G. Rader, "A Revolutionary Moment in Recent American Sports History," *Journal of Sport History* 36, no. 3 (Fall 2009): 319.

29. Terry Boers, "Bulls Pull Magic Act," *Chicago Sun-Times*, June 8, 1991; Clifton Brown, "Extra! Bulls Rally Then Down Lakers in Overtime," *New York Times*, June 8, 1991; Jack McCallum, "His Highness," *Sports Illustrated*, June 17, 1991, 31; Phil Jackson and Hugh Delehanty, *Eleven Rings: The Soul of Success* (New York: Penguin Books, 2014), 109.

30. Smith, *Jordan Rules*, 345.

31. Mike Downey, "There's Magic to Michael's Air of Conquest," *Los Angeles Times*, June 13, 1991.

32. Halberstam, *Playing for Keeps*, 281.

33. Sam Smith, interview by Jack Silverstein, December 24, 2011, A Shot on Ehlo, https://readjack.substack.com/p/the-making-of-the-jordan-rules.

34. Jackson, *Eleven Rings*, 109; Bryan Smith, "Inside the Start of the Chicago Bulls' Championship Run," *Chicago Magazine*, April 11, 2011.

35. Jeff Coplon, "Legends. Champions?," *New York Times Magazine*, April 21, 1996; Michael Leahy, *When Nothing Else Matters: Michael Jordan's Last Comeback* (New York: Simon & Schuster, 2004), 246–248.

36. Leahy, *When Nothing Else Matters*, 247.

37. Smith, *Jordan Rules*, 329.

38. Halberstam, *Playing for Keeps*, 308; Pippen, *Unguarded*, xxi.

39. Bruce Jenkins, "Jordan's Seven Years of Frustration End with Tears of Joy," *St. Louis Post-Dispatch*, June 14, 1991; Smith, *Jordan Rules*, 350.

40. Ailene Voison, "As Semi-Shock Waves Settle over L.A., Jordan Disappears," *Atlanta Journal-Constitution*, June 13, 1991.

41. Jeff Pearlman, *Showtime: Magic, Kareem, Riley, and the Los Angeles Lakers Dynasty of the 1980s* (New York: Gotham Books, 2014), 409–410.

42. Downey, "There's Magic to Michael's Air of Conquest."

TWELVE: ALONE AT THE MOUNTAINTOP

1. Sam Smith, "Jordan on No-Show: My Life Not Just Rose Garden," *Chicago Tribune*, October 4, 1991.

2. Lacy Banks, "The Air Defense: Jordan Rejects His Critics' Shots," *Chicago Sun-Times*, August 25, 1991; Jere Longman, "A Prisoner of Public Perception," *Philadelphia Inquirer*, September 22, 1991; George Castle, "Air to the Throne," *Sport*, January 1991, 29.

3. Jack McCallum, *Dream Team: How Michael, Magic, Larry, Charles, and the Greatest of All Time Conquered the World and Changed Basketball Forever* (New York: Ballantine Books, 2013), 82–88.

4. Jay Mariotti, "Jordan Strictly Bush League in His White House Snub," *Chicago Sun-Times*, October 2, 1991.

5. Andrew Hermann, "PUSH Rips Reports, Column on Jordan," *Chicago Sun-Times*, October 5, 1991; Chinta Strausberg, "PUSH Backs Jordan," *Chicago Defender*, October 7, 1991.

6. Bradley Considine, "Jordan's No-Show," *Chicago Tribune*, October 9, 1991; "The Jordan Issue—Reader's Voices, Jordan's Choices," *Chicago Sun-Times*, October 10, 1991.

7. Smith, "Jordan on No-Show"; Bob Verdi, "Let's Be Realistic: Jordan *Is* Special," *Chicago Tribune*, October 5, 1991.

8. Sam Smith, *Second Coming: The Strange Odyssey of Michael Jordan* (New York: HarperCollins, 1995), xii–xv, xviii–xix.

9. Mark Heisler, "Magic Johnson's Career Ended by HIV-Positive Test," *Los Angeles Times*, November 8, 1991; Rick Du Brow, "TV's Surprise Reality Show," *Los Angeles Times*, November 9, 1991; *The Announcement*, directed by Nelson George (ESPN Films, 2012).

10. "World Press Hails Magic as a Hero, 'Genuine Idol,'" *Toronto Star*, November 9, 1991; Paul Attner, "It Was Magic," *Sporting News*, November 18, 1991, 9; Jack Kroll, "Smile, Though Our Hearts Are Breaking," *Newsweek*, November 18, 1991, 70; Frank Deford, "A Magical Mystery Tour," *Newsweek*, December 23, 1991, 59–60; Robert Lipsyte, "Magic as Hero: It's Not the Most Comfortable Fit," *New York Times*, November 15, 1991; Lou Cannon, "Basketball Star Magic Johnson Retires with AIDS Virus," *Washington Post*, November 8, 1991.

11. "Magic's Show," *Nation*, December 2, 1991, 691; Thomas Heath and Christine Spolar, "Magic Johnson's World: A Life of Temptations," *Washington Post*, November 24, 1991; "Therefore, Magic Owes Us?," *Advocate*, December 17, 1991, 8; Edwin Diamond, "Magic and the Media," *New York*, December 2, 1991, 30; Charles Stewart, "Double Jeopardy," *New Republic*, December 2, 1991, 13; John Gallagher, "Johnson Disclosure Brings AIDS Issues to Middle America," *Advocate*, December 17, 1991, 14–16.

12. Magic Johnson with Roy Johnson, "I'll Deal with It," *Sports Illustrated*, November 18, 1991; Sally Jenkins, "Where's the Magic?," *Sports Illustrated*, November 25, 1991.

13. Diamond, "Magic and the Media," 30; Dave Anderson, "Sorry, but Magic Isn't a Hero," *New York Times*, November 14, 1991; Dorothy Rabinowitz, "Television: The Magic Circus," *Wall Street Journal*, November 18, 1991; Charles Pierce, "The Magic Act," *GQ*, February 1993, 125.

14. Pierce, "Magic Act," 125; Ira Berkow, "Magic, TV, and Kids," *TV Guide*, March 21–27, 1992, 13.

15. Jesse Katz, "Master of Illusion," *Los Angeles Magazine*, October 2003; David Rowe, "Accommodating Bodies: Celebrity, Sexuality, and 'Tragic Magic,'" *Journal of Sport & Social Issues* 18, no. 1 (February 1994): 15–16; Magic Johnson, "My Life," *People*, October 19, 1992, 119–124; Laura B. Randolph, "Magic and Cookie Speak Out for First Time on Love, Marriage, and AIDS," *Ebony*, April 1992, 100–107; "Magic Johnson Seeks Olympic Gold with Support of Wife and Baby," *Jet*, July 20, 1992, 50–55.

16. Greg Boeck and Mike Dodd, "Life on the Road: The Game Is Sex," *USA Today*, November 14, 1991; Harvey Araton, "Players, Temptations and AIDS," *New York Times*, November 10, 1991; Jay Mariotti, "Athletes, Sexual Restraint Strange Bedfellows Indeed," *Chicago Sun-Times*, November 10, 1991; John Elson, "The Dangerous World of Wannabes," *Time*, November 25, 1991, 77, 80; E. M. Swift, "Dangerous Games," *Sports Illustrated*, November 18, 1991; E. Jean Carroll, "Love in the Time of Magic," *Esquire*, April 1992, 138.

17. Carroll, "Love in the Time of Magic," 138.

18. Johnette Howard, " . . . An Alarm Clock for a Lot of People," *Sport*, June 1992, 82; Mark Vancil, "Playboy Interview: Michael Jordan," *Playboy*, May 1992; Mary G. McDonald, "Michael Jordan's Family Values: Marketing, Meaning, and Post-Regan America," *Sociology of Sport Journal* 13, no. 2 (1996): 350, 357–360; Lynn Norment, "Michael and Juanita Jordan Talk About Love, Marriage and Life After Basketball," *Ebony*, November 1991, 68.

19. Norment, "Michael and Juanita Jordan Talk," 72; Selena Roberts, "Jordan and His Image Have Lost Air and Come Back to Earth," *New York Times*, December 15, 2002; Lois Romano, "Jordan, in Her Court," *Chicago Tribune*, January 30, 2002; Roland Lazenby, *Michael Jordan: The Life* (New York: Little, Brown, 2014), 348.

20. Shia Kapos and Mickey Ciokajlo, "Woman Suing Jordan No Stranger to Civil Actions," *Chicago Tribune*, December 1, 2002; Michael Leahy, *When Nothing Else Matters: Michael Jordan's Last Comeback* (New York: Simon & Schuster, 2004), 332–334. In October 2002, Jordan filed a suit against Knafel in Cook County, Illinois, alleging she was trying to extort $5 million from him, the amount that Knafel claimed Jordan owed her as part of an oral agreement that she would not publicly disclose their sexual relationship or file a paternity suit against him. In November, Knafel countersued, asking the court to enforce the alleged oral agreement, but the judge dismissed the case.

21. *ESPN SportsCentury*, "Michael Jordan," aired December 26, 1999, on ESPN; Smith, *Second Coming*, xix.

22. Peter Richmond, *Phil Jackson: Lord of the Rings* (New York: Penguin, 2013), 163.

23. Jay Mariotti, "Book Depicts Tyrant Jordan and Irrita-Bulls," *Chicago Sun-Times*, November 11, 1991; Michael Miner, "The Mariotti Rules," *Chicago Reader*, November 21, 1991.

24. Miner, "Mariotti Rules"; Sam Smith, "And Now, a Word from the Author," *Chicago Tribune*, November 20, 1991; Peter Vecsey, "Book on Bulls Bona Fide," *USA Today*, November 26, 1991.

25. Sam Smith, interview by Jack Silverstein, December 24, 2011, https://readjack.substack.com/p/the-making-of-the-jordan-rules; Isaac Chotiner, "How the N.B.A. Has Changed since 'The Jordan Rules,'" *New Yorker*, July 20, 2020.

26. Bryan Curtis, "'The Jordan Rules' Was the Mother of All Woj Bombs," *Ringer*, June 9, 2017.

27. Sam Smith, *The Jordan Rules: The Inside Story of One Turbulent Season with Michael Jordan and the Chicago Bulls* (New York: Simon & Schuster, 1992), 125–127, 166, 212–213, 305.

28. Richard Roeper, "Controversial Book? No, It's Lighter Than Air," *Chicago Sun-Times*, November 19, 1991.

29. Vancil, "Playboy Interview: Michael Jordan."

30. Mike Mulligan, "Krause Gives Book a Bum Review," *Chicago Sun-Times*, November 19, 1991; Roland Lazenby, *Mindgames: Phil Jackson's Long Strange Journey* (Chicago: Contemporary Books, 2001), 176; David Halberstam, *Playing for Keeps: Michael Jordan and the World He Made* (New York: Random House, 1999), 313; Rick Telander, "The Sleuth," *Sports Illustrated*, March 15, 1993, 69; Mark Vancil, "Enraging Bull," *Chicago Magazine*, April 1992, 75–76.

31. Halberstam, *Playing for Keeps*, 322–323.

32. Phil Jackson and Hugh Delehanty, *Sacred Hoops: Spiritual Lessons of a Hardwood Warrior* (New York: Hyperion, 1995), 179; Vancil, "Playboy Interview: Michael Jordan."

33. Vancil, "Playboy Interview: Michael Jordan."

34. Ted Gup, "Scourge of the Senate," *Time*, May 30, 1988, 48; Sidney Blumenthal, "Republican of Fear," *New Republic*, November 12, 1990, 15; Donald Baer, "The Race in Black and White," *U.S. News & World Report*, July 23, 1990, 27–29; Charles Whitaker, "Harvey Gantt," *Ebony*, April 1986, 96; Laurence Barrett, "Race-Baiting Wins Again," *Time*, November 19, 1990, 43; Peter Applebome, "Helms Kindled Anger in Campaign, and May Have Set Tone for Others," *New York Times*, November 8, 1990; Smith, *Second Coming*, xix; Sam Smith, "The Story Behind One of Michael Jordan's Misunderstood Quotes," NBA.com, April 15, 2020.

35. Smith, *Second Coming*, xix; Susan Kauffman, "Gantt Says Jordan Backing Welcome," *Chapel Hill News*, September 17, 1990; Jim Naughton, *Taking to the Air: The Rise of Michael Jordan* (New York: Warner Books, 1992), 215; William Rhoden, *$40 Million Slaves: The Rise, Fall, and Redemption of the Black Athlete* (New York: Crown

Publishers, 1996), 203–204; Sam Smith, *There Is No Next: NBA Legends on the Legacy of Michael Jordan* (New York: Diversion, 2014), 12; *The Last Dance*, directed by Jason Hehir, aired from April 19, 2020, to May 17, 2020, on ESPN.

36. Myles Brown, "LeBron James, Michael Jordan, and Two Different Roads to Black Empowerment," GQ.com, August 6, 2018; Howard Bryant, "What 'The Last Dance' Reveals About Michael Jordan's Legacy," ESPN.com, June 28, 2020.

37. E. M. Swift, "Reach Out and Touch Someone," *Sports Illustrated*, August 5, 1991, 58; Arthur Ashe and Arnold Rampersad, *Days of Grace* (New York: Ballantine Books, 1993), 178–179; Mike Mulligan, "Brown Chastises Jordan," *Chicago Sun-Times*, August 11, 1991; Lacy Banks, "Air Defense"; Ira Berkow, "Jordan Tries, So Don't Be Stoopid," *New York Times*, September 2, 1991; Phillip Hersh, "Michael: A Symbol of Excellence," *Chicago Tribune*, January 17, 1999; Vancil, "Playboy Interview: Michael Jordan"; *Last Dance*; Tom Sorenson, "Life's Biggest Overmatch: 1-On-1 Against the Best," *Charlotte Observer*, May 31, 1986; Larry Platt, "Michael Jordan: Icon," *GQ*, October 2007.

38. Wright Thompson, "Michael Jordan: A History of Flight," ESPN.com, May 19, 2020.

39. "Charles Barkley, MJ, and Oprah Discuss Giving to the Homeless," YouTube video, accessed April 6, 2023, www.youtube.com/watch?v=vbmOtFfvzHg.

40. Robert D. Putnam, "Bowling Alone: America's Declining Social Capital," *Journal of Democracy* 6, no. 1 (January 1995): 67–68.

41. David Remnick, "The Joshua Generation," *New Yorker*, November 8, 2008. In his virtual lecture on Jordan, historian Damion Thomas also places him in the context of the Joshua Generation. See Damion Thomas, "Michael Jordan: A Re-evaluation," Smithsonian lecture, May 17, 2020, YouTube video, www.youtube.com/watch?v=ms9KkvqC6FY&t=1s.

42. Terrence Moore, "Count Jordan Among Those Afraid of Saying He's Black," *Atlanta Journal-Constitution*, June 23, 1991; Ken Green, "Should Black Athletes Speak Out on Issues?," *Chicago Defender*, August 12, 1991; Ken Green, "Criticisms Wearing on Jordan?," *Chicago Defender*, August 26, 1991; Banks, "Air Defense."

43. Mark Mulvoy, "From the Publisher," *Sports Illustrated*, December 23, 1991, 4; Daniel Boorstin, *The Image: A Guide to Pseudo-Events in America* (1962; New York: Vintage Books, 2012), 13; Megan Garber, "Boorstin's Image in the Age of Pseudo-Reality," *Atlantic*, December 1, 2016.

44. Jack McCallum, "Alone on the Mountaintop," *Sports Illustrated*, December 23, 1991, 66; David Halberstam, "A Hero for the Wired World," *Sports Illustrated*, December 23, 1991, 76.

45. Bob Greene, "Of Bulls, Beatles, and Flares in the Night," *Chicago Tribune*, October 30, 1991.

46. Reid Hanley, "Jordan Scoring in Another Sport," *Chicago Tribune*, July 25, 1990; Vancil, "Playboy Interview: Michael Jordan"; Bill Brubaker, "Jordan Finds Being Best Worth the Gamble," *Washington Post*, May 10, 1992.

47. Brubaker, "Jordan Finds Being Best Worth the Gamble."

48. John Day and Joseph Menn, "Convicted Drug Dealer Calls Seized Money Loan from Jordan $57,000 for Golf Driving Range, N.C. Man Says," *Charlotte Observer*, December 14, 1991.

49. Bill Brubaker, "Jordan's Gambling Undergoes Intense Scrutiny Again," *Washington Post*, August 1, 1993.

50. Brubaker, "Jordan Finds Being Best Worth the Gamble"; David Jackson, "Jordan's Acquaintances in Shadowy World," *Chicago Tribune*, March 29, 1992; Clifton Brown, "N.B.A. Won't Discipline Bulls' Jordan," *New York Times*, April 1, 1992.

51. Brubaker, "Jordan Finds Being Best Worth the Gamble"; Sam Smith, "Jordan's Gambling Under Increasing Scrutiny," *Chicago Tribune*, November 22, 1992. In 1978, only one state permitted casino gambling. But by the end of the 1990s, twenty-seven states allowed commercial gaming. See William R. Eadington, "The Economics of Casino Gambling," *Journal of Economic Perspectives* 13, no. 3 (Summer 1999): 173–192.

52. Thompson, "Michael Jordan"; Wright Thompson, "Michael Jordan Has Not Left the Building," *ESPN The Magazine*, February 22, 2013.

53. Donald Katz, *Just Do It: The Nike Spirit in the Corporate World* (New York: Random House, 1994), 13, 251.

EPILOGUE: THE LAST DANCE

1. The White House, Office of the Press Secretary, "President Obama Names Recipients of the Presidential Medal of Freedom," press release, November 16, 2016, https://obamawhitehouse.archives.gov/the-press-office/2016/11/16/president-obama-names-recipients-presidential-medal-freedom.

2. Alexander Wolff, *The Audacity of Hoop: Basketball and the Age of Obama* (Philadelphia: Temple University Press, 2016); Barack Obama, *Dreams from My Father* (New York: Three Rivers Press, 2004), 79–80.

3. Scott Fornek, "Contribution from MJ Helps Obama Campaign," *Chicago Sun-Times*, March 5, 2004; "Michael Likes Obama Too," *Chicago Sun-Times*, March 8, 2004; Wolff, *Audacity of Hoop*, 119.

4. Mike Wise, Jerry Bembry, and Martenzie Johnson, "Jordan Speaks Out on Shooting of African-Americans, Police," *Undefeated*, July 25, 2016.

5. Wise, Bembry, and Johnson, "Jordan Speaks Out."

6. Myles Brown, "LeBron James, Michael Jordan, and Two Different Roads to Black Empowerment," GQ.com, August 6, 2018.

7. Melissa Isaacson, "Bulls Agonize Over L.A. Turmoil," *Chicago Tribune*, May 2, 1992; Howard Bryant, *The Heritage: Black Athletes, a Divided America, and the Politics of Patriotism* (Boston: Beacon Press, 2018), 130.

8. Bryant, *Heritage*, 171.

9. Dave McMenamin and Ian Begley, "How NBA Stars Made It to the ESPY Stage," ESPN.com, July 18, 2016; Jasmine C. Lee et al., "At Least 88 Cities Have Had Protests in the Past 13 Days over Police Killings of Blacks," *New York Times*, July 16, 2016.

10. Wise, Bembry, and Johnson, "Jordan Speaks Out."

11. Elizabeth Hinton, *America on Fire: The Untold History of Police Violence and Black Rebellion Since the 1960s* (New York: Liveright, 2021), 288; Larry Buchanan, Quoctrong Bui, and Jugal Patel, "Black Lives Matter May Be the Largest Movement in U.S. History," *New York Times*, July 3, 2020; Mark Medina, "George Floyd Protests: Michael Jordan Says 'We Have Had Enough,'" *USA Today*, May 31, 2020.

12. William Rhoden, interview by Craig Melvin, MSNBC, *Craig Melvin Reports*, October 11, 2021; William Rhoden, *$40 Million Slaves: The Rise, Fall, and Redemption of the Black Athlete* (New York: Crown Publishers, 2006), 200, 215.

13. *The Last Dance*, directed by Jason Hehir, aired from April 19, 2020, to May 17, 2020, on ESPN.

14. Marc Stein, "Meeting the Michael Jordan We Didn't Know," *New York Times*, May 20, 2020; Jason Guerrasio, "How an Executive Producer on 'The Last Dance' Got Michael Jordan Involved in the Hit Docuseries," *Insider*, July 17, 2020.

15. Mike Fleming Jr., "Mike Tollin on ESPN Docu-Series 'The Last Dance,' a Citizen Kane-Sized Rendering of Michael Jordan's Legacy," Deadline.com, April 17, 2020.

16. Marc Stein, "Michael Jordan and the 'Last Dance' Argue the Bulls Are the Best Ever," *New York Times*, April 20, 2020; Stein, "Meeting the Michael Jordan We Didn't Know"; Will Leitch, "'The Last Dance' Is Awe-Inspiring. But It Has One Big Problem," *Washington Post*, April 26, 2020; Jason Guerrasio, "Michael Jordan Said He Would Only Appear in 'The Last Dance' Docuseries if He Always Had the Final Word," *Insider*, April 27, 2020; Scottie Pippen with Michael Arkush, *Unguarded* (New York: Atria, 2021), xiii.

17. Wesley Morris, "In 'The Last Dance,' Michael Jordan and the Bulls Still Dominate," *New York Times*, May 10, 2020.

18. Leitch, "'The Last Dance' Is Awe-Inspiring"; Jacob Rosenberg, "Republicans Watch Documentaries, Too," *Mother Jones*, May 6, 2020.

INDEX

Johnny Smith is the J. C. "Bud" Shaw Professor of Sports History and associate professor of history at the Georgia Institute of Technology. He is the author of five books, including *Blood Brothers: The Fatal Friendship Between Muhammad Ali and Malcolm X* (written with Randy Roberts). He lives in Atlanta, Georgia.